Gearing Up for Patents

The Indian Scenario

Gearing Up for Patents

The Indian Scenario

Prabuddha Ganguli

Universities Press

Universities Press (India) Limited

Registered Office
3-5-819 Hyderguda, Hyderabad 500 029 (A.P.), India

Distributed by
Orient Longman Limited

Registered Office
3-6-272 Himayatnagar, Hyderabad 500 029 (A.P.), India

Other Offices
Bangalore / Bhopal / Bhubaneshwar / Calcutta / Chandigarh
Chennai / Ernakulam / Guwahati / Hyderabad / Jaipur
Lucknow / Mumbai / New Delhi / Patna

First published 1998
Reprinted 1999

ISBN 81 7371 105 4

Typeset by
OSDATA, Hyderabad 500 029

Printed at
Sree Kalanjali Graphics, Hyderabad 500 029

Published by
Universities Press (India) Limited
3-5-819 Hyderguda, Hyderabad 500 029

This book is dedicated to my parents and teachers who kindled and nurtured the spirit of learning in me.

"In a time of change it is the learners who inherit the future. The learned find themselves living in a world that no longer exists."

Eric Hoffer.

Contents

Foreword

It is a matter of great pleasure for me to be writing the Foreword for this singularly important book. As a technologist convinced of the viability of the Indian genius in any competition, the spread of patent literacy and the establishment of a flourishing patent culture has been an article of faith with me.

The global context of organizing industrial enterprise and conducting trade and business has radically changed since the advent of the WTO, of which India is a member. The attitudes and habits that served us in an era of sheltered existence have become irrelevant and the sooner they are jettisoned, the better it will be for the country to find its rightful place in a technology-led world marked by intense competition. In this world, it is the intellectual wealth of a country that alone counts, and to be able to take advantage of it, rights over intellectual property have got to be claimed and protected in accordance with the internationally accepted Intellectual Property Rights (IPR) protection regime.

There are several kinds of intellectual property, e.g. patents, designs, trademarks, copyright. The book deals with all these. However, patents are the most important intellectual property in the industrial technology domain and pose the greatest challenge. It is no exaggeration to say that there has been no culture of patenting in India, and even the awareness about the need and significance of patenting has been abysmally low, not only in the lay public but even among the researchers and technologists who create intellectual property, and the law professionals who would be drafting, defending and challenging patents. Skills in filing, reading and exploiting patents will be most crucial in the years to come. Thus, a Patent Literacy Mission will have to be launched in India with a sense of urgency.

The Indian contribution to the pool of international patents is negligible. There are over 32 million patents published world-wide and over half-a-million applications are added every year. Our R&D efforts have not taken cognizance of this enormous intellectual wealth, available on tap as it were, waiting to be utilized for a number of purposes. Patents could give valuable information for planning R&D, planning strategic protection, blocking competitors, identifying emerging technologies, research areas and business opportunities, identifying possible collaborators, forging strategic alliances based on technological and geographical strengths, etc. We have so far failed to exploit these opportunities because of our neglect of patents.

It is imperative to develop outstanding capabilities in the reading and writing of patents. At the moment, we are capable neither of properly protecting our inventions nor of understanding the implications of patents granted to our competitors. We may have a good invention but we cannot effectively protect it by patents filed abroad as many of the patents written by our professionals can be effectively circumvented. Also, in a world of preemptive strategies, it is difficult to get entry in fortified domains even with a worthy invention.

How do we create within our system a cadre of top class professionals, who will wage and fight these battles to safeguard the nation's intellectual property? Manpower planning for IPR protection has to be handled on a priority basis. IPR must be made a compulsory, or at least a higher elective course in the curriculum for a law degree in Indian universities. Similarly, our graduates from engineering and technology streams have no idea about IPR and yet, these are the professionals who will generate and exploit intellectual property. It is necessary to introduce key elements of IPR in their courses. One could also think of a system of national accreditation of patent attorneys for those who successfully complete a custom-made higher professional examination consisting of papers in science, engineering, law, patent drafting, patent infringement and other key elements of IPR.

The book by Prabuddha Ganguli comes at a time when it is most needed. In fact, there is hardly anything available in the market to help the Indian reader who has stakes or interest in learning about IPR protection with specific reference to the Indian context. The prodigious experience and learning of the author in the area of patents acquired from his vantage position in Hindustan Lever Limited goes to make the book comprehensive and authoritative. Approaching the patenting activity in India from a historical perspective, the author discusses with rare clarity and lucidity the provisions of the Indian Patents Act, 1970, the changes that have become obligatory to be introduced in the Indian Patents Act following our accession to the WTO, essential patent documents, opposition to patents and enforcement of patents, patents as a source of information and as a strategic tool, harmonization of patent systems, etc. A very welcome chapter is devoted to debatable issues. Should researchers be allowed to use a patented process for research work without a license ? Who should get the patent—the first to file or the first to invent ? How to reconcile the Trade Secret Law with employees' service contracts, material transfer agreements and research collaborations ? How is software best protected — by copyright or by patent ? Controversies regarding manufacture of generic drugs and protection of living forms are dealt with, the latter including problems of having an appropriate legal system with respect to farmers' rights, researchers' rights, protection to hybrid and high-yielding seeds, transgenic plants and microbes, plants containing patented genes, protection to genes sequence, protection of new varieties of plants and issues related to biodiversity.

One great strength of the book is the large number of case studies to illustrate different issues being discussed. The book contains a wealth of other information. I have no doubt that it would eminently succeed in its stated objective to prepare the user of the book for carrying on an effective dialogue with IPR professionals including patent attorneys and information experts to exploit what the system has to offer. It has indeed been a delightful experience for me to go through the book as it took shape. My warmest congratulations to the author and the publisher for this timely and excellent contribution at a crucial stage in our development.

(R. A. Mashelkar)
Director-General,
Council of Scientific and
Industrial Research; and
Secretary,
Department of Scientific and
Industrial Research

Preface

In recent times, issues related to intellectual property rights (IPR), specifically patents, have been debated in various forums in India. The rapidly changing scenario and India's continuing progress towards globalization through liberalized policies make it imperative that the potential beneficiaries of the IPR system familiarize themselves with the basic elements of IPR to maximize their exploitation.

IPR does not find a meaningful place in our education system, neither has its importance received due recognition in the corporate world. This neglect has resulted in a hiatus in the appreciation of the basic concepts and their utilization by the researchers in academic/industrial laboratories, among business executives, planners, government officials, and other professionals.

Though trademarks find extensive application within industry in India, the role played by patents, copyrights, etc., has been comparatively small. This may be attributed to the lack of familiarity with the system and its relevance to commercial and scientific activities.

There are a number of treatises, books, and articles on IPR, patents, trademarks, copyrights, etc., but most of them are addressed to experts in the field. The need of the hour is a simple, reader-friendly presentation which is adequate to help professionals familiarize themselves with the basic elements and processes of the IPR system.

The present book attempts to satisfy such a need. The material has been developed in the last few years as a part of presentations made at various patent familiarization courses/workshops, seminars for professionals drawn from diverse fields organized in India by ASCI, Hyderabad and a number of Government of India departments, which include the Technology Information Forecasting and Assessment Cell (TIFAC), the Department of Scientific and Industrial Research (DSIR), and the Council of Scientific and Industrial Research (CSIR).

The user of this book would be able to carry on an effective dialogue with IPR professionals, including patent attorneys and information experts, to exploit what the system has to offer. It describes the present patent system and operational procedures in India, the issues evolving as a result of the General Agreement on Tariff and Trade (GATT) and the formation of the World Trade Organization (WTO).

If this book succeeds in making all those concerned with inventions and innovations pause and think seriously about patenting and exploiting their patents profitably, it has more than achieved its purpose.

PRABUDDHA GANGULI

Acknowledgments

This book has evolved over several years. A number of people have contributed to it—through discussions, material, participation and questions which have come up during workshops and seminars on IPR conducted at various places in India. My participation in these courses and workshops was possible due to the constant encouragement and support I received from the Patents Division of Unilever and my colleagues in Hindustan Lever Limited. I am grateful to them for their support.

I am thankful to Mr Louis Virelli, Head, Patents Division, Unilever for his valuable comments on the draft of the book. Acknowledgments are also due to Dr Enno Dekker, Mr David Butler of the Unilever Patents Division, Dr S. Venkatramani of Hindustan Lever Research Centre and Mr A. Dey, former Assistant Controller of Patents, Mumbai Branch of the Patent Office, for providing me with important literature on the subject. Some of the literature searches presented in the book were done with the help of Mr Makarand Waikar. I thank him for his help.

I have also drawn professional support from Mr S. Majumdar, Patent Attorney and IPR consultant, who painstakingly read the manuscript at various stages and enriched it with his experience and knowledge of the subject. I am indebted to him for sparing his time.

The suggestion to reorganize all my course material in the form of a book came from Dr B. Bowonder, Dean of Research, Administrative Staff College of India (ASCI), Hyderabad, who has been a constant source of encouragement. But for him, this book would not have come into being. His support in the form of ASCI library facilities and providing me opportunities to test the material in the courses conducted at ASCI have been invaluable. I would also like to thank Mr S.V. John Peter of ASCI for his contribution to Appendix IX.

Dr R. A. Mashelkar, Director-General of the Council of Scientific and Industrial Research (CSIR), and Secretary, Department of Scientific and Industrial Research, spared his valuable time to review the draft and very willingly accepted to write the Foreword to the book. His views and suggestions, together with those of Mr N. R. Subbaram, former Advisor, Patent Management Division of the CSIR, have helped to widen the perspective. I am indeed grateful to them.

It has been a pleasure to work with Universities Press, and the cooperation of the editorial staff in particular is much appreciated. Thanks are due to AICRA info mates (P) Ltd. for generating the illustrations.

My final thanks are to my family. Working on this book over the weekends and at times keeping late hours, did mean less time for family activities. Much of this work would not have been possible without the constant cooperation and participation of my family members: my wife Subhra and daughters Mishty and Lily. They have also contributed to computerizing the manuscript, which ensured its completion on time. I cannot thank them adequately.

PRABUDDHA GANGULI
Mumbai

1

Intellectual property rights: An imperative

Growth of business in an era of shortening product lifecycles and aggressive competition requires not only speedily available innovative inputs and rapid access to international markets but also measures for the protection of new technologies and products through

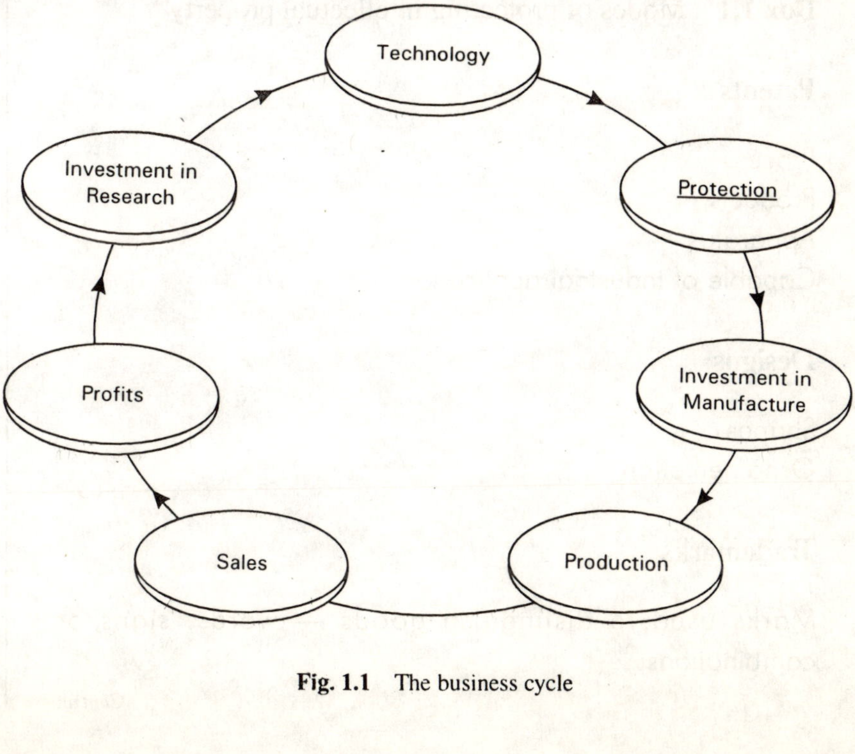

Fig. 1.1 The business cycle

appropriate intellectual property rights (IPR). The course of a business cycle is more or less similar to the representation in Fig. 1.1. The General Agreement on Tariff and Trade (GATT) discussions which concluded in 1995 with the formation of the World Trade Organization (WTO) made this amply clear. They impressed upon the members the urgent need to reassess their national IPR laws, specially with respect to the Trade Related Intellectual Property Rights (TRIPS). Copyrights, trademarks, geographical indications, industrial designs and patents, integrated circuits and trade secrets are the major branches of TRIPS.

These branches of intellectual property encompass different types of intangible property. The laws governing each of them are also distinct as their rights and enforcement varies. The property components falling under the purview of each IPR are given in Box 1.1.

However, any intellectual creation, whether it is a product/process, or a work of literature or art, a computer program, a sculpture, or even a logo, for example, can be protected by a judicious combination of the various IPR tools.

Box 1.1 Modes of protecting intellectual property

Patents

Process
Products
Apparatus
Capable of industrial application

Designs

Shapes
Ornamentation

Trademarks

Marks used to distinguish goods — words, signs or combinations

Continues

Continued

Copyrights

Musical work
Artistic work
Literary work, e.g. books, periodicals, lectures, plays, maps, art reproductions, models, photographs, computer software

Hence a thorough understanding of these rights is necessary to build up an IPR armory necessary for the protection of a given intellectual property. Box 1.2 provides a brief glimpse of the rights accruing with respect to the aforementioned intellectual properties.

Box 1.2 Intellectual properties and accompanying rights

Intellectual property	Accrual of rights
Patents	On registration: rights enjoyed for 14 and seven years, subject to renewal. Non-renewal leads to irretrievable loss of rights. Rights not divisible. Enforceability: only civil, at District Court and High Court levels.
Designs	On registration: rights enjoyed for 15 years, subject to renewal. Non-renewal leads to irretrievable loss of rights. Rights not divisible. Enforceability: only civil, at District Court and High Court levels.
Trademarks	Use/registration: perpetually subject to renewal. Non-renewal leads to cessation. Re-registrable.

Continues

Continued

	Rights divisible territorially or otherwise. Enforceability: civil, at District Court and High Court levels; and criminal, before magistrate.
Copyrights	On completion of work; no renewal required; valid for 60 years after author's death. Parallel rights may exist for same work prepared independently. Enforceability: civil at District Court and High Court levels; and criminal, before magistrate.
Passing off	Use of trademark/tradename or other distinctive features attached to trade which has acquired a distinctive identifiability. Passing off, traditionally a part of the trademark law, also finds applications in other branches wholly unconnected with trademarks.
Geographical indications	There are certain products which are easily identified as typical of a geographical region either by tradition or by practice. Examples of this are: Basmati rice, the product and its characteristics are identified as originating from India or Pakistan; Scotch, identified as coming from Scotland; Champagne, a typical produce of France; etc. This gives the right to producers only from those regions to name the produce by these names. Produce from any other region cannot be named by these geographical indications.
Trade secrets	A trade secret is information that is either a secret, or is not generally known in the industry related circles and gives its owner an advantage over competitors. Trade secret protection exists as long as the information is kept secret or confidential by its owner and is not lawfully and independently obtained by others. Examples of trade secrets include formulae, patterns, methods, programs, techniques, processes or compilations of information that provide one's business with a competitive

Continues

Continued

advantage. The owner of a trade secret may recover damages resulting from the improper disclosure or use of its trade secret by another.

A familiar misconception, even among professionals, is that only innovations in high technology fields are patentable. A commonly used tool like a pen, for instance, can be protected by:

- patents for novelties in various functional features such as the nib, a ballpoint or any other part ensuring effective/optimal flow of ink while writing. Innovations in enhancing the effectiveness of the clip, caps, etc., can each be individually patented;
- designs for features which involve the shape of the body, appropriate "grooves", slots, etc;
- names and distinctive signs, logos, package designs which are registered through "trademarks";
- write-ups, package design, advertisements which are protected through "copyrights".

These IPR tools can help to preserve the rights of the innovator against wrongful use by others.

Here are a few more examples. Various features of the Gillette's non-electric razor are protected by 17 patents, which are displayed on the pack. Gillette, as a name, is a registered trademark in several countries. Similarly, the US-based Golden Valley Microwave Food Inc.'s Microwave Popcorn is protected by a number of US patents, which are mentioned explicitly on the pack. Numerous examples of daily use items, such as toothpastes, toothbrushes, soaps, creams, lotions, lighting equipment, umbrellas, suitcases, etc., are all protected by such IPR tools.

Contrarily, some fundamental discoveries which can be considered as major scientific contributions may not qualify for patents. Examples abound: discovery of penicillin, laws of gravity, laws of thermodynamics, etc., could not be patented. Credit for discoveries, scientific principles is normally based on peer evaluation through publications in refereed journals, and presentations at scientific and technical conferences, workshops, and meetings. However, devices, processes or products based on the application of these principles have resulted in a large number of patented inventions.

inventor or to his assignee giving exclusive rights to make, use, exercise and vend the invention for a limited period in exchange for disclosure in a patent specification.

An asset

The patent system has an economic basis and is an avenue for disclosure of new technology. Further, it offers monopoly for a limited period, and defines areas of monopoly which are new and non-obvious, with provisions in national laws to balance public versus private benefits.

In a few countries, the **Utility Models System** is operative and is designed to "protect" innovations which are new and useful but fail to qualify for grant of a patent as per the patent system. This system was introduced to foster "small innovations" of demonstrable practicability. It does not exist in India, but is functioning in selected countries in Europe (France, Italy, Spain, Germany, Poland, Portugal), Asia (Philippines, Korea, Taiwan, Japan), Mexico and South America (Uruguay, Brazil). The system affords "protection" to innovations without the rigorous examination required in the patent system. This protection is restricted and the period of validity varies from six to ten years.

The intellectual asset is becoming a crucial factor in establishing dominance under patent dispute suits in business. This is particularly true in USA, Japan and the industrially advanced countries in Europe, where enforcement of patent rights is fairly strong. In India, enforcement of patent rights is yet to gain the importance it deserves. Globally, patent-related disputes and their settlements are on the rise. Consider the semiconductor industry alone. A sum of $800 million was exchanged in 1994 by way of licensing fees compared to $300 million in 1991: a staggering increase of about 165% in just three years. Texas Instruments, between 1987 and 1991, earned over $1.2 billion through licensing of their intellectual property. Honeywell, in the first quarter of 1992 earned $16.80 million and also made a historic settlement of $127 million with Minolta over a patent infringement suit on "autofocusing". Stanford University reported that one basic biotech patent will have earned them approximately $87 million in licensing fees by the time the patent expires in 1997.

In 1994–95, the US chemical industry experienced many litigations and settlements on patent-related issues. Mobil won $ 91 million from Amoco in a patent suit for violation of its three patents related to the production of paraxylene.

Genentech and EliLilly reached a settlement on the use of their mutual patents. Genetic Institute sued Orthopharmaceutical alleging infringement of a US patent on purified erythroprotein (EPO). Roche and Abott agreed to license each other's patents covering diagnostic applications on gene amplification technologies. Calgene exited the biotreatment market through a licensing deal with Sybron Chemicals, UK. Mosanto filed a suit against DNA Plant technology (DNAP) for infringing two of its patents related to the genetic engineering of crops. Similarly, Chiron's German and European Hepatitis C Virus (HCV) patents were granted by a District Court. The court discovered that two subsidiaries of International Murex Technologies infringed the patents by their sale of HCV immunoassays. Chiron, together with its joint diagnostic business partner, Ortho-Diagnostic System, filed a suit in the US against United Biomedical for infringing Chiron's US HCV patent. Another interesting aspect of this case is that a researcher named Daniel W. Bradley filed a suit against Chiron and Ortho-Diagnostic System to invalidate their US patent. Bradley claimed to be a co-inventor of the patent covering HCV immunodiagnostic tests. Chiron contested stating that Bradley had agreed to a settlement under which he had received payments and that he had surrendered the rights to any claims.

Patent opposition proceedings at the various patent offices have also been spiralling.

CASE STUDY

Eastman Kodak
VS
Polaroid

- In 1948, Erwin H. Land invented a camera that would develop a picture almost immediately after it was taken.
- The first film was made by Kodak for Polaroid.
- Instant camera technology had been developed largely by Polaroid, supported by a number of patents.
- Kodak entered into an agreement to produce the colour negative for Polaroid. The agreement lasted till 1969.
- In 1976 Kodak decided to move on its own into "instant" camera and film by working around the Polaroid patents.
- Immediately after Kodak entered the market in April 1976, Polaroid filed an infringement suit on Kodak for 12 of its instant camera patents.

- On 12 October, 1990 the court ordered Kodak to pay Polaroid $ 454,205,801 in compensation for the 10 years its instant camera products were in the market. An additional $ 455,251,766 was added on as interest. This was against Polaroid's demand of $ 13.5 billion as damages.
- Kodak moved out of the instant camera market.

In most countries, software is protected through copyrights and is considered as a "non-patentable" item. However, in the USA, patents have been issued for innovations in software. More than 3,200 software patents have been granted in the USA and the rate is continuously accelerating. Patentability of "software objects" and "object-oriented programming" has been an intensely debated subject. Infringements, litigations, challenging of claims, licensing, etc. are fairly common. The examples in Box 1.4 illustrate some of the issues and their impact on the information technology business. There have been a number of interesting settlements in this industry involving copyrights and patents.

Box 1.4 Examples of a few software-related cases

- Cadtrak Corporation, California was granted the US Patent No. 4197590 on computer screen display.
  Result : Anyone who wants to put a cursor on a computer screen either pays Cadtrak or gets into infringement problems.
  More than 300 hardware and software companies, including IBM, Texas Instruments, and Fujitsu pay royalties to Cadtrak to license the patent.
- The US Patent Nos. 4486857 and 4736308 were granted to Paul Heckel for developing a system which displays records or strings of information and then allows the operator to scroll or browse through them.
  Apple Computers was sued on the basis that their hypercard program infringed these patents.
  Result: Apple Computers took a license from Paul Heckel for the use of these patents for their products.

Source: The Patent Wars, Fred Warshofsky, John Wiley & Sons Inc., 1994.

Though India's copyright laws are on par with international laws, academic and business institutions are yet to exploit them fully. However, issues are now being addressed and sensitive areas discussed on television and other media.

Issues related to "information ownership in cyberspace" have surfaced in recent times but views on this subject are vague and uncertain. Clear-cut directions on copyright issues regarding "unlimited information, access/use", etc., are not available and are still under debate. Use of digitally procured information from virtual libraries, organized sharing of information, information repackaging, etc., will figure among the dominant issues needing serious readdressing. Disputes resulting from the unauthorized use and production of computer software, multimedia tools and distribution of pirated software and CD-ROMs, etc., have become hot subjects in international trade negotiations.

It is significant that both the examples cited in Box 1.4 are awards by non-Indian courts. The low patent awareness and concern coupled with a highly restricted patent regime and inadequate enforcement of patent rights in India have contributed to keeping patent-related activity at a negligible level. This is true of academic institutions, industry and even legal circles, including Indian courts.

Geographical indications

Article 22 entitled "Protection of geographical indications" deals with the following matters:

According to the TRIPS agreement, geographical indications are "indications which identify a good as originating in a territory of a member, or a region or locality in that territory, where a given quality, reputation or other characteristic of a good is essentially attributable to its geographical origin."

Some products which have been protected for their geographical identity are Champagne and Scotch whisky.

Business Line (Chennai, June 7, 1997) reported that the Agricultural Products Exports Development Authority (APEDA), India, won a suit against the US commodity firm Rice Tec. Inc. in Greece which had filed for registration of Texmati, Kasmati and Jasmati trademarks on rice varieties claimed to be analogs of the Basmati varieties grown in India. The decision in favour of India was taken by the statutory Trademark Authority Administrative Committee (TAAC) in Greece. A similar suit has also been filed by APEDA against Rice Tec. Inc., in the UK.

Experts have all along held that premium product's like Basmati rice, Darjeeling tea and Alphonso mangoes should be as "fiercely protected by India as Scotch whisky and Champagne wines are protected in their countries of origin".

Such issues will get raised at the WTO as one attains familiarity with the statutes governing them.

2

Patents in historical perspective

Protecting innovations — a retrospective

The nucleation and expansion of human settlements brought in the need for organized activity related to food collection, shelter, implements, etc. The structuring of such communities into "duty" or "responsibility" based groups or classes generated a system of evolution of skills within them. These skills were transferred from one generation to another essentially through hands-on experience and training, resulting in the process of "learning by doing". Initially, this "knowledge" or "skills base" was protected, as this knowledge was confined to a small group or class of people. With the formation of a number of settlements in different parts of the world, and improved mobility and communication, information and knowledge got transferred across these societies.

There were informal ways of recognizing and rewarding the innovators. Goods with novel features fetched higher returns and thus had more value. However the need for a formal system of assuring "protection" to inventors for their innovations was essential to encourage further technical developments, fair trade-practices and competition.

This need gave birth to a platform from which monarchs during the Middle Ages conferred rights and privileges to innovators (their subjects) by means of "open letters". These were documents on which the royal seal was not broken when they were opened. The public had access to these documents. The term "open letters" comes from the Latin term *litterae patentees*.

A brief history of patents

The exact origin of the patent system is not well established. There are reports of the introduction of a patent system around the fifteenth century in Italy. According to a published report (R. Baker, New and Improved British Library Board, UK, 8, 1976), the first patent known to be granted was to Filippo Brunelleschi in the Republic of Florence in 1421. He was given a three-year monopoly for his invention relating to special hoisting gear used on barges. Subsequently, an ordinance relating to patents was enacted in Venice in 1474. It is also recorded that one of the earliest patents in England was given to John of Utynam in 1449. He was granted a twenty year monopoly for developing a process for making stained glass.

From such unstructured beginnings, the patent system attained some formal status, and from time to time, systems with specific statutes got formalized in various countries. See Box 2.1.

The modern patent system was catalyzed with the onset of the industrial revolution, when exploitation of inventions for commercial benefits became fairly common. The patent system underwent changes to keep pace with the rapid advances in science and technology and the evolving international trade practices. This demanded that trading partners have a rational and harmonized patent system, which saw the setting up of various regionalized patent conventions such as the Paris Convention, the European Patent Convention, the Patent Cooperation Treaty(PCT), etc. The rapid advancement in various fields such as biotechnology, information technology, speciality materials, etc., is a result of an intense cross-fertilization of ideas from a number of fields. For example, cloning techniques use methods from chemistry, physics, computer sciences, engineering, etc. In view of this, it is becoming increasingly difficult to clearly identify what is "obvious" and/or "novel" while deciding on patentability criteria. In addition, issues on "morality and societal responsibility", and "religion" are emerging debates which are expected to influence matters related to IPR in due course.

As the number of innovations grew at a faster pace, covering a wider range, the demand for protection through "letters of patents" also grew. One had to then evolve a rationale for granting of such privileges to private individuals. The administrators had to consider a way of balancing the benefits of individual innovators with that of the state's interests. Hence conditions for "patentability" and

Box 2.1 Calendar of patents

• First introduced in the fifteenth century	Italy	
• First known grant by a "state" to an inventor	Republic of Florence	1421
• Patents Ordinance	Venice	1474
• Granting rights and privileges to inventors by Queen Elizabeth I	Great Britain	
• Statute of Monopolies proposing grant of exclusive rights to inventors for new inventions for a period of 14 years	Great Britain	1623

In 1623, Great Britain proposed granting exclusive rights for new inventions with a term of 14 years through an act of the Parliament, known as the Statute of Monopolies Act of 1623. It was only towards the end of the eighteenth century and during the nineteenth century that comprehensive patent statutes got formalized in various countries, including France and the USA.

Statutes on patents

USA	1770	Canadian Provinces (2)	1823/1826
France	1791	Mexico	1832
Netherlands	1809	Texas	1839
Austria	1810	Brazil	1840
Russia	1812	Chile	1846
Bavaria	1812	Great Britain	1852
Prussia	1815	India	1856
Sweden	1826		
Spain	1826		

In 1859 the law was introduced in the rest of Italy in stages up to 1870

Germany	1877

Source: The New Encyclopaedia Britannica, 15th edition, vol. 30, p. 1071.

monopoly were introduced. This brought in a system of refusing grant or monopoly to inventors unless the inventions were "new and were also not contrary to law".

The state-run patent systems as it has evolved, has a deeply rooted economic basis, provides a formal avenue for disclosure of new technology which is "novel", "useful" and "non-obvious" *vis-à-vis* what is known at that point in time, and gives the inventor a "monopoly" on it for a limited period.

3

Science and technology and IPR: The Indian context

The development of science and technology in India is closely linked to the rise and decline of advanced settlements since 2500 BC. Innovative approaches to unravelling the mysteries of nature and exploiting them for societal benefits are well documented in the archives related to the Harappan and Vedic cultures. However, "IPR" as a concept was never considered significant. With the introduction of western education in India by the British, the growth of science and technology made formal and institutional beginnings. Organizations, such as the Trigonometrical Survey of India, the Geological Survey of India and the Botanical Survey of India, were established largely to aid British rule. This was followed by the setting up of schools in physical sciences like chemistry, physics, biology and mathematics.

The basic elements of IPR were introduced in India with the framing of the Act on Protection of Inventions based on the British Patent Law of 1852 enacted in India in 1856.

Box 3.1 presents in chronological perspective the major stages in the development of Indian IPR.

Box 3.1 Calendar of events of Indian IPR

Patents

1856	The Act on Protection of Inventions based on the British Patent Law of 1852. Certain privileges granted to inventors of new manufactures for a period of 14 years.

Continues

Continued

1859	The Act modified as Act XV; patent monopolies called exclusive privileges (making, selling and using inventions in India and authorizing others to do so for 14 years from date of filing specification).
1872	The Patents & Designs Protection Act.
1883	The Protection of Inventions Act.
1888	Consolidated as the Inventions & Designs Act.
1911 – 47	The Indian Patents & Designs Act (under management of the Controller of Patents & Designs) came into force from 15 August, 1947.
1959	Justice Ayyangar Report.
1967	The Patent Bill introduced in Parliament.
1972	The Patents Act (Act 39 of 1970) came into force on 20 April, 1972.
1994	On 31 December, 1994, ordinance framed to amend the Patents Act, 1970 and the concept of exclusive marketing rights introduced as pipeline protection.
1995	Rejected by the Upper House in the Parliament on 23 March, 1995. Bill to be reintroduced by the Government.

Designs

Evolved to afford protection to textiles, linens, cottons, calicos and muslins.

Extended to patterns and prints made by modeling, casting or embossment or ornament or article of manufacture.

Concept of novelty introduced for use/publication prior to registration not allowed.

1872	The Patents & Designs Protection Act.
1888	Consolidated.
1911	The Indian Patents & Designs Act.
1970	The Indian Patents Act, 1970. The Designs Act of 1911 retained without changes.

Trademarks

1940	11 March, 1940 legislation for protection of the Trademarks Act; brought into force from 1 June, 1942.

Continues

Continued

	Prior to this, such protection was possible by a passing off action under the Indian law of torts based on the principles of the English common law relying on the guidelines of established British case laws.
1959	On 25 November, 1959, the Act of 1940 amended as the Indian Trade & Merchandise Marks Act, 1958.
1992	Amendments proposed for a "New Act" in line with internationally accepted norms. Debates continuing.
1994 – 95	The Amendment Bill, introduced in Parliament was passed by Lok Sabha (Lower House) but rejected by Rajya Sabha.

Copyrights

Closely associated with the British Copyright Law.

1914	Copy of the British Copyright Act of 1911 with suitable modification for British India.
1957	Adopted many principles of the British Copyright Act of 1956; came into force on 21 January, 1958 to cope with new problems in the law of copyright created by technological advances in the fields of communication, broadcasting, microfilming, photolithography, movies, cinemas and talkies.
1983	Amendments to availing the benefits arising from the revision of the Berne Convention and the Universal Copyright Convention to which India adheres.
1984	Amendments to discourage and prevent piracy prevailing in video film and records.
1992	Amendment to increase protection time to Author's lifetime + 60 years.
1994	Amendment to give effect to the obligations arising from the GATT. Copyright protection extended to new areas of creative work, including the computer industry. Special rights introduced to cover the performing arts.

The national R&D policies and their implementation has influenced the development of IPR in India. The Industrial Policy Resolution of 1950 focused on building an industrial base as well as a research system to support the industries. The science policy statement of 1958 stressed on the "internal development of science and technology for economic and political needs". Similarly, the basic objectives outlined by the technology policy statement of 1983 included the development of indigenous technology, and efficient absorption and adaptation of imported technology appropriate to national priorities and resources. The science and technology infrastructure was accordingly planned and implemented by setting up organizations such as the Department of Science and Technology (DST), the Council of Scientific and Industrial Research (CSIR), the Indian Council of Medical Research (ICMR), and the Indian Council of Agricultural Research (ICAR). Intermediary bodies such as the Department of Scientific and Industrial Research (DSIR), and the National Research Development Council (NRDC) were also set up to assist in the process of technology absorption and transfer, licensing agreements, and establishment of systems for efficient and smooth transfer of technology from various national/foreign institutions to the evolving industries in India.

A chronological history of IPR in India shows that the Indian laws in this respect were a direct fallout of the then existing British system. The Patents Act of 1970 was designed after an extensive review of the 1911 Act, specifically with respect to inventions which were not patentable in India. These changes were perceived by the policy makers to be more conducive to rapid industrialization and development of indigenous technology and at the same time fostering R&D activities in India in areas of national significance which would result in immediate import substitution. The strength or weakness of a country's system of intellectual property protection appears to have a substantial effect on the kind of technologies transferred, particularly in high technology industries. With India's joining the WTO in 1995, the context has again changed and the Patents Act of 1970 is due for revision.

However, protection of trademarks for products has been common in India and has remained the dominant IPR activity in the Indian industry.

In the wake of the open policy adopted by the Indian economy, organizations in India are now experiencing major restructuring. A pragmatic approach to IPR should underline this restructuring to make it more fetching. The formation of the WTO and India's liberalization process have already stimulated enhanced filing of patents in India.

The average of approximately 3,500 patents filed in a year increased to about 5,500 in 1995 and to about 8,000 in 1996. All associated activities such as patent opposition, enforcement, infringement/ revocation litigations, licensing, etc., will also gain momentum in due course.

It is, therefore, imperative that the entire process of patenting and its enforcement, including the possible changes to be introduced in the Indian Patents Act as a part of the harmonization program be appreciated by businessmen, educationists, scientists, engineers and administrators so that the patent system can be effectively exploited. This would enable incorporating IPR management into work systems and prove an encouraging reward to productive project working teams. Trademarks have been routinely used by industry in all parts of the world and hence its various facets are more widely familiar.

4

Patenting in India: An overview

The recent relaxation of tariff barriers has increased the flow of goods from various countries into the Indian market, thereby intensifying competition. If India has to survive this onslaught of global competition, she has to reinforce her inventiveness as well as strengthen and efficiently use the IPR system.

Patenting trends in India are illustrated in Figs. 4.1 to 4.5.

Source : Annual Reports of the Controller General of Patents, Designs and Trademarks (CGPDT). A few salient features to note are:

- The total number of filings in India is extremely low though there is a gradual increase since 1994. In most developed countries the average number of filings will exceed 10,000 per year. Japan stands out with over 300,000 patent filings every year.
- Approximately 80% of the patents filed in India are by foreigners.
- The number of patents in force (i.e. actually active and valid) has been spiralling down from approximately 30,000 in 1970 to below 10,000 in 1996. This indicates that a large number of patents are not being kept in force by payment of the annual fee.
- The number of patents filed and granted in foods is negligibly small.
- On an average, about 40% of the patents filed in chemicals get granted as compared to a rate of over 60% for foods, drugs, electrical and mechanical engineering, and general goods.

Further there is a big gap between the number of patents filed and granted in India.

These features need to be understood in terms of R&D activities in India and the prevailing IPR status.

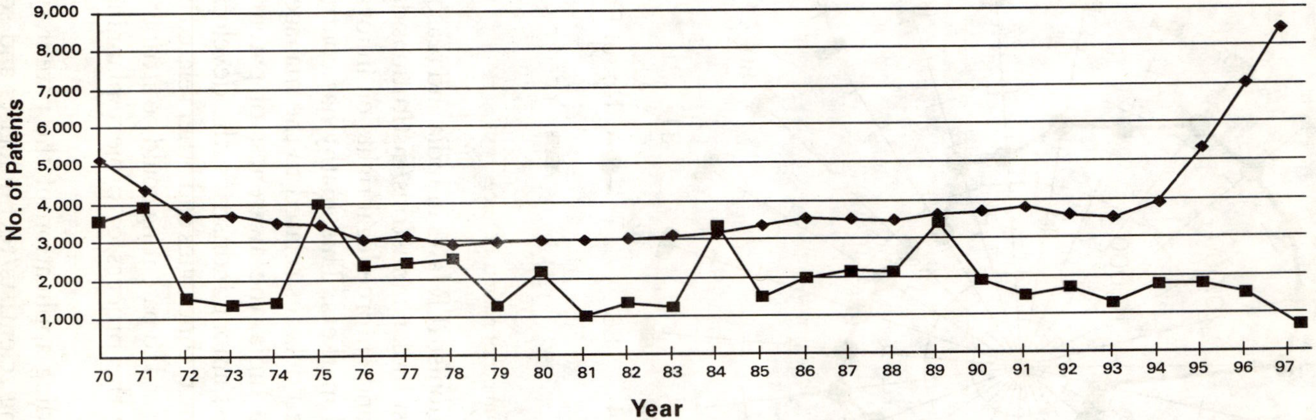

Year	Filed	Granted	Year	Filed	Granted	Year	Filed	Granted
70	5,142	3,532	79	2,932	1,281	88	3,457	2,104
71	4,345	3,923	80	2,980	2,173	89	3,598	3,380
72	3,659	1,510	81	2,954	1,019	90	3,661	1,890
73	3,639	1,342	82	2,989	1,357	91	3,764	1,491
74	3,491	1,416	83	3,085	1,227	92	3,552	1,676
75	3,406	3,944	84	3,145	3,319	93	3,467	1,272
76	2,996	2,320	85	3,319	1,469	94	3,869	1,746
77	3,104	2,390	86	3,526	1,951	95	5,330	1,759
78	2,870	2,514	87	3,489	2,126	96	7,036	1,533
						97	8,562	907

■granted ◆ filed

Fig. 4.1 Patenting in India—a profile

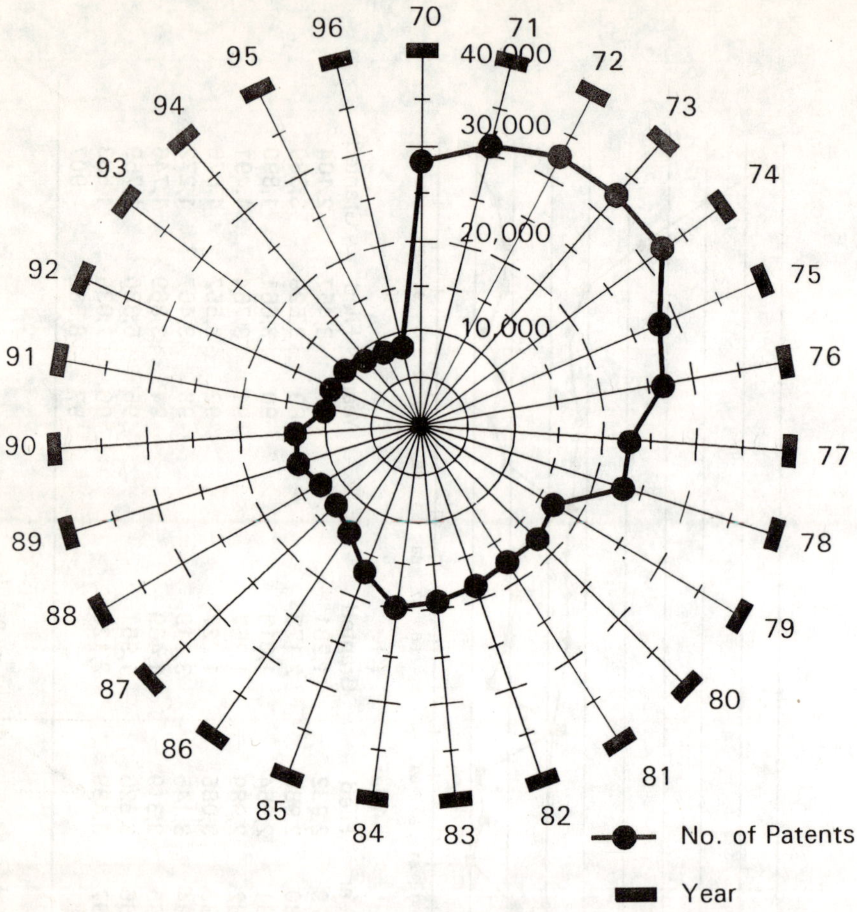

Fig. 4.2 Number of patents in force

In view of the over-protectionist IPR laws in India and reasonably assured internal markets, most Indian industries/institutions did not feel the pressure to protect and enforce legal rights on innovations and compete in the external markets. This apathy has continually raised a number of unresolved debates related to the management of science and technology in India, the awareness of patents and their use, the competitiveness among industries, the development and implementation of the new technologies and other related issues.

The apathy in India with regard to patenting could be attributed to:

- inadequate focus during the process of project planning and execution;
- the non-awareness regarding application of the patent system and its significance among scientists/technologists and science managers;

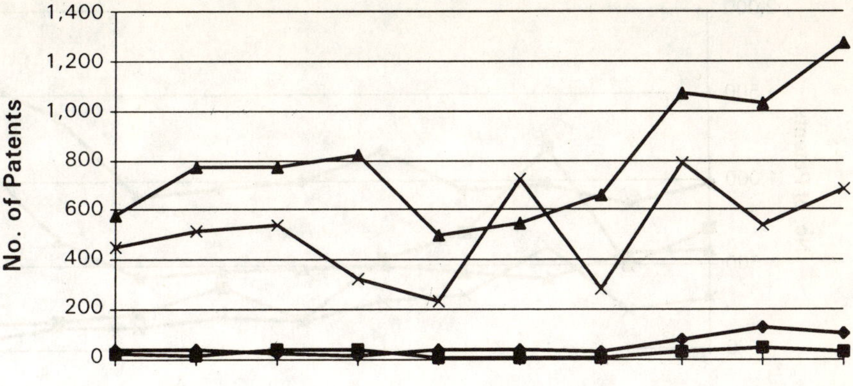

Year	1986–87	87–88	88–89	89–90	90–91	91–92	92–93	93–94	94–95	95–96
foods(fl)	34	39	21	13	41	38	29	82	125	104
foods (gr)	21	15	44	44	10	10	12	30	49	34
gen (fl)	579	772	772	821	502	544	659	1,071	1,030	1,268
gen (gr)	448	517	541	321	235	726	282	788	540	682

gen–general; fl–filed; gr–granted

Fig. 4.3 Patents filed and granted in foods and general

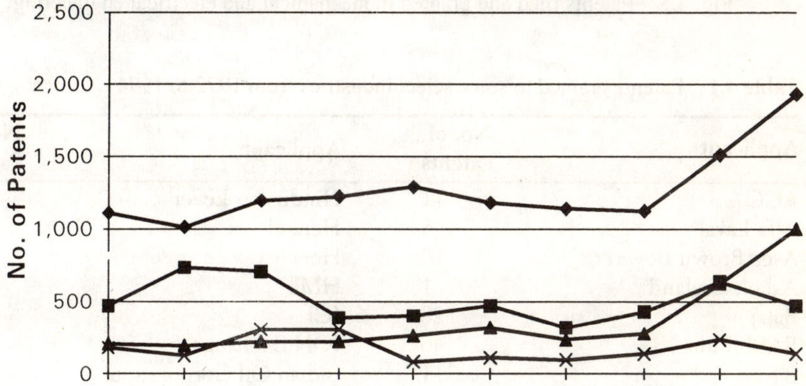

Year	1986–87	87–88	88–89	89–90	90–91	91–92	92–93	93–94	94–95	95–96
chem (fl)	1,112	1,020	1,191	1,225	1,297	1,185	1,138	1,122	1,516	1,934
chem (gr)	474	731	704	389	399	474	318	436	642	470
drug (fl)	214	198	221	216	258	323	234	273	629	1,000
drug (gr)	185	124	300	300	87	118	94	145	232	132

chem–chemicals; fl–filed; gr–granted

Fig. 4.4 Patents filed and granted in chemicals and drugs

- insufficient institutional infrastructure to support patenting, including non user-friendly patent information systems, etc.;
- restrictive patent laws as compared to many other nations;
- insufficient enforcement of patent rights.

Further, reading of patent literature has rarely found a place in our educational system.

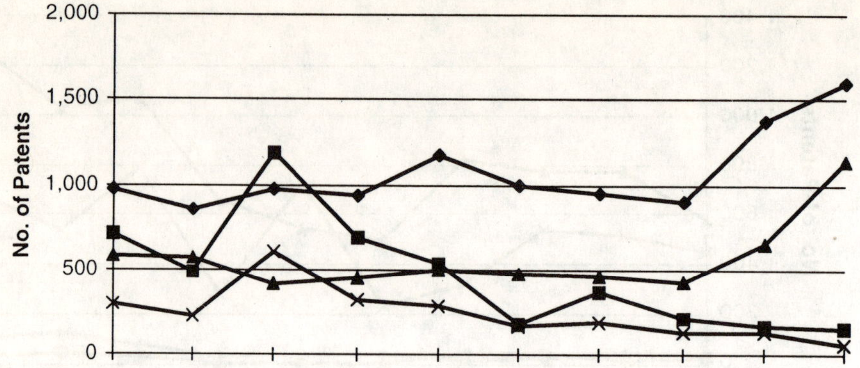

Year	1986–87	87–88	88–89	89–90	90–91	91–92	92–93	93–94	94–95	95–96
mech(fl)	972	847	974	932	1,173	994	946	895	1,377	1,599
mech (gr)	705	489	1,183	692	535	181	372	215	161	159
elc (fl)	577	563	419	454	492	468	461	426	653	1,131
elc (gr)	293	228	608	322	285	167	194	132	135	56

mech–mechanical; elec–electrical; fl–filed; gr–granted

Fig. 4.5 Patents filed and granted in mechanical and electrical engineering

Table 4.1 Patents granted to some select industries from 1972 to 1994

Applicant	No. of Patents	Applicant	No. of Patents
ACC	11	Hindustan Lever	435
Alfa Laval	5	Henkel	23
Asea Brown Boveri	10	Hoechst	547
Ashok Leyland	1	HMT	3
Bajaj	128	ICI	20
BASF India	46	ION Exchange	24
Bayer	311	Indian Oil Corporation	10
BHEL	122	Indian Petrochemicals	4
Britannia	1	Johnson & Johnson	66
Brooke Bond Lipton	4	Kirloskar	28
Castrol	4	Kimberley Clark	6
CIBA	150	Larsen & Toubro	38
Coca Cola	5	Lucas	399
Colgate–Palmolive	146	Nestle	92
Color Chem	7	Philips	17
Crompton Greaves	18	Pfizer	253
Cynamid India	7	Ranbaxy	4
Garware	3	SAIL	4
Glaxo	8	Sandoz	96
Godrej	7	SPIC	10
General Foods	19	TATA	31

Source : *Indian Patents Database* (INPAT)

A scan of the patents granted in India to various firms from 1972–94 (see Table 4.1) reinforces the point that major players in the patenting scene in India have been transnational companies. Even very successful Indian companies dealing with drugs, chemicals, consumer products, etc., have not patented the results of their R&D activities. Public sector undertakings in spite of their elaborate R&D facilities and manpower, have so far not taken to patenting in any significant way. Defence and space research comprise a substantial part of national expenditure in India. Though they have made notable innovations, these institutions have not considered it necessary to patent their achievements. This is in sharp contrast to the attitude of the corresponding government departments in USA, who have pro-actively patented their innovations and continually reaped commercial benefits from them. However, new trends are setting in with a few Indian companies initiating their Patents Activities in the last two years.

India has a chain of 40 laboratories under the CSIR. One of the objectives of the CSIR is to tackle applied problems and establish capability and generate technological know-how across a wide spectrum of science and technology areas to assist Indian industry in technology development. The CSIR is also expected to evolve technologies which finally can find their way into industry through effective technology transfer schemes. Patenting trends of the CSIR from 1983 to 1994 are shown in Fig. 4.6. The contribution of some laboratories is also presented. The number of patents filed by the CSIR laboratories started increasing after 1988–89. Patents from the CSIR laboratories working in chemicals, materials and pharmaceuticals have registered a noticeable increase. This increase coincides with a shift in the CSIR policy, which required that the laboratories earn a significant portion of their budgets through research sponsored by industries.

Recent policy changes in the CSIR are directed at inducing the laboratories to create a favourable climate and attract industrial sponsorships or even "sponsored collaborations" so that the pace of technology development and transfers is enhanced. Recently, the CSIR has also formulated its IPR policy and widely publicized it among its laboratories. A number of Indian and foreign companies have already signed Memorandums of Understanding (MoUs) with the CSIR for joint activities. Patentable inventions are expected to increase and the patent filing scores will improve as a consequence.

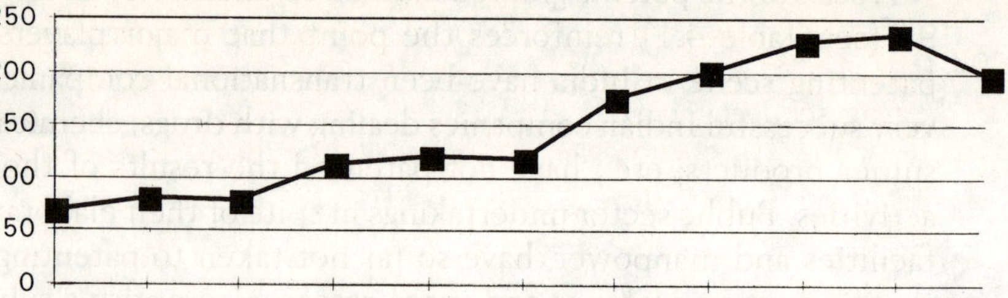

NUMBER OF PATENTS GRANTED TO SELECTED LABS

	1983–84	84–85	85–86	86–87	87–88	88–89	89–90	90–91	91–92	92–93	93–94
CDRI	14	5	3	15	11	6	8	16	34	21	12
CECRI	1	11	6	7	9	12	10	20	23	33	10
ICT	2	5	3	7	4	3	14	11	12	6	10
NCL	10	12	13	8	20	26	39	41	56	42	49
NML	4	3	11	6	3	14	15	25	12	16	9
RRL(BHU)	7	11	4	13	8	3	9	5	7	10	4
RRL(JT)	2	2	3	7	16	3	5	6	12	21	10
■ TOTAL	69	82	79	113	120	119	175	202	230	232	196

The graph refers to the total number of patents granted to the CSIR

Fig. 4.6 CSIR patenting trend

The NRDC, a corporation under the DSIR, has also started helping Indian firms and other institutions to file patents abroad. In 1992–93, they had only three foreign filings while in 1994–95 they totalled 40.

India's exports of software items, pharmaceutical, primary commodities such as tea, coffee, sugar, rice and wheat, fruits, processed foods and engineering goods are also going up gradually. Apart from delivering quality products and services, protecting innovations through the appropriate IPR tools will be essential for competitiveness in the global market.

Global R&D has to respond to the phenomenon of "compressing the process of innovation into even shorter time-frames".

Today the reality is:

- As one technology is announced, often a successor with improved benefits is already anticipated or realized.
- Knowledge and patents have become necessary to establish market dominance.

Research efforts in Indian institutions need to be innovative with a focus on simultaneously creating dominance through well-coordinated collaborative working between the academic institutions and commercial organizations. This will require a reorientation, ensuring comprehensive technology planning supported by an efficient process of technology mapping, and forecasting. A strong patent information system and a rigorous patenting infrastructure will have to back up these efforts.

Building IPR management into project working

Proper management of the patent portfolio can be of significant commercial advantage to any organization. To incorporate IPR management and innovation strategy into company policy requires:

- mapping prior knowledge;
- identifying protected zones;
- evaluating vulnerability of barriers raised via claims;
- evolving bypasses;
- formulating research proposals and work plans;
- competitor monitoring;
- planning oppositions; blocking moves;
- collaboration if necessary, e.g., cross-licensing of patents;

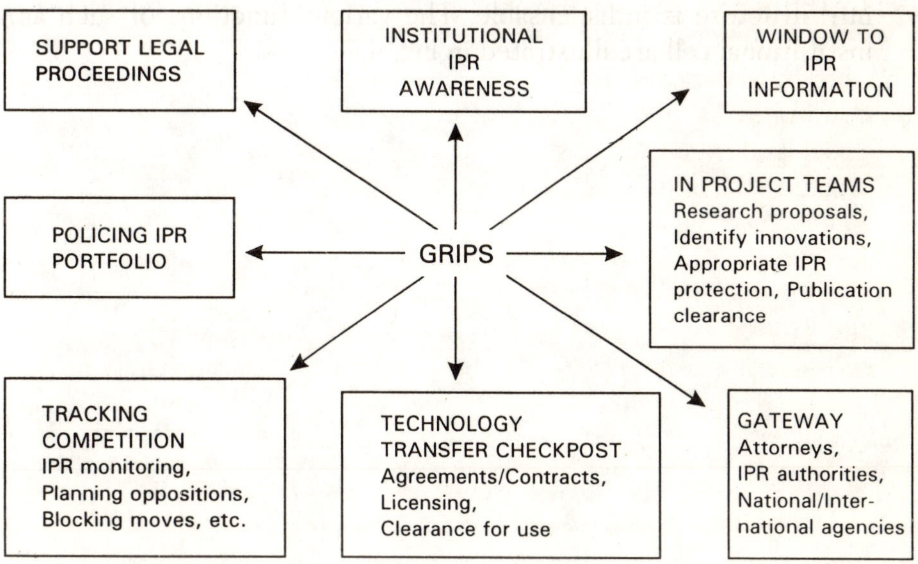

Fig. 4.7 Group Intellectual Property Services (GRIPS)

- geographical areas for coverage, strategic alliances/collaborations to exploit expertise/facilities, cost-optimization and the number of patents in force.

The number of patents filed and granted and in force shows that in the last 25 years patenting as a tool has not been effectively used in India unlike other industrially developed countries. The Patents Act, 1970 which came into effect in April 1972 had a significant impact on the number of patents filed and granted after 1972. The numbers have declined since 1970 and 1971. Over the years there has been a systematic fall in the number of patents that have been renewed, reflecting the low confidence in the Indian Patent System. In 1995, there were only about 10,000 patents in force in India. However, with India signing the GATT and simultaneously opening up its economy, the trends are already changing.

A host of new questions and problems will emerge on how to deal with "sponsored collaborations" between academic institutions, funded research organizations and industries, especially with respect to decisions on issues related to ownership of the "fruits of joint activities". Lessons from systems prevailing in other countries should help to evolve an appropriate mode of managing these issues.

In this dynamic state of flux an institutionalized patent support infrastructure is indispensable. The various functions of such an institutional cell are illustrated in Fig. 4.7.

5

Indian Patent Office: Structure and jurisdiction

Patents, designs and trademarks in India are the charge of the Controller General of Patents, Designs and Trademarks (CGPDT) functioning under the control of the Department of Industrial Development, Ministry of Industry. The Ministry of Human Resources is in charge of the Copyright Board.

Figure 5.1 presents the structure and jurisdiction of the Indian Patent Office and Indian Trademark Office which are under the CGPDT.

The institutions located in states/union territories falling within the jurisdiction of a zonal branch are required to file their patents in the respective branch offices. For example, the CSIR has its Registered Office in Delhi. Therefore, all the constituent laboratories of CSIR fall under the jurisdiction of the Delhi Branch of the Patent Office. Thus, the application for patents originating from the CSIR are filed at the Patent Office Branch in Delhi. Similarly, a company which has its registered office in the western region is required to file all its applications for patents at the Mumbai Branch of the Patent Office. Organizations registered in the south, fall within the jurisdiction of the Chennai Branch and those registered in the eastern part of the country, at the Calcutta Patent Office. All patent prosecutions, (i.e. examination of the patent by patent examiners) and oppositions have to be filed at the office in which the application for the patent has been filed.

The Head Office in Calcutta has additional exclusive responsibilities. They include;

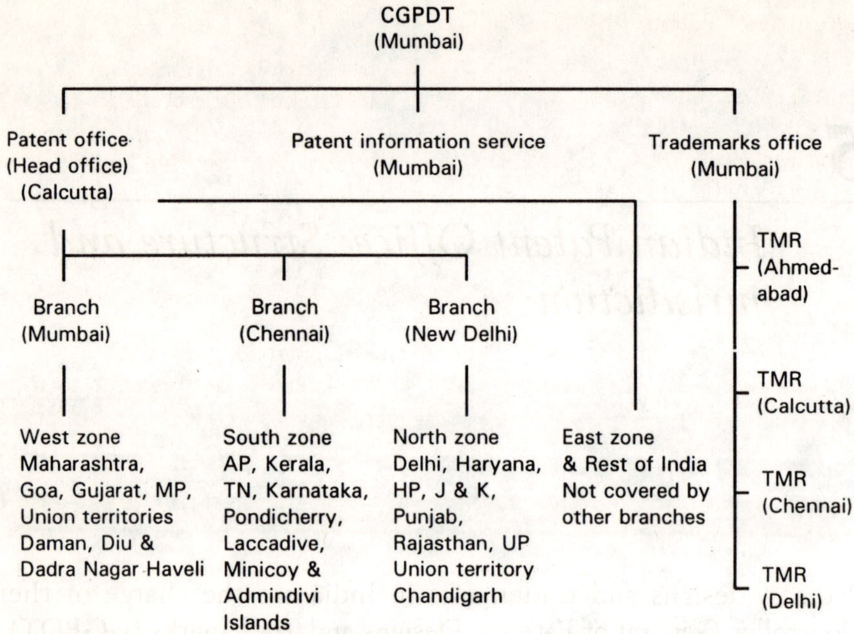

Fig. 5.1 Jurisdiction of Indian Patent Office and Indian Trademark Office

- granting and sealing of patents;
- amendment of patents granted to deceased applicants;
- power of the Controller to give directions to co-owners;
- grant of the patent to the true and first inventor where it has been obtained by another by fraud;
- application for restoration of lapsed patents;
- revocation of patents or amendment of complete specifications on directions from the Central Government in cases pertaining to atomic energy;
- registration of assignments, transmission, etc.;
- making entries in the register of patent agents;
- providing information pertaining to patents when formally requested;
- loss or destruction of patents.

The activities listed above are well defined in the various sections of the Indian Patents Act, 1970. Infringement or revocation proceedings are within the jurisdiction of the High Courts. However, the decisions on revocation or any amendment of specification issued by the court have to be implemented at the Patent Office. All revoked patents are to be entered in the Register of Patents at the Calcutta Head Office.

Addresses of Patent Offices in India

1. The Controller of Patents,
   The Patent Office Branch,
   Todi Estates, III Floor,
   Lower Parel (West),
   Mumbai 400 013.
   Telefax : (022) 4925094
   Telephone : (022) 4924058 & 4925092

2. The Controller of Patents,
   The Patent Office (Head Office),
   "Nizam Palace",
   2nd M.S.O. Bldg.,
   5th, 6th and 7th Floor, 234/4,
   Acharya Jagdish Bose Road,
   Calcutta 700 020.
   Telefax : (033) 2473851
   Telephone : (033) 2474401

3. The Controller of Patents,
   The Patent Office Branch,
   Unit No. 401 to 405, III Floor,
   Municipal Market Building,
   Saraswathi Marg, Karol Bagh,
   New Delhi 110 005.
   Telefax : (011) 5716204
   Telephone : (011) 5716209

4. The Controller of Patents,
   The Patent Office Branch,
   61, Wallajah Road,
   Chennai 600 002.
   Telefax : (044) 841014
   Telephone : (044) 845324

Other offices dealing with patent-related activities

Patent Information System,
3rd Floor, Block "C",
CGO Complex, Seminary Hills,
Nagpur 400 006.
Telefax : (0712) 528186
Telephone : (0712) 525670

Office of the Controller General of
Patents, Designs & Trademarks,
101, Maharishi Karve Road,
Mumbai 400 020.
Telefax : (022) 2053372
Telephone : (022) 2039050

The Address of the Copyright Board
Copyright Board,
Ministry of Human Resources Development,
West Block No. 2, Wing No. 6, Sector 6,
R. K. Puram, New Delhi 110 066.

6

Patents: Some basics

A patent may be defined as a grant by a sovereign or state to an inventor or to his assignee giving exclusive rights to make, use, exercise and vend the innovation for a limited period in exchange for disclosing it in a patent specification. This gives the owner the right to exclude others from using the invention. It is relevant here to introduce the concept of a "qualified right".

Qualified right

A qualified right enables the owner to exclude others from using his invention, but does not necessarily give him the right to practise the invention. To elucidate, let us consider the following example. Suppose a patent has been granted to an invention of a four-legged chair. Then, any subsequent improvement on it, such as converting it into a rocking chair could also be patented, but the inventor of the rocking chair would not have the ability to practise his invention as it would infringe the rights of the owner of the chair's patent. Consider another example, for instance an invention related to the "ball" of the ballpoint pen. The owner of the patent for the ballpoint pen would not be able to practise his invention as he would need ink for the pen, which could have been patented by someone else. In the same way, the owner of the patent for the ink would not be able to practice his invention without infringing the patent on the ballpoint pen.

To summarize, the main feature of a qualified right includes the granting of a patent, but, does not automatically give the owner the right to use the invention.

However, a patent is no substitute for statutory approvals such as:

- registration for medicines;
- permission from the authorities to build a plant, or even;
- a license from another inventor.

For example, one may have a patent with respect to a drug granted to him. Though he now has the patent rights, he cannot introduce the drug into the market without procuring other statutory clearances from the FDA, registering the medicine, etc. Similarly, a patent may be granted to an inventor for some innovation related to a chemical process or equipment. If practising the invention would require some statutory clearances, for example, pollution/safety clearances, they have to be obtained from the appropriate authority. Any license if required (refer the ballpoint example) from another inventor must be obtained before putting one's invention into practice.

The purpose of patenting is to enable one to build upon the inventions of others and thereby advance the state of technology in countries having a patent system.

National rights

Patents are national rights and there is no such thing as a "world patent", or an "international patent" in the true sense of the term.

Although there is nothing like an "international patent", a Patent Cooperation Treaty (PCT) application is called an "international application". Therefore patents must be applied for in each of the countries where one seeks to have the innovation protected. The right accrues only when the patent is granted. A brief discussion on the EPC and PCT is given in Chapter 15 on Harmonization of patent systems.

The following are the major prerequisites for patenting in India:

- Invention must be new, i.e. not previously published in India or elsewhere.
- Should be new/non-obvious with respect to "prior art".
- Not previously used in India.
- Invention must be useful.

Non-patentable inventions

There are many categories of "non-patentable" inventions. Their selection varies from nation to nation depending on the state of industrial and technological progress. However, the recently concluded GATT attempts to harmonize and set a few minimum guidelines which its members are expected to follow. Box 6.1 gives a list of such non-patentable categories.

Box 6.1 What is non-patentable in India?

- Frivolous claims contrary to well-established natural laws.
- Anything contrary to law or morality, or injurious to public health.
- Mere arrangement or rearrangement or duplication of known devices, each functioning independently of one another in a known way.
- A method or process of testing applicable during the process of manufacture for rendering the machine, apparatus or other equipment more efficient or for the improvement or restoration of the existing machine, apparatus or other equipment or for the improvement or control of manufacture.
- A method of agriculture or horticulture.
- Inventions related to atomic energy.
- Computer software.
- Aesthetic creations.
- Discoveries, scientific theories, mathematical methods.
- Schemes, rules or methods for performing mental acts playing games or doing business.
- Presentations of information.
- Methods of treating humans or animals through surgery, or therapeutical diagnostics.
- Animals and plants, and biological methods for rearing/growing them. (However, micro-organisms are patentable in India).
- Products made by chemical synthesis—foods, medicines.

Proper enforcement of patents in any society demands a national system which promotes innovation and has provisions to punish infringers.

"Invention" as per the Indian Patents Act, 1970 includes any new and useful :

- art, process, method or manner of manufacture;
- machine, apparatus or other article;
- substances produced by manufacture, including any new and useful improvements of any of them and an alleged invention.

Not all inventions are patentable even if they are new, non-obvious and useful. In general, the non-patentable items include discoveries, principles, mathematical methods, presentation of information, mere schemes or plans, literary, dramatic, musical or artistic work. There are a number of requirements for patenting. In India, as in many other countries, under the Patents Act, certain classes of inventions are not considered patentable. These Special Provisions of the Indian Patents Act which outline the type of inventions not patentable are described in Chapter 7.

What is patentable ?

Thus, "art", "process", method or "manner of manufacture" must relate to the making of something which could be a substance, an article, or a machine. It can utilize known principles, substances, equipment, etc., but ultimately the "invented process" must result in either a "more efficient" or a "cheaper" way of making the material or could even lead to a "purer" product or "more useful" end result. In most cases, inventions are "incremental improvements" of existing practices or products but to be patentable they must satisfy the basic requirements stated above. The following example would illustrate the meaning of the term "invention" within the framework of a patent.

The example considered is a simple item of everyday use—an umbrella. Even this seemingly simple device has been a very popular subject of patents the world over. In the case of an umbrella, innovations can be made in various ways to enhance its utility as a device for protection against rain/sun. The practical problems in its use relate to the mutually conflicting requirements of:

- firmness, strength and resistance;
- compactness;
- rapid and reliable capability to be opened when needed.

In addition, one can create improvements with extended useful applications which are new and non-obvious with respect to the prior art in that field. Such innovations can be patented if they satisfy all the tests of patentability. Examples satisfying such criteria are numerous:

- Extraction of specific ingredients from naturally occurring materials such as minerals from ores, compounds (pure or mixtures) from naturally occurring sources such as plants/ microbes/animals.
- Drying of substances by various means: the drying process could produce the article/substance without altering its desired characteristics. At the same time it could enhance the products shelf-life, use less energy or raw materials or reduce losses during manufacture, or merely convert it into a semi-processed form. Examples of this can be found in the process for drying of polymers, food ingredients, silicas, cement, etc. In the case of silicas/zeolites, for instance, the invented drying process may ensure retention of the particle size distribution, particle shapes, porosity, bulk density, as they influence the functional features of such materials. There are a number of patents covering the drying of milk, soup formulations, etc., to obtain useful products with enhanced dispersion, solubility, retention of texture, taste, and flavour.

An invention does not have to arrive at a "complete" manufacturing process or even disclose a "complete technology" to be patentable. Any manufacturing process is normally a combination of a number of steps/unit processes. There could be innovations in one or many of the steps such as in "conveying the raw materials to a reacting chamber," "mixing of the ingredients," "arriving at optimum conditions of the reaction/mixing", "ways of isolating/separating products" or creating favourable "conditions" for taking the reaction to completion for best yields, purity, or conveying the desired product into packing lines, etc. The invention may address any one or a combination of these steps but to be patentable it must satisfy the criteria mentioned earlier.

Thus, different components of a "complete" manufacturing process may be protected by a number of patents and most often not necessarily owned by the same set of inventors. In such a case, the person who develops the "complete" technology may have to take licences from the owners of these patents to utilize their inventions as part of his "total technology package" depending on how he utilizes them.

At this stage, it would be useful to study a patent to appreciate some of the features discussed here. Appendix I has been included as an example. A reading of this patent will help the reader to get a feel of the type of information that is included in a patent.

Who can apply for patents ?

- First and true inventor of the invention.
- An assignee of the first and true inventor.
- Legal representative of any deceased person who was entitled to make such an application before his death.
- The true and first inventor can have others as joint applicants (see Box 6.2.)

Box 6.2 Inventor

- In all countries except USA, the first to file is entitled to a patent; who first invented is not the criteria.
- A consideration in USA—first to invent is entitled to a patent; who first filed is not a consideration.
- Proper maintenance of records in chronological order in an accepted format is essential to establish inventorship.

Selection patent

When considering a patentable subject matter it is quite possible that a complete class of materials/compounds or mixtures have been disclosed in open literature or in previous patents. However, if in later studies, one identifies specific innovations in terms of positive and definitive advantages within the class or sub-class, this may qualify for a "selection patent". There are well-laid down criteria to decide whether the "claim" for the selection patent is justified or not.

Some of the key questions with regard to selection patents are:

- Does the prior art disclose the subject matter in any way so that the "selection" becomes obvious and does not qualify as an invention?
- Is there a clear advantage or usefulness in the selection over the prior art?

While drafting a selection patent one has to be very careful not to impinge on a patent in the prior art with fairly broad claims. This could lead to an infringement when the patent is practised. Thus while filing an application for a selection patent it is necessary to provide strong evidence by appropriate experimentation to differentiate the invention clearly from the closest prior art. Such claims should be very tightly drafted to be a true selection of the existing broad protection claimed by the prior art.

CASE STUDY

Ethyl Corporation (Cooks) vs Chevron Research Company

This is a well-known judgment in the opposition of Ethyl Corporation (Cooks) Patent by Chevron Research Company (1970 RPC, pp. 227–233) in UK.

In the opposition proceedings, the Examiner upheld a prior claiming objection against certain claims relating to a tetramethyl lead antiknock composition comprising *inter alia* ethylene (or propylene) dibromide, the position being that ethylene dibromide was referred to in the body of the cited patent containing similar compositions. The Examiner however held that the objection was not made out against a claim for such a composition which included hydrocarbons in a limited range of 10 to 15 % by weight; this range falling within the range of the earlier patent. The applicants (Ethyl Corporation) contended that it was clearly alleged in their specification that the range claimed by them had a great advantage over anything disclosed in the cited specification, and that they should be given rights to this selection.

Chevron appealed against the Examiner's decision.

The Patents Appeal Tribunal agreed with the Examiner's views and decided in favour of Ethyl Corp, as the judge observed that the range of 10 to 15% by weight in Specification No. 946268 has great advantage over anything disclosed by the prior patentee in his Specification No. 941742.

The earlier patent had disclosed an example with the use of hydrocarbon as low as 16.6%, but no emphasis was placed on the figure as giving a cost and effectiveness advantage alleged by Application No. 949268, in which they claimed a slightly lower range of 10 to 15%.

The judges commented: ". . . The earlier patentee clearly did not appreciate that there was a range of 10 to 15%, where the cost and effectiveness advantages were outstanding and that if he had appreciated it, he could not have failed to have mentioned it and given an example in that range."

Ethyl Corporation was awarded a selection patent. (This case is summarized in Appendix II.)

This illustrates the point that inadequate disclosure in a patent specification can be of disadvantage in a competitive world. Thus drafting must take into consideration all aspects of the invention.

Patent of addition

Patent of addition can be claimed on an "improvement" or a "modification" of a "main patent" which is already granted and is in force by payment of renewal fees or is even pending acceptance. This provision gives the patentee of the main patent the opportunity to seek protection on additional features invented subsequently but, on evaluation of patentability, does not meet all the requirements for an independent patent. In other words, an improvement over an existing invention of the same source which is usual but not inventive can be covered under the "patent of addition". For that reason, the term of a patent of addition is linked with the main patent.

The application for a patent of addition can be made:

- only by the applicant who has also been the applicant for the main patent;
- any time before the expiry of the main patent.

The main features of a patent of addition are:

- the Fee must be paid on grant;
- the term ends with that of the main patent;
- if the main patent is in force no renewal fee is required for the patent of addition;
- validity of the patent of addition is not affected if the main patent is revoked. In this case the patent of addition can be converted to an independent patent.

Where, however, the improvement or modification is itself inventive, it is advisable to go for a regular patent rather than a patent of addition. Where again the improvement, whether inventive or not, comes into being at a point of time when the main patent application is unpublished, one should opt for a regular patent. In the regular patent the claims should be carefully drafted such that there is no overlap with the earlier patent.

Let us look at an example of a main patent and a patent of addition. (Specifications in Appendices IIIa and IIIb.)

Patent No. 170499 was filed on 18-06-90 under the Application No. 157/Bom/1990 and was accepted on 04-04-92. The title was "An improved composite indentation hardness tester with built-in base for rubber and the like substances such as soft or hard plastics and textile wound packages." As this was being examined at the Mumbai Patent Office, a patent of addition with the same title under the Application No. 354/Bom/1991 was filed on 29-11-91. This was accepted and published on 11-12-93 and was given the Patent No. 172840. The abstract of the patent of addition reads as follows:

> "An improved indentation hardness tester with built - in base for rubber and the like substances as claimed in my Main Patent No. 170499 dated 18-06-90 the improvement/modification being in replacing the simple clamping pressure spring (11), working in compression by two or more spiral springs (14) provided vertically, in between the top base (5) and the flange of the bush (12), to give constant load of buckling at all the stages of pressure thereby assuring an absolute constant clamping load on the specimen."

The main patent application described only one spiral spring and with this arrangement it was observed that absolute constant clamping load on the specimen was not possible, as the load goes on increasing with compression of the spring and to achieve the desired load on the fixed value, a mechanical stopper such as a setting nut is to be used. This made the hardness tester cumbersome, costly and also created calibration problems. The invention in the patent of addition overcame these problems.

A patent of addition has both advantages and disadvantages. The advantage is that even small improvements which are new and useful, though lacking in inventiveness *vis-à-vis* one's own earlier main patent on the same invention, can be protected. The disadvantage is that the term of the patent expires with that of the main patent even though the patent of addition was granted at a later date than the main patent.

By formulating the appropriate patenting strategy on what should be covered in a master patent (which is normally the broadest) and subsequent innovations either by further patents with narrower claims or through selection patents or patent of addition, one can plan the breadth, type and period of protection one is seeking in the fields of research and business.

Priority date

Priority date of a patent is the date on which the first patent application is made in India or anywhere else in the world subject to the countries notified as "Convention Countries" by the Central Government. It is a very important "date" as many patent-related issues are decided based on it.

Some of the important aspects of a priority date are stated below:

- This is the first date on which the inventor makes a disclosure of his invention to the patent office.
- From this date the inventor can put the invention into practice or even make a public disclosure through conferences, publications, etc. The product can also carry the notification "patent applied", "patent pending", etc.
- The state of knowledge, i.e. prior art, prior to that date will be considered while deciding on the novelty of the invention.

In many countries, their national patent laws may require that inventions made in that country must be first filed nationally before being filed in other countries. The "conventions"allow a period of twelve months from the priority date to file the same patent in the other member countries of the convention.

The patentee can use the invention after the "priority date" in any of the convention countries and also file a patent in these countries within twelve months of the first filing without affecting the novelty of the invention.

Prior to the WTO, India had reciprocity arrangements with UK, Australia, Ireland, Sri Lanka, New Zealand and Canada. As per this arrangement, these countries offered to applicants for patents in India or to citizens of India, similar privileges which are granted to their own citizens in respect of the grant of patents and protection of patent rights.

However, with the formation of the WTO from 1 January, 1996, and a special notification by the government, the term "members" of the convention countries has been broadened to include all the countries which are members of the WTO. Thus applicants from all these countries can take advantage of the "priority date" while filing "convention applications" in India. Similarly inventors in India can take advantage of the "priority date" of the Indian filing and plan their patent filings in other countries. One can also plan product launches in the WTO countries immediately after first filing the patent in India. (A list of the convention countries is given in Appendix VI.)

As per this convention, an applicant in any one of these countries can file a convention patent application within 12 months of filing the first patent application in any one of the convention countries and retain the priority of the first application. In actual practice this means the following:

If someone has filed a patent in USA in June 1995 then the person can file a patent application in India till May 1996 claiming the US priority date. Thus even if the product or process has been exploited or made public in USA after filing the patent in USA and before filing the patent in India, this will not interfere with the priority of the patent application in India.

India is a member of the World Intellectual Property Organization (WIPO) and of the WTO but not of the Paris Convention. Hence a patent first filed in India cannot be filed as a PCT application in any of the Paris Convention countries using the priority of the Indian patent application. Similarly, a PCT application cannot be filed in India using the PCT priority.

It should also be noted that all patent applications in India by foreigners need not be convention applications. An applicant may choose to file a patent in India without claiming the priority of the first filing in a convention country. In such a case, the application is given a date as per the Indian filing. Under these circumstances, it is essential to ensure that the invention has not become public in any form anywhere or been exploited in India before the filing of the patent in India to satisfy the novelty requirements of the Indian Patents Act.

The significance of the priority date may be understood as follows:

- Mr X has filed a patent, say, on 01-01-96 in India. The priority date for this patent is then 01-01-96.
- He can then proceed to publish a scientific paper, present papers, disclosing the invention from this priority date.
- The invention can also be exploited (process put into practice, product marketed or even publicly tested) in India or in any of the convention countries (USA, UK, etc.) without its novelty being affected.

- The same patent should be filed in the other WTO Convention countries (USA, UK, etc.) within 12 months, i.e., up to 31-12-96 without affecting its novelty.
- Mr X should however be careful to check whether he has business interests *in any country other than those included in the WTO list*, for example, China or Switzerland, etc. In such cases, patent applications should be filed in these non-convention countries before the said patent application is published anywhere.
- Similarly if Mr X finds someone practising the same invention in any of the convention countries after his priority date, he can bring to the notice of the alleged infringer that a patent has already been filed. Such a notice could be the starting point of negotiating licensing agreements between the parties which could significantly save time and cost of litigations that may arise at a later date after the patent is granted.
- The inventor during these twelve months known as the "convention period", can also negotiate joint ventures by making full disclosures of the invention without the fear of being strangled by provisions concerning "anticipation" affecting the novelty criteria for patentability.

In view of these and many other advantages, it is important to file a patent for any invention at the earliest to retain one's priority. No public disclosures of the invention in the form of announcements, publishing papers, conference proceedings, advertisements, market trials, etc., should be done before filing the provisional specification to avoid problems of such actions being considered as prior art. It is always recommended that the consumer panel which is selected for any trials should be bound by a formal secrecy agreement.

A mandatory requirement under the Patents Act is that the applicant undertakes to disclose details of "prosecution" of corresponding foreign applications of the patent filed in India by the applicant. All relevant details of the foreign application, including the serial no., date of filing, and the name of the country, are to be disclosed. Up to the date of acceptance of the application in India, the patentee is also expected keep the Controller informed from time to time of the prosecution status and details of the foreign applications.

As patents have a definite life, they have to be kept alive in every country by payment of a prescribed annual fee. Failure to pay such a fee can lead to lapse of rights on the patent. Patents, like other assets, can be licensed, sold, mortgaged, etc. (See Box 6.3.)

Box 6.3 Patent as an asset

PATENT =	PROPERTY (e.g. House)
Use	Live
Sell	Sell
License	Rent
Mortgage	Mortgage
Abandon	Abandon

It should be appreciated that the term (life) of a patent in India is well defined with respect to the "date of the patent". In some categories the term is also measured with respect to the "date of sealing" of the patent. For an invention claming that the method/or process of manufacture of a substance whose intended use is or is capable of being used as food/medicine or drug:

- the term of the patent is five years from the date of sealing the patent or seven years from the date of the patent, whichever period is shorter; for all the other inventions the term is 14 years from the date of the patent;
- the date of the patent is the date on which the complete specification is submitted;
- the date of sealing is the date when the patent is sealed by the Controller and the entry is made in the Register of Patents at the Head Office in Calcutta. (See Box 6.4.)

Box 6.4 How to keep patents alive?

- To keep patents in force, a yearly fee has to be paid.
- The fee goes up with the age of the patent.
- Failure to pay fees within the prescribed time leads to lapse of the patent.
- Patents cannot be renewed at the end of their lifetime when they lapse.
- The patent then becomes open to all and can be used by anyone without the fear of infringement.

7

Special Provisions of the Indian Patents Act, 1970

Over and above what has been listed in terms of patentable/non-patentable inventions, it should be appreciated that the Indian Patents Act, 1970 further limits the type of inventions that can be patented in India. These are defined in Sections 3 and 5 of the Act. (See Boxes 7.1 and 7.2.)

Box 7.1 Section 3 of the Indian Patents Act, 1970

Section 3 of the Indian Patents Act, 1970 stipulates that inventions are non-patentable if they are:

- a mere new property or a new use of a known thing;
- a mere admixture resulting in aggregation of properties or process of producing it;
- a process for medicinal, surgical, curative, prophylactic or other treatment of human beings, animals and plants to render them free from diseases or to increase their economic value or that of their products.

The Government of India by a notification (Ministry of Health Notification No.1-20/60-D dated 03-06-61) specifies the following substances as non-patentable:

Box 7.2 Section 5 of the Indian Patents Act, 1970

As per Section 5, only inventions which are methods or processes of manufacture are patentable.
Restricts patents from:

- claiming substances in India for use or capable of being used as food or as medicine or drug; or
- relating to substances prepared or produced by chemical processes (including alloys, optical glass, semiconductors and intermetallic compounds). In such cases, only methods or processes of manufacture are patentable.

- contraceptives;
- disinfectants;
- fluids made from coaltar oils, coaltar acids or similar acids derived from petroleum with or without hydrocarbons;
- fluids made from synthetic or naturally occurring substances other than those mentioned above by virtue of their composition possessing disinfectant properties or claiming to possess disinfectant properties. (See Box 7.3.)

Box 7.3 Section 2(1) (I) of the Indian Patents Act, 1970

Medicine or drug includes under its definition :

- all medicines for internal or external use of human beings or animals;
- all substances intended to be used for or in the diagnosis, treatment, mitigation or prevention of diseases in human beings or animals;
- all substances intended to be used for or in the maintenance of public health, or in the prevention or control of any epidemic disease among human beings or animals;
- insecticides, germicides, fungicides, weedicides and all other substances intended to be used for the protection or preservation of plants;

Continues

Continued

- all chemical substances which are ordinarily used as intermediates in the preparation or manufacture of any other medicines or substances above referred.

Product patents

There is considerable misunderstanding of the term "product patents" in India. The most common belief is that "products" are not patentable. A brief clarification would be most appropriate here in view of Sections 3 and 5 of the Indian Patents Act. Substances capable of being used as "food/medicine/drugs" and the entire class of materials that are a result of chemical reactions do not qualify as patentable subject matter. Thus, molecules which are products of chemical reactions are as such non-patentable in India. This restriction coupled with the restriction on mere admixtures resulting in aggregation of properties in which the components do not exhibit any synergistic behaviour, severely limit the items which can be patented in India. This implies that "actives" prepared by chemical synthesis are as such non-patentable in India even if they exhibit functional properties. Likewise standard drug formulations in which the ingredients behave as mere admixtures also do not qualify for patents in India. In such cases only the process, i.e. the method of making the product, is patentable.

However, if the "active" is part of a formulation whose function is enhanced as a result of synergistic interaction with the other ingredients, the formulation may qualify for a patent if all other tests of patentability are satisfied. Formulations with enhanced drug delivery, dispersion, etc. have been patented in India. Similarly, formulations of other "products" such as soaps, detergents, cosmetics, and speciality paints are patentable if the ingredients exhibit some synergistic behaviour with respect to one or more functions.

Similarly, the mere discovery of any new property or new use for a known substance or a mere use of a known process, machine or apparatus, unless such known processes result in a new product or employ at least one new reactant, is not a patentable invention in India. If one finds a new function for an existing drug or uses an "active" already known for some other purpose/activity, it will not qualify for a patent. For example, if a drug known for its action on, say, headaches has now been found to be active for healing wounds, will not qualify for a patent. However, in USA, this restriction has been relaxed.

Such clauses generally do not exist in patent laws of most advanced countries, where inventions are patentable if they are new, non-obvious with respect to prior art, and have some element of usefulness.

Examples to demonstrate some Special Features of the Indian Patents Act, 1970

The point being illustrated in the following examples is that a novel composition was patented in UK though it did not exhibit any synergy among the ingredients. In UK and most other countries novelty of the formulation is important. Synergy is not necessary. This composition is non-patentable in India; only the process for making the composition is. Accordingly, the corresponding patentable patent application in India was modified to patent only the process.

Example 1

A product patent filed and granted in UK and the corresponding process patent filed and granted in India.

UK Patent No.: GB 8618634

Title: Treatment of keratinous fibres

Object of invention : The invention relates to compositions for treating keratinous fibres, and more particularly to compositions for dyeing human hair. For the sake of clarity, the following description will be concerned with the dyeing of human hair, although it is to be understood that the composition according to the invention can be employed in the treatment of other keratinous fibres, such as wool or animal fur, in order to dye them or to impart other benefits.

Main claim: An aqueous single-phase composition, particularly for use in the treatment of keratinous fibres, which comprises:

- from 0.1 to 10% by weight of a cationic polymer or mixtures thereof;
- from 0.1 to 10% by weight of anionic monomer or mixtures thereof;
- a solubilizing agent chosen from amphoteric detergent active compounds, inorganic electrolytes and mixtures thereof, provided

that when the solubilizing agent is an amphoteric detergent active compound, it forms from 0.1 to 20% by weight of the composition, and when the solubilizing agent is an electrolyte, it forms from 1 to 30% by weight of the composition; the composition having an anionic to cationic charge ratio of from 0.2 to 1.0.

The corresponding Indian Patent No. is 166205

Title: Process for the manufacture of an aqueous single-phase composition particularly for use in the treatment of keratinous fibres

Object of invention : The present invention relates to a process for the manufacture of aqueous single-phase compositions, particularly for use in the treatment of keratinous fibres, and more particularly to compositions for dyeing hair. For the sake of clarity, the following description will be concerned with the dyeing of human hair, although it is to be understood that the composition according to the invention can be employed in the treatment of other keratinous fibres, such as wool or animal fur, in order to dye them or to impart other benefits.

Main claim : A process for the manufacture of an aqueous single-phase composition, particularly for use in the treatment of keratinous fibres, which comprises, in addition to water:

- anionic species including an anionic monomer, such as herein described, or mixtures thereof;
- cationic species, including a cationic polymer such as herein described, or mixtures thereof, and
- a solubilizing agent chosen from amphoteric detergent active compounds, inorganic electrolytes and mixtures thereof, the composition having an anionic to cationic charge ratio of 0.2 to 1.0; which comprises the step of mixing together the oppositely charged species in the presence of the solubilizing agent; the anionic monomer and cationic polymer forming a complex; the composition so formed comprising by weight expressed in terms of the total composition:
    - from 0.01 to 10% of the anionic monomer;
    - from 0.1 to 10% of the cationic polymer; and
    - from 0.1 to 30% of the solubilizing agent, provided that when the solubilizing agent comprises an amphoteric detergent active compound, it forms from 0.1 to 20%, and when the solubilizing agent comprises an electrolyte, it forms from 1 to 30%.

Example 2

UK Patent No. : GB 8623643

Title: Oral products

Object of invention: This invention relates to oral products, particularly oral hygiene products which can effectively combat dental caries.

Main claim: An oral preparation for inhibiting caries, which comprises a combined preparation; a first composition and a second composition for admixing in the mouth or for admixing immediately prior to introduction into the mouth, wherein

- the first composition contains a source of calcium ions;
- the second composition contains a source of fluoride ions;
- the first and second compositions being such that when mixed rapid precipitation of calcium fluoride occurs.

The Indian Patent No. is 166199 and is dated 01-10-87

Title : Method of preparing a two-part oral preparation

Object of invention : This invention relates to oral products, particularly oral hygiene products which are effective to combat dental caries.

Main claim : A method of preparing a two-part oral preparation for inhibiting caries, which comprises, as a combined preparation, a first composition and a second composition for admixing in the mouth, wherein the steps of preparing the oral preparation comprises providing the first composition containing a source of calcium ions as defined earlier; and providing the second composition containing a source of fluoride ions as herein before defined; the first and second compositions being such that when mixed rapid precipitation of calcium fluoride occurs.

In summary, "non-patentable product patents" in India are to be understood in terms of the restrictions defined in Sections 3, 5 and 2(1) (I) of the Indian Patents Act, 1970.

8

Stages of patenting

The patenting process is formally structured and the applicant for a patent has to strictly follow the guidelines laid down by the Indian Patents Act. (See Box 8.1.)

Box 8.1 Patenting: A twelve-point scale

1. Identification of patent opportunity during project progress. Is the invention: (a) novel; (b) non-obvious in view of what is already known.
2. Prior art search.
3. Filing of patent application in India with provisional specification before any public disclosure of the invention.
4. Consider matter for international filing.
5. Generate further examples to support the invention.
6. Filing of complete specification 12 months after provisional specification (extension to 15 months possible with late fee only in India).
7. Technical examination by Patent Office.
8. Acceptance of patent and publication in the Gazette.
9. Opposition by competitor, if any.
10. Grant and sealing of patent.
11. Maintenance of patent by payment of renewal fees.
12. Enforcement/revocation (possible litigation, if any).

As mentioned earlier, innovations that are new, non-obvious *vis-à-vis* prior art and useful can be considered for patenting, provided all other aspects of the Act are fully satisfied.

Need for policy

Every organization must formulate a patenting policy and strategy and the projects should be assessed for patentability at various stages of progress. The first step is to identify the patentable invention and also decide on the set of inventors. These can be arrived at after a formal consideration of a number of factors. There are several key questions that the inventor(s) must answer before the invention can be assessed for patenting.

Such questions should be standardized so that they are considered in a formal way. They can also serve as a tool to review projects at various stages of progress and function as a gateway for clearance for publication, disclosure, etc. This step also helps in designing experiments to fill possible gaps in the invention to satisfy various patentability criteria or even to get around prior art. It makes interaction with the information experts and patent agents/attorneys effective while designing prior art search. Therefore, it is important that organizations make their researchers sensitive to such a structured approach to identifying patentable inventions.

Evaluation of innovations for patenting

Evaluation involves answering the following questions satisfactorily.

Inventiveness

- What is the object of the invention? What are the problems or difficulties the inventor seeks to surmount? Have these difficulties been surmounted in reality?
- What are the new and additional features of this invention over what has been published, used or known?
- What is the relevant known information (literature, including publications, patents, productions, usage, etc.) related to this invention?
- Has a systematic and structured prior art search been done on local and international databases? (These searches can also be done manually or electronically based on the patent classification systems.)

- How does this invention differ from the prior art or from what is known in related fields?

Non-obviousness

- Can this invention be considered as an "obvious" extension of the present state of knowledge in this field or in related fields?
- Have any experimental trials or tests been conducted to show that the prior art does not adequately solve the problem being tackled by the present invention? (These aspects need to be debated from various points of view.)

Technical expectations/usefulness

- What is the expected technical value of this invention?
- Where can this invention be usefully exploited?
- What are the various aspects of usefulness (e.g., savings and costs, knowledge, materials, manpower, etc.)? Indicate possible commercial benefits.
- Provide examples from the experiments done to demonstrate the various aspects of the invention and its usefulness.
- Provide examples to show the framework of various parameters in which this invention works. Similarly, provide the limits of the parameters under which the invention will not work.

Inventorship

- Who first thought of the invention? (It is always useful to provide reference to any documentary record such as laboratory notebooks, reports, memos, project proposals.) Are there any co-inventors? If so, what are their contributions?

Assignments and disclosures

- Have the funding agencies or the institutions put down conditions on proprietary aspects of the inventions resulting from the funded projects? Check for any conditions laid down on the MoU in terms of disclosures, licensing, etc.
- Has the invention been disclosed in any form to the public? If yes, in what form and when?

Once such questions have been answered with clarity, the matter can then be taken to a patent attorney who can advise on all the other aspects that need to be considered to satisfy the various provisions of the Indian Patents Act. Documentation of experiments and their results in chronological fashion serves to establish inventorship.

Since 1 January, 1996, for the first time, records of inventive activities in countries outside USA can be used to establish the date of inventorship in USA. However, the records must keep to the format and procedure recommended and recognized by the US courts. (See Box 8.2.)

Box 8.2 Laboratory notebooks/manuals — some useful guidelines

Here are some guidelines on how to maintain laboratory records of inventive work so that they can be used to prove the date of the invention. Two concepts that need to be understood are: evidence and diligence. Evidence goes to establish the date of conception of the invention. This can be done by instituting a formal system of recording who conceived the idea and when. This can be documented as minutes of a research review meeting/project planning exercise, recordings of a brain storming session, etc. In many organizations there is a regular format system of monthly reports. The evidence should be signed and dated by both the inventor and a corroborating witness. Diligence is used to prove that the idea was actually put into practice. This requires one to keep records of the progress or even gaps in the activity. This is best done through well-established laboratory manuals or laboratory notebooks which should be maintained by the laboratory personnel.

A few essential features are given in the following paragraphs but the list is by no means exhaustive. The description is intended to only give a flavour of the issues involved.

The laboratory manual/notebook must be hardbound so that it cannot be tampered with and the pages numbered. It must have a little page showing when it was issued. Every laboratory notebook should be numbered. This is to be followed by a "preface" recording relevant details of the inventor such as his name, department, project commencement date, co-workers, record of previous notebooks where progress was recorded, etc. The title page lists the contents. A page

Continues

Continued

lists the contents. A page listing the abbreviations being used in the notebook is also recommended. Every page has to be dated and the entries signed by the inventor, with each page countersigned by an independent witness.

Entries have to be made in clear and legible script. Experimental results, their interpretations, experimental strategy and development of ideas are expected to be documented in the notebook with appropriate signatures and counter signatures. Acknowledging discussions with co-workers, presentation of the data made during reviews, references to submission of samples for analysis and their results have to be indicated in the appropriate pages. It is not necessary to paste the data or computer outputs in the notebook, but such materials must be kept in a separate file/box, which is systematicly indexed, allowing easy retrieval.

An institution is expected to have a section that is responsible for issuing note books, which is also responsible for maintaining records of the issues. Similarly, a system should be created to archive the completed notebooks should they be required at a future date to serve as legal documents for any patent related litigation.

Needless to mention that proper training should be given to the laboratory personnel to maintain the notebooks as recommended.

Need for a patent agent/attorney

At this stage proper interaction with the patent attorney is of great significance. It is advisable to lay before him all the information available with the inventor on prior art such as, strengths/weaknesses of the prior art and the possible technical overlap of the present invention with the prior art, etc. An inventor must also outline the strengths and weaknesses of the invention *vis-à-vis* what is known so that the attorney is able to draft the patent specification with the most appropriate disclosures in the text and a set of claims covering the inventions. Most often, the quality of a drafted specification is dependent on the effectiveness of these interactions. After the specification is drafted the inventor must also play the "devil's advocate" and challenge the specification in as many ways as possible, especially on the grounds of "novelty", "obviousness" and "usefulness" *vis-à-vis* the prior art. He must also reassess whether the examples presented adequately support and demonstrate the invention. Such questioning exposes the weaknesses of the case and helps design further experiments or develop explanations to correct them.

As the Indian Patents Act does not allow patentability of mere admixtures, it is important to design experiments to demonstrate synergy of properties among the various constituents in formulations. Prior planning in this respect can be of advantage while tackling objections by examiners, opposition or litigation proceedings which may arise at later stages of the patenting process.

While consulting a patent attorney, it is advisable to consider the relevance and possibilities of patenting the invention in other countries. Accordingly, experiments can be designed to satisfy the patent laws of those countries. This also helps set up time targets for the research projects to generate the necessary examples so that the international claims can be filed within the priority period.

The provisional specification containing the broadest aspects of the invention should be filed at the earliest, keeping in mind that another twelve months are available to refine or generate further examples to support the invention and the claims.

Refer to Box 8.3 for a better understanding of the time-frame for each of the stages in patenting.

Box 8.3 Obtaining a patent in India: The time-frame

↑		Filing of provisional specification
	12 m	Filing of complete specification
	3 m	(late filing of complete specification with fine)
3 to 4 years		Start of examination
	15 m	Acceptance of application
	3 m	(late acceptance)
		Publication
↓	4 m	Notice of opposition

Continues

Continued

↑ 1 m (late filing of opposition)

Opposition filed | No opposition Grant of patent

1 to 2 years

Further periods for exchange of evidence between opponent and applicant

Hearing

Decision

↓ ↑

Appeal

1 to 2 years at least

Further proceedings

Grant of patent

Note:

- Examination of patents on inventions related to processes/methods of manufacture of drugs/foods, etc. taken up within six months of submission of the complete specification.
- The term of a patent in India is 14 years from the date of filing the complete specification. For processes in foods, drugs and related areas it is seven years from the date of filling the complete specification or five years from the date of sealing the patent, whichever is shorter.

9

Patent document

Structure

The patent document is technical literature structured to meet the requirements of the patent law. The conventions are more or less uniform in all the countries. English is the operating language at the Indian Patent Offices.

The patent document has a short title, the inventor's and assignees' names, addresses, and the abstract, followed by a well-defined text describing the invention supported by examples and a set of claims at the end of the text which define the boundaries of protection being sought. The document may also contain appropriate tables, drawings, figures, etc., which add documentary support to the invention and also describe it.

To summarize, a patent document includes:

- bibliographic information;
- text with the claims;
- drawings.

A patent application is made for one invention only. Every complete specification in it relates to a single invention. (See Appendix I.)

Text

The object(ive) of invention clearly defines the problems being tackled and the difficulties one is attempting to overcome. It also highlights the advantages and usefulness of the invention besides defining the invention and disclosing how the problems have been solved. (See Box 9.1.)

Box 9.1 The text

Text discloses details of the invention in a structured manner as:

- object of the invention
- prior art
- defination/description of the invention
- examples with supporting data
- claims defining the monopoly (This helps in finding what constitutes infringement)
- paper size 33cm × 20.5cm or 29cm×21cm with at least 4cm margin on the left.

If necessary, diagrams/formulae could also be separately included in the specification, but not in the main text.

To recapitulate, an invention is patentable when it is new, non-obvious with respect to prior art and is capable of some industrial application. This requires the patentee to review the prior art relevant to the invention so that the state of knowledge at that point of time is well established. The patentee then discusses the weakness in the prior art and in this context defines the problems being addressed by this invention. (See Box 9.2.)

Various approaches to tackle the problem and the course taken by the patentee are briefly described below.

The patentee is obliged to disclose all the best methods of carrying out the invention and therefore has to make a proper and clear disclosure of the invention together with supporting examples. (See Box 9.3.)

Scientific principles on which the approaches are based and reasons for preferring a particular course may also be indicated. However, this is not absolutely necessary as it is not essential as per the Patents Act. Though, in certain cases, such a description may prove useful in highlighting the differences between the invention and the prior art, its appropriateness must be evaluated by the patent attorney while drafting the specification.

This is followed by a set of examples well supported by data obtained from experiments carried out by the patentee to achieve the set objectives. The examples are to be described in such a manner and detail, that a person trained in the field can repeat the experiments and obtain the results as described by the patentee. This would also help in enforcing the patent in case of any infringement or opposition or even in revocation proceedings.

Box 9.2 Prior art

Prior art is any form of disclosure available to the public at a point in time. Prior art includes:

- Literature
  - — patent specification
  - — textbooks
  - — brochures
  - — journals
  - — lectures
- Broadcasts
- Product sales

Prior art has to do with public (not private) knowledge and is meant for public use.

Box 9.3 Disclosure

- The invention must be described in a patent specification in such a way as to enable a person trained in the art to practise the invention.
- Beware of disclosing too little. It is a ground for refusal of the patent, opposition, or revocation.

It is mandatory to present a few examples to demonstrate the most preferred manner (process or formulations etc.) of practising the invention.

Very often the inventors fear that such a disclosure would harm their interests and would prefer not to disclose the best examples. This can be a self-defeating approach as any weakness in the text, examples and data leading to inadequate or improper disclosure by the patentee can be a ground for opposition or even revocation of the patent.

It is therefore essential that the inventor discloses all possible information, including prior art, positive and negative results, strengths and weaknesses of the invention and the complete set of examples while discussing the invention with a patent attorney. This openness enables the attorney to draft the specification with the required detail and specificity so that it satisfies all the criteria of patentability and at the same time to make provisions for defending it during processing of the application or during subsequent litigations.

Often the quality of a patent specification is dictated by the nature of information disclosed to the patent attorney at the time of the initial discussions. Thorough disclosures in the patent specification also assist the examiner at the Patent Office to differentiate the invention from the prior art during the examination process. This can also contribute to minimizing the time taken for the examination by anticipating obvious comments and objections by the examiner.

The inventor, however, is not required to (and should not) disclose the technology which is outside the patent regime. The inventor is entitled under law to withhold the technology, including know-how, which he may transmit by license or otherwise.

The Patents Act requires that the invention sought to be patented is adequately described and demonstrated with a set of the best worked examples so that anyone trained in the "art" can repeat them. For example, if the invention relates to a novel process for preparing silica with specific "pore-size range" it is adequate to present laboratory examples of the same process. It is not necessary to describe how the scale-up was done, what type of equipment was used, the plant layout, etc. These details are beyond the scope of the patent.

Claims

Claims are to be designed with much caution as they define the territory of protection desired by the patentee. Drafting good and well-balanced claims is an art. They comprise a main claim followed by a set of other claims defining the optimal aspects of the invention.

1. The main claim covers the invention in the broadest possible way and protects the salient features of the invention. Extreme care should be taken to ensure that the breadth of the claim should not cause an overlap with the prior art.

A very wide claim is likely to be drowned in the sea of prior art, while too narrow and specific a claim would be easy to work around. The determination of the right area of a claim is the job of a skilled patent attorney and the inventor should not attempt to tackle this part of the document. However, he should question the coverage and challenge the claim, to examine in how many ways it can be bypassed. (See Box 9.4.)

Box 9.4 Typical format of a patent document

Object of the invention

The invention relates to cosmetic compositions for promoting lightening of skin colour.

Prior art

Published information: Dermatol azelatic acid inhibits melanin biosynthesis. JP 59157009 : Ascorbic acid stearate + Hydroquinone (unsafe)

Definition of the invention

The invention provides synergistic compositions suitable for topical application to human skin, comprising dicarboxylic acids/esters/salts in a cosmetically acceptable vehicle.
This would be followed by the text.

Example

Compound A gives lightening by 23%.
Compound B gives 60% lightening.
Additive A+B would give 83% lightening if the compounds behave independent of each other.

Continues

Continued

Synergy between A and B in the composition causes 90% lightening of the skin as experiment result obtained by a formulation containing A and B in the ratio of 1:1.

Main claim

A cosmetic composition for lightening of skin colour comprising 1 to 25% dicarboxylic acid(s)/esters/salts, 1 to 20% ascorbic acid/esters/salts, 0.1 to 5% vitamin E or its derivatives by weight of composition.

2. The invention could have one or more subclaims which provide protection to specific and optional features of the invention. However, the subclaims must have a bearing on the main claim. This is essential as the subclaims when read together with the main claim exactly define the extent of protection the patentee is entitled to when the patent is granted.

Any ambiguous claim which is not supported by description in the text can be a ground for either witholding the grant of a patent or for opposition/revocation. The main claim should not be too broad and attempt to claim more than what can be justifiably supported by disclosures including the examples in the specification.

Broad claims are always susceptible to challenge. Based on the weakness of the specification it may be possible to find a selection and pierce the claim by demonstrating certain specific benefits (not disclosed in the prior art) and claiming protection for that restricted area through a proper selection. The example of the Ethyl Corporation patent cited earlier (see p. 37) illustrates this point.

Thus a mere description of the invention in the specification does not give protection to the patentee. All the aspects of the invention must find their way into carefully drafted claims.

Therefore, it pays to remember that what is not claimed is in fact disclaimed and is open to the public for its use.

Drawings

Drawings are to be included in the patent specification as per the rules laid down by the Patents Act. Models or samples are not included in a patent specification and are to be furnished only if required by the Controller during the examination of a patent application.

Some of the essential features regarding the way in which drawings are to be presented in the specification are summarized below:

- To support the invention. This could include circuit diagrams, flowcharts, etc.
- Paper size for drawings: 33 cm × 20.5 cm or 30 cm × 41 cm with a margin of 1/2 cm off.
- If there are a large number of figures, two or more sheets are to be used instead of a larger sheet.
- One copy of the drawings should be on tracing cloth/transparent/semi-transparent sheet/plastic/fiberglass film.
- Mounted drawings are not permitted.
- Letter, numerals, symbols used in conjunction should be bold, distinct and 0.3 cm in height.
- Drawings should contain the name of the applicant.
- Number of sheets and signature of the applicant should be put in the right-hand corner.
- Title of invention should not appear on the drawings.
- No dimensions are to be given on the drawings.
- If scale is given it is to be drawn and not expressed in words.

No drawings, sketches, formulae or photographs should appear in the descriptive part of the specification.

Inclusion of photographs is also not permitted in the main text; however, they can be included as diagrams. Only black and white photographs are permitted. See Box 9.5.

Box 9.5 Processing of an application (Main features)

(A) Complete specification submitted within 12 to 15 months of filing the provisional specification.

↓

(B) Complete specification taken up for examination by the Controller who refers it to the Examiner.

↓

(C) The Examiner submits report within 18 months of receiving the complete specification from the Controller.

Continues

Continued

↓

(D) The Controller conveys list of objections to the applicant on receiving the report from the examiner.

↓

(E) Applicant to reply to objections and put application in order within 15 months of communication (step D).

↓

Three months extension possible on application.

(1)	(2)
Applicant amends application to satisfy Controller.	Applicant also given opportunity to be heard. Applicant given at least 10 days notice after fixing date of hearing. Applicant notifies Controller whether he will attend hearing. Applicant allowed extension of time for hearing (maximum extension allowed 3 months).

↓

After Controller is satisfied that all objections are satisfactorily cleared by the applicant, the specification is accepted and published in the Gazette of India, Part III, Section 2. (See Box 9.6.)

Post-acceptance proceedings

Section 25

Opposition of patent under Section 25 is done by giving formal notice of opposition.

Box 9.6 Options before grant

The Controller has powers to direct some changes. *Continues*

Continued

Division of application

Splitting of application if claims relate to more than one invention. The applicant can apply for this to the Controller any time before the acceptance of the specification or agree to the division in response to objections raised by the Controller.

Post-dating of application

The application can be post-dated on request by the applicant before acceptance of complete specification. The complete specification can be treated as a provisional application. Maximum post-dating by six months is allowed. This can also be directed by the Controller so that the applicant can meet the objections during the examination or introduce amendments as part of opposition proceedings.
Post-dating gives the applicant more time to meet the requirements of the Controller. It will enable the patentee to extend the term of the patent by the period of post-dating. However, as the priority date shifts forward, there is always a possiblity of some prior art appearing in the meanwhile.

Substitute names of applicants

The name of the applicant can be substituted if as a result of assignment, agreement, or by operation of law, the interest of the applicant in the invention is transferred to another. This can be affected by the "claimant" making an application to the Controller. If satisfied, the Controller may order substitution of names in the patent application.
In case of death of a joint applicant for a patent, the survivor(s) with the consent of the legal representative of the deceased, may apply to the Controller to proceed with the application in the name(s) of the survivor(s). The Controller has powers to allow the application if he is satisfied with the matter.
In case of disputes between joint applicants for a patent, the Controller may give directions as he thinks fit to proceed with the patent application in the name of one or more of the parties alone or regulate it in a manner in which it should

Continues

Continued

proceed. This has to be formally initiated by the applicant(s) by making an application to the Controller to resolve the matter.

Inserting or deleting references

The Controller can direct insertion of reference to another patent if it is considered as a relevant anticipation or if it appears that the invention for which the application is made cannot be performed without the risk of infringing the other patent. A request for deletion of a reference can also be made.

Amendment of specification

During examination the applicant may amend the patent specification, provided the amendment is made to enter some correction, disclaimer, or to clarify the invention. These have to be done by formally applying to the Controller as per the conditions laid down in the Act.

Section 27

If the invention, as claimed, has been published before the priority date of the claim, the Controller can refuse grant unless the specification is amended to his satisfaction

Such documents can also be brought to the notice of the Controller at any stage before the grant of the patent by any party who feels that this patent should not be granted in view of the cited prior art. This is not equivalent to an opposition proceeding. Apart from pointing out documents to the Controller, the interested party has no *locus standi* in the matter. This implies that the Controller can invite the interested party to attend a hearing between the Controller and the applicant only as an observer. The interested party is not allowed to participate in the proceedings.

10

Patent opposition

India follows the system of pre-grant opposition, while Europe, USA and Japan follow the post-grant opposition system. In the latter system, if the opposition is successful, the patent retroactively loses its effect.

After a patent application is accepted by the Patent Office, the information is published in *The Gazette of India*, Part III, Section2, published weekly from New Delhi. The basic information given includes the title, inventor, names of assignees, patent number, the main claim and a few relevant diagrams. It is then possible to obtain a copy of the complete specification and the provisional specification from the Patent Office by paying a prescribed fee.

If the patent application is in an area of interest of another organization and has the potential of being a threat to the planned or on-going R&D activities or to the business by blocking/competing with the present or future activities of the organization, or if one considers that it has been wrongfully given by the Patent Office, then the acceptance of the patent could be opposed. The opponent however must be an interested party, i.e. someone who is likely to be affected by the grant of the patent. (See Box 10.1.)

The opposition procedures are also very well defined and the proceedings can be initiated by raising the objections after meeting a few requirements laid down by the Indian Patents Act, 1970. (See Box 10.2.)

If a patent is to be opposed, a notice of opposition under Section25 has to be submitted at the appropriate Patent Office in that branch where the patent application was filed and prosecuted.

Box 10.1 A few grounds for opposition under Section 25

- Invention wrongfully obtained.
- Prior publication before the priority date of the patent application in India or elsewhere.
- Prior claiming in India.
- Publicly known or publicly used in India.
- Obviousness and lack of inventiveness.
- Insufficiency of disclosure.
- Failure to disclose information regarding foreign applications.
- Subject of the patent application is not patentable in India.
- A convention application was not made within 12 months of making the application in the convention country.

Box 10.2 Opposition proceedings

Publication of accepted patent application in *The Gazette of India*, Part III, Section 2.

- Four months given from date of publication for filing notice of opposition (Form14). Additional one month grace allowed to file opponent's full written statement.
- Applicant should file reply within one month (extensions possible on application with consent of the Controller).
- Opponent to file evidence within one month (extensions possible on application with consent of the Controller).
- Applicant to file evidence within one month (extension possible on application with consent of the Controller).
- Hearing at the Patent Office.
- Appeal in the High Court on decisions by the Controller possible. Matter can subsequently be taken up to the Supreme Court if required.

If extension of time by one month (over the permitted period of four months from the date of advertisement of the accepted patent application in *The Gazette of India*) is desired by the prospective opponent, an application for extension is to be made at the appropriate Patent Office.

In India, opposition has not been very frequent. However, with enhanced competition and awareness of its significance, this activity is likely to pick up. Oppositions filed at various Patent Offices in India in the last three years are shown in Box 10.3.

Box 10.3 Oppositions filed at various patent offices in India (1991–94)

	1993 – 94	1992 – 93	1991 – 92
Oppositions filed during the year	7	24	34
Opposition matters pending at the beginning of the year	74	78	76
No. of cases disposed of during the year	17	28	32

To initiate an opposition

The complete specification of the patent application to be opposed can be obtained from the Patent Office by quoting the patent application number.

The patent specification is to be studied carefully to identify all the grounds on which it can be opposed. A prior art search should be conducted to obtain the relevant documents to substantiate the objections being raised. Each ground of opposition needs to be referred to individually and elaborated. Arguments are to be built up carefully supported by documentary evidence. The attempt should be to knock down the patent on as many grounds as possible by attacking the text, claims, prior art or even on the basis of non-conformity with the requirements of the Patents Act. One should attempt to cite as many documents as possible which teach the invention or even lead to the invention without requiring substantial inventive work or exercise. All the grounds on which a patent is to be opposed have to be raised separately, looked into and documented in the initial written statement of opposition. No new documents would normally be permissible at later stages of the proceedings. At the evidence stage, a technical expert is expected to file an affidavit in support of some or all the arguments. While framing the notice of opposition, it is always advisable to consult a patent attorney for citations from previous judgments on similar patent cases where similar oppositions/revocations were upheld.

To counter an opposition

As indicated above, a statement of opposition attempts to attack the patent application on as many grounds as possible. While countering the opposition, the applicant has to consider each and every point raised by the opponent. The documents cited by the opponent need to be examined carefully to distinguish the invention in as many ways as possible from the cited prior art. If the cited documents are patents, the text, examples and the claims have to be dissected and effort should be made to qualitatively, and where possible quantitatively, identify weaknesses in them especially in terms of differentiating their teachings from one's own invention. It is important to identify judgments on similar patent cases where patents granted were declared valid and/or opposition/revocations were turned down. Once the technical aspects are in place, the patent attorney with the help of the scientists prepares techno-legal arguments to defend the patent. Among other approaches, it is also important to find out whether the opponent has attempted "mosaicing" (putting together separate steps from different documents) of separate steps to show anticipation. Mosaicing cannot be used to prove an anticipation. Similarly, one has to build arguments against objections on "obviousness", subjecting the patent to all the possible tests on "obviousness". As this aspect of law has varied interpretations, it is necessary to study a large number of previous judgments while constructing the counter argument. In the reply statement it is always useful to rely on as many documents as possible. It is advisable to submit the reply in the form of an affidavit from one of the inventors who is a technical expert. (See Box 10.4.)

Box 10.4 Opposition as per Section 25 (Main features)

Complete specification accepted and published in *The Gazette of India,* Part III Section 2.

↓

Any time within four months, the person interested in opposing can give a notice of opposition. Extension by an additional month possible by applying to the Patent Office within the four-month period.

↓

The notice of opposition is to be filed in the Patent Office which examined the patent specification.

↓

Reply statement to be filed by the applicant within one month of receiving the notice of opposition.

↓

Extension time for filing reply statement possible through a petition to the Controller.

↓

This extension is at the discretion of the Controller.

↓

Evidence of the opponent.

↓

The opponent to file evidence in duplicate within one month of receipt of reply statement from the applicant (patentee). One copy also to be delivered to the applicant. Extension of time possible through petition to the Controller but at his discretion.

↓

The applicant to file evidence within one month of receipt of the opponent's evidence.

Continues

Continued

↓

Extension of time possible through petition to the Controller, but at his discretion.

↓

Reply evidence by the opponent.

↓

Reply evidence by the opponent within one month of receipt of the applicant's evidence.

↓

Further submission by the applicant can be filed but, strictly with the leave or direction of the Controller.

↓

Hearing fixed by the Controller giving not less than ten days' notice to both parties.

↓

Parties desirous to be heard to give intimation to the Controller.

↓

Adjournment and rescheduling of dates possible on application to the Controller and with consent of the other party.

↓

Hearing takes place.

↓

Controller gives decision.

↓	↓
Parties accept Controller's decision, therefore patent is either granted (with amendments if necessary) or is rejected.	Either of the parties does not accept the Controller's decision. ↓ Files petition in High Court. At this stage further proceedings

Continues

Continued

are in the High Court till a decision is taken. These decisions can be further appealed against in the Supreme Court. The final judgment is conveyed to the Controller in the Patent Office.

Examples of opposition proceedings at the Indian Patent Offices

Headnotes and summaries of a few judgments by the Controllers are reproduced to illustrate features of grounds of opposition and how they are handled.

CASE STUDY

Thermax Private Limited (Opponents)
vs
Deccan Sugar Industries (Applicants)
25th July, 1986
(1987 – PTC – 137)

Summary

Opposition to grant of patent in respect of "system for concentration of distillery spent wash and method of disposal of spent wash concentrate" — preliminary objection that the applicants being a trust are not juridical persons in law — inspection of documents — further evidence — petitions — claims as claimed in complete specification — prior publication, public knowledge, obviousness, disclosure of information, etc. Section 25 of the Patents Act, 1970, Rules 38, 39, 40, 41, 44, and 115 of the Patent Rules 1972:

As regards the preliminary objection of the opponents regarding locus standi of the applicants to hold patent in their name, it is held that the applicants being a society registered under the Act enjoy the status of (a) legal entity and as such are capable of suing or being sued as well as capable of entering into a contract, and accordingly the preliminary objection raised by the opponents is rejected. The evidence called for by the opponents from the applicants being not in accordance with the procedure laid down by the Rules, cannot be taken note of. With regard to grounds of opposition as stated in Clauses (a) to (h) of Sub-section (1) of Section 25 of the Act, it is held that the opponents have failed to establish ground (a) regarding wrongful obtaining of invention. Similarly, the opponents having failed to substantiate grounds (b), (c), (d) and (e) by way of documentary evidence, the same are also rejected. As regards ground (f), it is held that since subsequent claims do not have any independent status and have to be construed in conjunction with claim 1 and the opponents having failed to analyse the claim of the applicants, this ground also fails. Regarding ground (g) relating to unfair description, the opponents having been successful in establishing the deficiencies in the description, it is ordered that no patent should be granted to the applicants.

CASE STUDY

M/s. Scooters India Limited (Opponents)
vs
M/s. Jaya Hind Industries Limited (Applicants)
23rd September, 1986
(1987 – PTC –204)

Summary

Opposition to grant of patent on the ground of prior publication, prior public knowledge or prior public use, obviousness, not qualifying as an invention and unfair description. Preliminary objection — exhibits in language other than English — non-filing of attested translation — effect on affidavit filed — absence of seal of the Notary Public and his name — Section 25 of the Patents Act, 1970, Rules 42 (2) and 111 of the Patent Rules 1972:

In view of the preliminary objections raised by the applicants regarding taking on record exhibit "A" in Italian language, an affidavit sworn before a Notary Public under Rule 111 (4) of Rules must contain his name and seal and moreover the affidavit being in a language other than English, and not accompanied by an attested English translation, cannot be taken on record. As regards the grounds of opposition relating to prior publication and prior public knowledge being based on the exhibit "A" and the affidavit which have not been taken on record, the same are rejected. Similarly the opponents having not proved the ground relating to obviousness, the same is also dismissed. The opponents having also failed to prove grounds "not an invention" as well as "unfair description", as there is no inconsistency in the statement of prior art and the statement of the object of the invention and the fact that the description is sufficient to describe the invention, the opposition is hereby dismissed with orders that the patent be sealed.

CASE STUDY

Mechelonic Welders Pvt. Ltd (Opponents)
vs
Paul Opprecht (Applicant)
17th February, 1988
(1988 – PTC – 126)

Summary

Registration of patent in respect of applicant's invention of "Electrical Resistance Steam Welding Machines" — opposition on the ground of prior art, prior use, obviousness, etc. — disclosure of information — arguments in respect of grounds not pleaded — amendment of claim — Sections 25 and 59 of the Patents Act, 1970:

Held that the opponents' reliance on ground specified in clause (b) of Section 25 as to prior art is irrelevant as the applicant's invention when compared with the opponents' invention is different. Moreover, there being no evidence that the "dogs" and "pawls" in respective inventions are the same, it is held that the opponents have failed to establish the ground of prior art. As regards grounds — specified in clause (d) as to prior use etc. — there being no evidence that the applicant's invention was publicly used in India before the date of filing the application for patent, the opponents' ground is rejected. Similarly the ground as specified in clause (g) is also rejected as the opponents have produced no evidence; moreover the opponents cannot raise matters which are not pleaded. The ground specified in the clause being based on mere statement is also rejected as no evidence has been produced on this ground also. As regards the disclosure of information as to abridgement of the US patent, it is held that since the matter has not been pleaded, the same cannot be raised at the hearing; even otherwise the invention in the US patent is not substantially the same as the applicant's invention; the opponents fail on this ground also. In these circumstances, the opposition is dismissed and it is ordered that the patent be sealed, subject to amendments in the applicant's specification as allowed.

CASE STUDY

M/s. Gujrat Reclaim & Rubber Products Ltd. (Opponents)
vs
M/s. Kamani Metallic Oxides Ltd. (Applicants)
17th March, 1983
(1983 – PTC – 105)

Summary

Opposition to grant of patent on the grounds of prior publication, prior public knowledge and prior public use, obviousness, lack of inventive step and insufficiency of description — petitions to condone the delay for filing further evidence and evidence in reply — justification — the Patents Act, 1970:

Keeping in view the facts and circumstances of the case that the opponents having neither cared to file the further evidence or even evidence in reply nor having filed the same or even to inform the Controller as to their desire to file the same, the petitions for filing further evidence and evidence in reply cannot be allowed at the eleventh hour particularly when their non-filing the same is due to their own fault and negligence.

As regards the grounds of opposition to the grant of patent, it is held that the opponents being engaged in the manufacture of reclaimed rubber in which cracked waste of automobile tyre and such other rubber waste are used and have a manufacturing unit, the opponents are held as "persons interested" as stipulated in Section 25 (I) of the Act. As regards the ground of opposition relating to prior publication, the opponents cannot be allowed to rely upon the documents in a language other than English in view of mandatory provisions contained in Rule 42 (2) of the Rules which implies the filing of an attested English translation. Even otherwise, the steps involved in the process claimed in the complete specifications are not found in the documents relied upon by the opponents, particularly when the applicant's invention is not anticipated in these documents. In the circumstances, the opponents failed to establish the ground of prior public knowledge and prior public use as the documents relied upon by the opponents were not relevant as they do not anticipate the applicant's invention. The opponents have failed to provide any other evidence in support of their contention of obviousness and lack of inventive steps. This ground is also rejected. Similarly, there being no force in their other grounds of opposition, the opposition is hereby dismissed and the patent is ordered to be sealed.

11

Other aspects

Granting and sealing of patents

If no opposition is filed by any interested parties within the statutory period under Section 25 or there are no proceedings under Section 27, then the patent is granted in favour of the applicant. Under these circumstances, the applicant is expected to apply for sealing of the patent not later than six months from the date of advertisement of the acceptance of the complete specification. The Controller is obliged to have the patent sealed and have it entered in the Register of Patents.

However, during the six months, it is always possible that various types of proceedings may be initiated. Some of these proceedings could be:

- opposition of the patent application under Section 25 is in progress;
- objections raised by the Controller under Section 27;
- application for amendment of the specification is pending;
- High Court matter related to the patent is pending.

If, after the expiry of the six months from the date of advertisement of the acceptance of the complete specification, there are proceedings with respect to the application pending at the Controller's office or in the High Court, then, in case the matter is decided in favour of the applicant, the request for sealing should be done within two months of completion of all the proceedings.

A patent of addition cannot be sealed before the sealing of the main patent.

- For a "patent of addition", the request for sealing of the patent should be submitted within six months from the date of advertisement of acceptance of the complete specification.

- Request for converting a patent of addition to an independent patent can also be made.
- Extension of time for sealing can be applied for at the Patent Office. Maximum extension allowed is nine (3+6) months with payment of prescribed fees.
- In case a patent has been granted to a deceased applicant or to a corporate body which has ceased to exist before the patent was sealed, an application for substituting the name of the person or organization (provided other legal formalities are satisfied) can be submitted by paying the prescribed fee within 12 months of the date of death of the applicant.

Amendment of applications and specifications

An applicant for a patent has the option to amend the complete specification at various stages. Only amendments which are either by way of a disclaimer, correction or explanation are allowed. Therefore the amendment should not claim or describe matter not in substance disclosed in the original specification. Also, the amended claims should fall wholly within the scope of a claim in the specification as it stood before the amendment. Thus, no new matter can be incorporated or claimed which will have the effect of broadening the scope of the invention or even changing the meaning of the invention as originally filed.

Box 11.1 Amendments to specifications (1991–94)

Year	Total amds.	Before accept.	After accept.	After sealing	Action taken
1993 – 94	315	279	34	2	245
1992 – 93	393	297	89	7	325
1991 – 92	384	293	86	5	294

An application has to be made to the Controller to introduce any amendment. Such amendments on application can be made during the examination of the patent application, or as part of opposition, revocation or even infringement proceedings.

When any amendment of the specification is allowed by the Controller or by the High Court after the advertisement of the accepted complete specification, the amendments become a part of the complete specification. This must again be advertised in the official gazette in public interest as it would enable anyone in the public to raise objections to the allowed amendments.

The records of the Indian Patent Office show this activity to be prevalent during various stages of the patenting process.

Amendments to the specifications during the last few years are given in Box 11.1.

Restoration of lapsed patents and surrender of patents

Patents which are granted and sealed are to be kept in force by payment of the annual renewal fees within the prescribed time. A patent is declared lapsed if the renewal fee is not paid on time or at least within the extended period. The period for renewal of fees can be extended maximum by six months by making a request to the Controller along with the appropriate extension fee before the completion of this period. See Box 11.2.

Box 11.2 Keeping patents alive

- Pay the yearly fee; the fee goes up with the age of the patent.
- A patent cannot be renewed at the end of its lifetime when it lapses.
- Failure to pay fees within the prescribed time leads to lapse of the patent.
- The patent then becomes open to all and can be used by anyone without fear of infringement.

However, it is possible to restore patents which have lapsed on account of failure to pay the annual fees. This can be done by formally applying to the Patent Office. Application for restoration of a patent can be done within one year of the lapse of the patent by payment of the prescribed fee. The restoration application can be opposed by an interested party within two months.

A patent can also be voluntarily surrendered provided a formal notice of offer to surrender a patent is filed at the Patent Office. This can also be opposed by any interested party within three months.

Most organizations that have a large portfolio of patents in various countries institute a regular audit by doing a cost-benefit analysis of their patent portfolio. Based on their business interests and competitor strategy, they decide to maintain patents in specific countries. Accordingly, some patents of low or no interest are allowed to lapse in some countries.

Appeals

The Patents Act provides opportunities to appeal in the High Court against any of the following decisions, orders or directions of the Controller:

- Rejection of patent applications.
- Division, post-dating, insertion of reference, substitution of applicants by virtue of assignment of an application.
- Decisions in opposition proceedings.
- Refusal of an application or requiring an amendment of specification without opposition on the ground of prior publication.
- Mentioning name of inventor.
- To sell or lease a patent.
- Refusal of a patent of addition.
- Restoration of a patent.
- Amendment of a complete specification.
- Surrender of patents.
- Registration of title (assignee, license, etc).
- Correction of clerical errors.
- Application for a compulsory license.
- Application for endorsement of "license of right".
- Terms of a "license" for patents endorsed with license of rights.
- Revocation of a patent for non-working.
- All matters of granting licenses to customers, amending any existing license, directive depriving a patentee of the right to use the inventions, revoking existing licenses and a spectrum of issues related to licensing and/or use of patents.
- Application for a license in respect of related patents.
- Granting a license in respect of a patent notified by the central government.

Appeals related to the above issues can be made within three months of the date of the order and may be extended by the High Court.

Extension of time

Extension of time is allowed for the following:

- Delay in filing of the complete specification within 12 months. However, it must be filed within 15 months of filing the provisional specification.
- Delay in responding to all objections of the Controller within the specified period of 15 months. Application for extension of time can be made to respond to objections. A maximum of 18 months from the date of the first statement of objections is given to put the application in order.
- Extension of time to pay renewal fees not being more than six months from the prescribed period.
- Application for extension of time by one month to file notice of opposition.
- Application to mention inventor as such in a patent at request, not later than two months after the date of advertisement of acceptance of complete specification or with extension of maximum one month for such an application by the inventor.
- Application for extension of time to file amendments as suggested by the Controller to a maximum of two months. This is for extensions beyond the prescribed period of two months after intimation of the suggested amendments by the Controller.
- Application for extension of the period for making a request to seal the patent (maximum by three months).
- For review of decision by the Controller or setting aside the order of the Controller. A maximum of one month extension is allowed to apply for review.

12

Enforcement of patents

The patent system strives to provide a platform for innovators to disclose their innovations and in return "seek protection for their inventions" from the state. The competitive world of today is a dynamic one, continuously converting and transforming existing information and knowledge to "new, usable and value-added knowledge". This asset finds expression in novel technologies, processes and products. This is also exchanged at a cost either in currency or traded in kind. Protection of this asset in the form of patents plays a deciding role in transfer of technologies, know-how, etc. Enforcement of patent rights is therefore very important.

The patent system can be effective only if the national legal system provides a facilitating climate for its enforcement. This is an aspect outside the jurisdiction of the Patent Offices and is handled by the civil courts.

Patent rights

Grant of a patent confers the exclusive right on the patentee, his agents or licensees to make, use, exercise or distribute the invention in India, subject to certain other provisions in the Patents Act. It is relevant to recall that the "qualified right" only gives the owner the right to exclude others from using his invention but does not necessarily give the owner the right to practise the invention. The limitations as discussed in Chapter6 need to be clearly understood.

Transfer of patent rights

Patent rights can be transferred partly or wholly by the patentee to other persons/organizations using provisions in the statute through:

- assignments (legal, equitable);
- mortgages;
- exclusive or non-exclusive licenses (express and implied or statutory).

A **legal assignment** is an agreement between the patentee and the assignee through a deed. This entitles the assignee to get his name entered in the Register of Patents and for all purposes he acquires the rights as an owner of the patent. This agreement has to be registered with the Controller of Patents as per the Patents Act.

An **equitable assignment** can be a document in which two parties agree to share the patent. An equitable assignee, unlike the legal assignee, cannot have his name entered in the Register of Patents. However, the equitable assignee is allowed to get "the notice of his interest in the patent" recorded in the Register of Patents.

Mortgage in the context of patents has its usual meaning, i.e. a transfer of rights partly or wholly as security for payment of a loan or debt that becomes void when the debt is repaid. The mortgagee cannot get his name entered in the Register of Patents. As in the case of an equitable assignee, he can have "the notice of his interest in the patent" entered in the Register of Patents.

A patentee can license the invention to one or many licensees. An **express license** permits the licensee to make, use or exercise the invention within the framework of the license. A license [with all its associated documents enlisting the terms and conditions] has to be registered with the Controller of Patents in the Patent Head Office in Calcutta. Once the Controller is satisfied that all documents are written as per the Act, he allows registration of the license.

An **implied license** normally is linked to purchase of patented articles sold with or without restriction. When an article is bought, an implicit license is implied on its use, resale or any further dealings with respect to the article. If there are any restrictions, these should be made known by the patentee to the purchaser of the article at the time when the article is purchased.

Statutory licenses such as compulsory license and license of right which relate to use of a patented invention for or by the Central Government are elaborated in later sections of this chapter.

Three relevant Sections of the Patents Act are reproduced below as these explicitly lay down the requirements for transfer of patent rights.

Section 68 — assignments, etc., not to be valid unless put down in writing and registered

An assignment of a patent or of a share in a patent, a mortgage, license or the creation of any other interest in a patent shall not be valid unless the same were in writing and the agreement between the parties concerned is reduced to the form of a document embodying all the terms and conditions governing their rights and obligations and the application for registration of such document is filed in the prescribed manner with the Controller within six months from the commencement of this Act or the execution of the document, whichever is later, or within such further period not exceeding six months in the aggregate as the Controller on application made in the prescribed manner allows.

Provided that the document shall, when registered, have effect from the date of its execution.

Section 69 — registration of assignments, transmissions, etc.

1. Where any person becomes entitled by assignment, transmission or operation of law to a patent or to a share in a patent or becomes entitled as a mortgagee, licensee or otherwise to any other interest in a patent, he shall apply in writing in the prescribed manner to the Controller for the registration of his title or, as the case may be, of notice of his interest in the Register.
2. Without prejudice to the provisions of Sub-section (1), an application for the registration of the title of any person becoming entitled by assignment to a patent or a share in a patent or becoming entitled by virtue of a mortgage, license or other instrument to any other interest in a patent may be made in the prescribed manner by the assignor, mortgagor, license or other party to that instrument, as the case may be.
3. Where an application is made under this Section for the registration of the title of any person, the Controller shall, upon proof of title to his satisfaction, entitle

(a) that person to a patent or a share in a patent, register him in the Register as proprietor or co-proprietor of the patent, and enter in the Register particulars of the instrument or event by which he derives title; or

(b) that person to any other interest in the patent, enter in the Register notice of his interest, with particulars of the instrument, if any, creating it:

Provided that if there is any dispute between the parties whether the assignment, mortgage, license, transmission, operation of law or any other such transaction has validly vested in such person a title to the patent or any share or interest therein, the Controller may refuse to take any action under clause (a) or, as the case may be, under clause (b), until the rights of the parties have been determined by a competent court.

4. There shall be supplied to the Controller in the prescribed manner for being filed in the Patent Office copies of all agreements, licenses and other documents affecting the title to any patent or any license thereunder authenticated in the prescribed manner and also such other documents as may be prescribed relevant to the subject-matter:

Provided that in the case of a license granted under a patent, the Controller shall, if so requested by the patentee or licensee, take steps for securing that the terms of the license are not disclosed to any person except under the order of a court.

5. Except for the purposes of an application under Sub-section (1) or of an application to rectify the Register, a document in respect of which no entry has been made in the Register under Sub-section (3) shall not be admitted by the Controller or by any court as evidence of the title of any person to a patent or to a share or interest therein unless the Controller or the court for reasons to be recorded in writing, otherwise directs.

Section 70 — power of registered grantee or proprietor to deal with a patent

Subject to the provisions contained in this Act relating to co-ownership of patents and on also to any rights vested in any other person of which notice is entered in the Register, the person or persons registered as grantee or proprietor of a patent shall have power to assign, grant licenses under, or otherwise deal with the patent and to give effectual receipts for any consideration for any such assignment, license or dealing:

Provided that any equities in respect of the patent may be enforced in a like manner as in respect of any other moveable property.

Infringement of patents

Infringement of a patent would constitute any action by which these rights are violated or interfered with. No suit or other proceedings can be initiated for any infringement committed before the date of acceptance of the complete specification.

The user of a patent may ascertain that an infringement is not being committed by checking against the following three questions:

- Do the features of the accused product fall within the claims of the patent?
- Can the patent holder use the "doctrine of equivalents" to cover the accused product even if its features fall outside the literal terms of the claim?
- Can the defendant use the "reverse doctrine of equivalents" to avoid liability even though there is literal infringement?

Though the above statements appear fairly clear and unambiguous, courts have taken diverse views while arriving at decisions on infringement of patents.

Patents rights are also not considered to be infringed when the invention is used on foreign vessels, aircraft or land vehicles, temporarily or accidentally in India. Any use of the patented article or process beyond the limits of territorial waters is also not considered as infringement.

If the invention is used in :

- the body of the vessel, aircraft or land vehicle; or
- the machinery, tackle, apparatus or other accessories thereof, so far as the invention is used on board the vessel, aircraft or land vehicle and for its actual needs only; or
- the construction or working of the aircraft or land vehicle or of the accessories thereof as the case may be,

it is not considered as infringement.

This immunity clause does not apply to vessels, aircraft or land vehicles belonging to foreigners from countries which do not give corresponding rights to vessels, etc., owned by Indians while in their territorial waters or within the jurisdiction of their courts.

A few special provisions have been introduced in the Act to protect public interest. These deal with the grant of patents under certain special conditions for use by or on behalf of the government or researchers/teachers.

While deciding on infringements a number of other factors are considered. Some of them are given below :

- Determining the scope of the monopoly by virtue of the claims of the patent in question and deciding on whether the alleged infringement literally falls within the scope of the claims.
  Thus, to constitute an infringement, the article must take each and every one of the essential integers of the claim. Non-essential integers may be omitted or replaced by mechanical equivalents by an infringer, resulting in insignificant differences. There will still be infringement.
- It is also important to establish whether the infringing article or process is a "non-obvious" or "non-colourable" variant of the patented invention. The courts now tend to adopt what is known as triangular tests to establish infringement:
  — to determine whether the claim can be read as new and non-obvious from prior art;
  — to determine whether a hypothetical claim covering the abused device or process can be read to be obvious from the claimed invention; and
  — to determine whether the hypothetical claim can be read to be new and non-obvious from the prior art.

Other considerations

- All persons facilitating the act of infringement can be construed as alleged infringers. They could directly or indirectly be connected with the manufacture of an infringing product using a "patented process", patented machine/patented intermediates or involved in sale or distribution of the infringing product.
- Any unauthorized selling of a patented apparatus/machine/device as a whole or even in parts which can simply be put together to obtain the patented machine is an act of infringement.
- Repairing of patented products for purposes of "mere repair" is not infringement. However interpretation of the expression "mere repair" and making of a "new one" as a consequence of repair have been subjects of debate and varied interpretation. There are a number of features in deciding infringement and the courts in various countries differ in their judgments even on similar issues.

Thus, while defining the scope of protection, the interpretations can vary from court to court depending on whether they have used the non-obviousness tests together with limiting equivalents or non-limiting equivalents of patenting inventions. (See Box 12.1.)

Box 12.1 Doctrine of equivalents

The doctrine of equivalents

An accused product or process will infringe though it is outside the literal terms of the claims, if it does the same work in substantially the same way to accomplish substantially the same result as the patented product or process.

Reverse doctrine of equivalents

Even where an accused product falls within the literal terms of a patent, if the accused product is so far changed in principle from the patented product, that it performs the same function in a substantially different way, infringement liability is unwarranted. Selection patent is an example of reverse doctrine of equivalents.

Court proceedings on infringement matters are long and protracted and consume considerable time and money. One of the ways of informing the public of a patented invention is by marking the good with the words "patent pending", "patent applied for" or "patented", giving the serial number of the patent and the country where it is granted. It should be noted that any "false markings" or "mis-information" is considered to be a criminal offence in most countries, including India.

One of the recommended ways of "warning infringers" is to formally bring to their notice the "alleged infringement". If as a result of such a warning the "infringer" stops the infringement, litigation proceedings can be avoided. In a number of instances the patentee after issuing a "formal" warning to the alleged infringer negotiates mutually acceptable terms for licensing, compensations, etc. instead of proceeding with litigation.

It is always advisable to do a complete cost-benefit analysis before opting for litigation.

However, all efforts to enforce one's patent rights must be done in earnest as it creates a positive image of the organization's concern to protect its own intellectual property.

In case the matter enters the court, one can attempt to obtain certain reliefs. Short-term relief such as an interlocutory injunction is possible under specific circumstances. Long-term relief is available on conclusion of the infringement suit, which can include a permanent injunction with payment of damages and costs. To exploit all the legal provisions it is essential to seek competent and efficient legal advice.

Special Provisions

Special Provisions in the Indian Patents Act which do not constitute infringement are when :

- *any machine, apparatus or other article* in respect of which the patent is granted, or any article made by using a process in respect of which the patent is granted *may be imported or made by or on behalf of the government for the purpose merely of its own use*;
- *any process* in respect of which the patent is granted *may be used by or on behalf of the government for the purpose merely of its own use*;
- *any machine, apparatus or other article* in respect of which the patent is granted *may be made or used*, and *any process* in respect of which the patent is granted *may be used by any person, for purposes merely of experiment or research, including the imparting of instruction to pupils*; and
- in the case of a patent in respect of any medicine or drug, *the medicine or drug may be imported by the government for the purpose merely of its own use or for distribution in any dispensary, hospital or any other medical institution maintained by or on behalf of the government or any other dispensary, hospital or other medical institution which the* Central Government *may, having regard to the public service that such dispensary, hospital or medical institution renders, specify in this behalf by notification in the official* Gazette.

In national and public interest there are provisions in the Act under which the government can:

- make or import a patented article or use a patented process for specific purpose without paying any royalty or fee to the patentee, and is not liable to any infringement proceeding;
- authorize agent(s) to use a patented invention on behalf of the government. In case of medicines, foods or drugs, the royalty or fee can be fixed not exceeding 4% of the net ex-factory sale price. The patentee would be kept informed from time to time on the purpose and extent to which the invention has been used by the government;
- acquire inventions in its own name by compensating the patentee through mutually agreed upon terms and conditions.

Compulsory license

There are other provisions in the Act under "non-working of patents" and "compulsory licenses" in which if a patented invention has not been put to practise by the patentee within three years from the date of sealing of a patent, the Controller has the powers to grant a "compulsory license" to any interested party if approached. The Controller must be satisfied that the patented invention is not available to the public at a "reasonable price" or that "reasonable requirements" of the public with respect to the patented invention have not been satisfied. The Controller must also consider the reasons why the invention has not been put into practice by the patentee or the efforts put in by the patentee to work the invention and also whether the applicant for the compulsory license has the capability of working the invention.

License of right

There are special provisions under the Patents Act 1970 under which certain patents are deemed to be endorsed with the term licenses of right (LOR) after three years from the date of sealing the patent. These are for inventions relating to:

- substances used or capable of being used as foods, medicines or drugs;
- methods or processes for manufacture or production of substances referred to above
- methods or processes for manufacture or production of chemical substances, including alloys, optical glass, semiconductors and intermetallic compounds.

License of right allows anyone interested in working the invention in India to negotiate with the patentee to grant him the license at a "reasonable price". However, if the two parties are unable to arrive at "mutually acceptable terms" the Controller can exercise his powers to fix the terms if approached by the applicant. In any case the royalty or fee will not exceed 4% of the net ex-factory price in bulk of the patented article.

The term license of right can also be endorsed on "any" patent by the Controller if:

- approached by the Central Government after three years of the sealing of the patent on the ground that "reasonable requirements" of the public with respect to the patented invention have not been met or that the patented invention is not available to the public at a reasonable price;
- the Controller "on his own" is satisfied that the "reasonable requirements" of the public with respect to the patented invention have not been satisfied or the invention is not available to the public at a reasonable price.

Any patent of addition also gets endorsed as a license of right if the main patent falls under this classification.

In India, reasonable requirements of the public are deemed to be not satisfied when:

- a patentee is not exploiting the invention to the fullest extent possible extent;
- a patentee is unable to manufacture the article for adequate supply on reasonable terms;
- a patentee refuses to grant licenses on reasonable terms, thereby obstructing existing trade, commercial activities, industry, and their development in India;
- the demand in India is met through importation of the patented article by:
  - — the patentee or persons under him; or
  - — persons directly or indirectly purchasing from him; or
  - — other persons against whom the patentee is not taking, or has not taken, proceedings for infringement;
- the working of the patented invention in India on a commercial scale is being prevented or hindered by importation of the patented article by the patentee or the other persons referred above;
- the export demand of the patented article is not met by its manufacture in India.

All these provisions have seldom been exploited in India. As per the reports of the Indian Patent Offices there has not been a single application for compulsory license in the last five years. However, on a routine basis, the Patent Office does classify a number of patents by the term license of right. In 1993–94, the number of patents endorsed as license of right by the Indian Patent Office came down to 257 as against 787 in 1991–92.

The patent on request of the Government or any interested person can be revoked by the Controller on expiry of two years:from the date of granting:

- the first compulsory license;
- the license of right.

Every action under these Special Provisions is announced in the weekly Gazettes.

The records of the Patent Office reveal that these Special Provisions have not been substantially used in India.

These Special Provisions in the Indian Patents Act, 1970 are expected to be revised while considering possible amendments to the Act to meet the various provisions of the GATT. In the absence of product patents, many firms attempted only minor process improvements or process developments. The result was low levels of R&D, leading to no product innovations in drugs, chemicals, polymers, food processing and new materials. This coupled with inadequate awareness of patents and patenting procedures made many firms neglect the importance of patent, design and copyright protection.

13

Revocation

The process of granting a patent is well-defined and there are in-built controls in the Act to check the patent specification for compliance with the conditions of patentability. It also provides opportunities to the public at various stages to challenge the Patent Office's decisions related to the "acceptance" of a specification through opposition proceedings and other options in the Act.

Grant of a patent by the Patent Office does not gaurantee the validity of the patent. It is possible to challenge the validity even after a patent is granted and sealed. In contrast to the pre-grant opposition cases which are initiated and contested at the Indian Patent Offices, revocation suits fall under the purview of the High Courts.

If objections are to be raised on any patent after the grant and sealing, they can be done in the form of revocation proceedings. A revocation suit can also be filed in a High Court even after the term of a patent has expired.

The *revocation petition* can be filed by any interested person or by the Central Government or may be taken up as a counterclaim in a suit for infringement of the patent. In normal practice, when an infringement suit is filed by a patentee on an infringer, the "alleged infringer" counters and challenges the validity of the patent by filing a counterclaim for revocation of the patent as a part of the same proceedings.

Revocation proceedings are mostly filed by defendants in patent infringement suits to establish *prima facie* invalidity of the plaintiff's patent and to thereby avoid a temporary injunction.

Revocation is also used as an offensive weapon to invalidate patents especially when one considers the patent under question as damaging to one's business interests. Such patents are identified by effective competitor patent monitoring systems. A revocation petition attempts to rely on as many grounds of revocation as possible to demolish the claims of the patent. Apart from vacating the claims, one uses revocation as a tool to create gaps in the "patents-web" for entry points into unprotected zones. In recent times, revocation proceedings have resulted in out-of-court settlements between the mega corporations, resulting in strategic alliances, joint ventures, cooperative research programmes, etc.

An independent revocation suit against a patent can also be filed in any High Court in India as the Act does not explicitly put down any conditions on deciding the jurisdiction of High Courts to entertain a petition for revocation of a patent.

A court may even revoke a patent which has already expired. While filing a revocation suit on a patent, the petitioner has to study the various grounds under which a patent is liable to be revoked. As in the case of opposition, the patent being considered for revocation is attacked using as many grounds as are available for revocation. It should be noted that additional grounds are available for revocation as compared to those available for patent oppositions. The approach is similar to that followed in the case of oppositions and is therefore not elaborated here. However, for revocation, it is advisable to form a team of patent attorneys, civil lawyers and technical experts.

All revocation proceedings when concluded are announced in the offical gazettes and the revocation is recorded in the Patent Register at the Patent Head Office in Calcutta. The grounds for filing a revocation suit are highlighted in Boxes 13.1 and 13.2.

Box 13.1 Grounds for filing revocation

A revocation suit on a patent can be filed on the following grounds:

- The claim already is a valid claim of an earlier priority patent granted in India.
- The patent is granted to a person not entitled to get a patent.

Continues

Continued

- The patent has been wrongfully obtained.
- This invention is not a patentable invention.
- The invention is not new with respect to prior art.
- The invention is obvious and lacks inventiveness with respect to prior art.
- The invention is not useful.
- The invention and its method is not clearly described.
- The scope of any claim of the complete specification is not clearly defined.
- The patent is obtained on a false suggestion.
- The invention is non-patentable under the Patents Act.
- The invention so far claimed in any complete specification was secretly used in India, on or before the priority date of the claim.
- Leave to amend complete specification is obtained by fraud.

Box 13.2 Grounds on which the Central Government can ask for revocation

The Central Government may ask for revocation in the following cases relating to inventions:

- in atomic energy;
- not in the public interest;
- not in the interest of the State;
- generally prejudicial to the public.

Examples of a few patent revocation cases with summaries of their decisions are given to illustrate how various grounds are taken and treated by the courts in India.

Patent Revocation in India

A few headnotes of the judgments are reproduced to illustrate some of the issues in matters on revocation as interpreted in Indian courts

CASE STUDY

Star Textile Engineering Works Ltd.
vs
James Mackie Holdings Ltd. and Others

O.O.C.S. No. 551 of 1977
Calcutta High Court, reported in 1978-IPLR-160

Summary In an application for revocation of three patents on the ground of insufficiency, the terms of two patents had expired pending the proceedings and the term of the third was about to expire. The applicants argued that a suit for infringement of a patent was maintainable even after the term of a patent had expired, if the applicant established a ground for revocation as provided in Section 64(1) of the Act.

Held, allowing the application: (i) that the complete specification of the patents did not sufficiently and clearly describe the respective method by which it is to be performed; (ii) that the said specifications by themselves were not sufficient to enable a person of average skill and knowledge to work the inventions; (iii) that as the applicants were entitled to protection, the patents would stand revoked; and (iv) that there would be no order as to costs.

CASE STUDY

Bishwanath Prasad Radhay Shyam
vs
Hindustan Metal Industries

Supreme Court of India, reported in 1983-IPLR-55

Summary The respondents, who were patentees of an invention relating to a means for mounting metallic utensils for the purpose of turning them before polishing, filed a suit for infringement of a patent against the appellant in the Court of the District Judge, Allahabad.

The appellant resisted the suit and made a counterclaim for revocation of the patent on the grounds that the method covered by the patent was well-known and openly in use since several years prior to the date of the patent; that the alleged invention of the plaintiff's was not on the date of the patent a manner of new manufacture or improvement, nor did it involve any inventive step or ingenuity and that the patent had no utility.

On transfer of both the suit and counterclaim from District Court to High Court, the matter was heard by a single judge who upheld the contentions of the appellant, dismissed the suit and ordered revocation of the patent.

The respondents appealed to the division bench of the High Court, who reversed the judgment and order of the trial judge, holding that the patented invention was unknown previously and hence it was new when the patent was granted. Against this decision the appellant appealed to the Supreme Court.

Held, allowing the appeal: (i) that the respondents' claim to novelty, ingenuity, inventive step, etc. for their invention could not be substantiated; (ii) that the subject matter might be useful, but mere utility could not sustain a patent; and (iii) that since the invention did not involve any matter of new manufacture, nor novel improvement, nor inventive step, the grant of patent to it was invalid.

CASE STUDY

Ajay Industrial Corporation
VS
Mr Shiro Kanao
Delhi High Court reported in 1983-IPLR-95

Summary Patent — Application for revocation — Prior use — Prior knowledge — Want of novelty — Locus Standi of applicant for revocation — Applications dismissed Appeal to Division Bench whether Court has jurisdiction to entertain suit — Appeal dismissed.

The appellants filed in the Delhi High Court applications for revocation of two patents — one for a manufacturing process i.e. "the method and apparatus for continuously producing a spiralled tube of plastic resin", and the other for the article i.e. "Flexible plastic hose" — on the ground of lack of inventiveness, prior knowledge and prior use.

The appellants appealed to the Division Bench. The respondent raised a preliminary objection that the Delhi High Court had no jurisdiction to entertain the appellants' applications on the ground that the respondent had filed a suit for infringement against the appellants in a Court in Ahmedabad and hence the appellants should have sought revocation of the patents by way of a counterclaim in the suit for infringement so that the suit and the counterclaim would have been transferred to the High Court, Ahmedabad for decision or alternatively the applications for revocation ought to have been made to the High Court at Calcutta within the jurisdiction of which the Patent Office at Calcutta where patents were registered, is situated.

Held, dismissing the appeals, (i) that Delhi High Court had jurisdiction to entertain an application for revocation of a patent. Section 64 conferred a separate right to seek revocation of the patent on any interested person whose commercial interests were adversely affected by the rights of the patent holder and such an application could be filed in the High Court within whose jurisdiction the commercial rights were so affected and this right was independent of the right of revocation by way of counterclaim in a pending suit for infringment, (ii) that the appellants could not be called "person interested", since they were not engaged in the manufacture or trade of the patented machinery or apparatus by which the patented article was obtained, (iii) that the learned judge had correctly dismissed the application and (iv) that, with regard to the relevant specifications and claims, which clearly showed that the patented article was of a distinct quality produced by a special process inspite of the superficial likeness of the finished article to other patented products of the same kind already existing, the patented article was a "new device" involving a new discovery or invention.

CASE STUDY

Polar Industries Ltd. (Petitioner)
vs
The Jay Engineering Works Ltd. and Anr. (Respondent)
Matter No. 2668 of 1988
Calcutta High Court, reported in 1991-IPLR-150

The respondent was the owner of a patent dated 20-02-81. The patent was for an alleged invention of a split-type socket by which the shaft of the motor of (the) ceiling fan was clamped to the lower end of the rod, the upper end being fixed to a hook in the ceiling. The petitioner applied for revocation of the patent on the ground that the use of a split socket for clamping was neither novel nor uncommon since such use was being made by ceiling fan manufacturers much before the date of the patent. . . .

. . . The subject matter of the patent in the instant case was not at all new to those who were experts in the field. Clamping of the rod for ceiling fans both at upper and lower ends was a common practice

followed since long and the modification of the socket introduced by the patent holder was merely a workshop improvement.

Allowing the application for revocation, the court held — that (i) for an improvement to be patentable, it was not enough to incorporate what was already known with some minor changes, combination or collection of components or things; (ii) in the given case the device or mechanism of clamping, did not involve any novelty but was only a workshop improvement, easily obvious to any skilled worker and, as such, the patent was not validly granted.

14

Patent information

With the rapid strides in R&D in industries and other public- and private-funded institutions, the volume of technical information generated is growing by leaps and bounds. The statistics are interesting:

- *Chemical Abstracts* alone publishes over 10,000 abstracts each week, over 15 million to date, with disclosures of over 13 million compounds; currently about 25% relate to patents, 60% of which are Japanese specifications.
- There are thousands of scientific journals documenting contributions from researchers all over the world.
- In addition to these, there are over 32 million patents published worldwide, growing at the rate of more than half-a-million new applications per year.
- 80% of these disclosures which are in the form of patent applications are not published elsewhere, i.e. in journals, periodicals, etc.

Disclosure of an invention in a patent document is well-structured. This is essential as any person trained in the "art" is expected to be able to reproduce the findings disclosed in the patent document. See Box 14.1.

Box 14.1 Patents as an information source

Patents as an information source enable planning of strategic protection, blocking competitors and ensuring freedom to use inventions.

- Technical information

Continues

Continued

- Emerging technologies
- Emerging research areas
- Emerging business opportunities
- Tool to identify potential opportunities and threats
- Tool to identify possible collaborators, business mergers, strategic alliances based on technological and geographical strengths.

Note: Useful both in business and in research.

Patent literature can be considered to be a very large and well-structured source of technical/scientific information. Information on patents is classified by an internationally accepted classification scheme. The various aspects such as the inventors, assignees, priority dates, countries in which it is first filed, subsequent filings with their dates and places, titles, abstracts, documents cited in the specification and also by the examiners, etc., are all systematically indexed and therefore searchable electronically. These are also maintained in the various patent office libraries and it is possible to retrieve information manually where electronic searching facilities are not available. Nowadays, even the legal status of a patent in various countries can be found from the databases.

Assuming that a project moves on from these early stages and produces a potentially innovative technical development, then further patent searching is essential before any decision is made on filing patent applications or on maintaining secrecy. Such searches should be directed to determining whether the development is likely to be novel and whether, on implementation, it is likely to infringe existing patents.

If a patent is applied for and granted, these searches should be updated regularly throughout this process to ensure that potential conflicts are identified early. Again, if disputes do arise, extensive patent and literature searches may be vital in determining the real strength of the relevant patents.

Hence, patent searches are valuable all the way through the process of initiating, developing and marketing a new product, process or other manufacture. (See Box 14.2.)

Indicator of future growth

Patent Searches are also useful in other ways, for example, they help competitor analysis, marketing, recruitment, etc.

Analysis of a particular company's patent activities over a period of several years can give useful pointers to future products that the company is currently working on. While being only one of a number of aspects that need to be considered in looking at the company's future activities, a substantial and increasing portfolio of patents is a strong indicator of a likely future commercial development.

Looking at the patent holdings of other companies can also be useful in marketing and identifying companies that might be end-users of a particular product or piece of equipment.

Analysis of the patent holding of specific inventors within a narrow research area can be used as an aid to recruitment, since it can identify a major player in the field, whose service could then be sought.

Box 14.2 Bibliographic information

- Country of publication
- National Patent Classification
- International Patent Classification
- Title
- Abstract
- Inventor
- Applicant
- Application No.
- Serial No.
- Date of application
- Priority date
- Priority No.
- Priority country
- Reference cited by Examiner

Gazette of India Part III, Section 2

The information on patent filings, accepted patents, opposition proceedings, lapsed patents, working/non-working of patents, etc., are documented in the weekly Gazette published by the Office of the Controller General of Patents, Designs and Trademarks, Government of India. (Extracts from this are presented in Appendix IV. See Box 14.3.) The reader is advised to follow Appendix IV critically to familiarize himself with the kind of information published in the Gazette. The Gazette publishes the titles, inventors, date of provisional filing and the name(s) of assignee(s) every week. Thus, the public has the opportunity to know the titles of provisional patent applications and convention patent applications filed in India within weeks of their filing through the Gazettes. The details of a patent application are published for the first time only after the patent has been accepted after examination by the Patent Office and are, therefore, available to the public only three to four years after the filing of the patent. (See Box 14.4.)

Box 14.3 Extracts from the Gazette of India Part III Section 2

Selected pages from different issues of the Gazette are enclosed to illustrate the type and format of the information provided :

Extracts	Information
1. Title page of Gazette of December 21, 1996 including pages 1033–35	• Patent office addresses and jurisdictions. • details of patent applications filed. 1597/CAL/96 indicates that application No. 1597 of 1996 was filed in Calcutta. MAS/CHE, BOM/MUM and DEL indicate applications filed in Chennai, Mumbai and Delhi, respectively.
2. December 21, 1996 pages 1037–38, 1042, 1050–51	Alteration of date under Section 16. Complete specifications accepted: • only text material; • also includes formula with text; • includes diagram with text.

Continues

Continued

3. December 21, 1996 pages 1057–58	• Amendment proceedings under Section 57. • Claims accepted under some special sections of the Act. • Cessation of Patents. • Renewal fees paid. • Patents sealed. • Endorsement with words "License of Right". • Registration of Designs.
4. December 7, 1996 page 984	Opposition proceedings under Section 25.
5. April 20, 1996 page 298	Commercial working of patented inventions listed as per various fields of engineering, such as Chemical, Industrial, Mechanical and Electrical Engineering, etc.
6. November 2, 1996 page 861	• Restoration Proceedings. • Alphabetical name index of application for patents filed in the Patent Office, Calcutta and branches, for specified months.
7. October 5, 1996 page 776	• Registration of Assignments, Licenses, etc.
8. December 14, 1996 page 1002	• Cessation of Patents.
9. January 20, 1996 pages 36–37	• List of Printed specifications published. • Application number index of complete specification accepted during the year 1994.

Box 14.4 Gazette of India Part III Section 2

Information provided on patents in the Gazette (Illustrated in Appendix IV)

On Provisional specification

- name of applicant;
- date of filing;
- title;
- Application No.

On Complete specification after acceptance

- name of applicant;
- names of Inventors;
- date of filing;
- title;
- Application No.
- main claim;
- drawing;
- first filing of provisional or complete specification;
- complete specifications accepted (oppositions invited within four months of publication date);
- filing of opposition to grant of patent and decision of the Controller thereon is notified;
- sealing of patent (identified by Patent No.);
- amendment proceedings;
- proposals for amendments (post-acceptance) under the Act; opposition to these proposals and decision of the Controller;
- compulsory license proceedings (licenses of right are identified by numbers and titles);
- non-working of patents;
- other notifications (change in name of inventor/ application/post-dating/ante-dating of applications, restoration proceedings, cessation of patents.

The Register of Patents

The Register of Patents is a vital document kept at the Head Office and at all the Branch Offices. However, only the Head Office at Calcutta has the authority to make any additions or alterations.

This information can be meaningfully exploited by utilizing it to establish "ownership", especially when negotiating licensing, acquisitions, setting up joint ventures, debating infringements, etc. It is always advisable to consult the Register of Patents to acquaint oneself with the latest status of the patent in question. See Fig. 14.1.

To consult the Register at any of the Patent Offices, a formal request has to be made to the concerned Patent Office along with payment of a prescribed fee.

Name, address, nationality of person to whom patent is granted	Updated information on matters related to validity, proprietorship, court orders	Title of patent	Renewal fees, status, category, classification, sealing as LOR, etc., removal of abandoned patents, altered address of service	Date of patent, Address of service of patentee	Notification of assignment, transmission, licence amendment, or revocation of patent

Fig. 14.1 · Information on sealed patent

Sources of patent information in India

In view of the growing demand and speed required to service the need of business, many private information searchers and brokers are offering professional help to organize the information and prepare specialist reports on demand. The functions of some of the major organizations providing such information are briefly outlined here.

1. *National Informatics Centre,*
   Patent and Know-how Information Division,
   A Block, CGO Complex,
   Lodhi Road, New Delhi 110 003.
   Telex : 031 61274
   e-mail : root@nicnet.nic.in; root@hub.nic.in; sio@nct.delhi.nic.in

Kind of Information	*Scope*	*Year*
Bibliographic:	Global	1986 (onwards)
• without abstract	(57 countries)	
	USA	1969 (onwards)

• with abstract and full text	European(EP)	1978 (onwards)
	PCT(WO)*	1978 (onwards)
	USA	1967 (onwards)
	Great Britain	1974–1993
	France	1974–1993
	Germany	1974–1993
	Canada	1974–1986

* For PCT(WO), only abstracts are available.

2. *Patent Management Division (CSIR),*
   14, Sansad Vihar Marg,
   Special Institutional Area,
   New Delhi 110 067.
   Tel: 6962560; Fax 6968819

INPAT - Database on Indian Patents

The patents unit developed a computerized database on Indian patents from 1972 onwards. The database provides the flexibility to retrieve information on any of the bibliographic items, namely Patent No., Application No. and date, publication date, applicant's and inventor's name, priority data, International Patent Classification, and Indian Patent Classification through keywords. Patent search facility from this database is available to interested members of the public on a chargeable basis.

This database is also available on-line through:

Indian National Scientific Documentation Centre (INSDOC),
14, Sansad Vihar Marg,
Special Institutional Area,
New Delhi 110 067.

3. *National Chemical Laboratory,*
   NICHEM/NCL,
   Pune 411 008.
   Telex: 0415 266
   e-mail: kri@ncl.ernet.in; nichem@ncl.ernet.in; ncl@iucaa.ernet.in

At the request of the client the unit conducts Value Added Patent Information Services (VAPIS) by doing searches of international databases on CD-ROMs and also on-line. Based on the customer's need, the information is also collated and reports prepared.

4. *National Research and Development Council (NRDC),*
   20-22, Zamroodpur, Kailash Colony,
   New Delhi 110 048.
   Tel : 6417821,6231879; Fax : 6231876

NRDC with its expertise in on-line — the access technology for global information—strives to provide a diverse range of information services.

This facility has been established in collaboration with DIALOG of USA, which has an extensive collection of worldwide information sources, providing access to more than 450 databases covering millions of documents from scientific and technical literature, full text of trade journals, newspapers, etc., since 1972. The coverage has been further extended to an additional 350 databases on account of DATASTAR, Europe's leading information service, merging with DIALOG.

This on-line search facility provides access to more than 15 million patents from 56 different patent authorities around the globe. These patent sources, which help identify prior inventions against which the applicant's will be evaluated, can be extremely useful in preparing the patent application.

There are also a number of databases for trademark scan covering Austria, Benelux, Canada, Denmark, France, Germany, Ireland, Italy, Liechstein, Monaco, Switzerland, USA, etc.

5. *Patent Information System (PIS),*
   CGO *Complex,*
   C *Block, Seminary Hills,*
   Nagpur 440 006.

This office was created in 1980 under the charge of the CGPDT, Ministry of Industries. PIS provides a number of search facilities and copies of patent specifications. The services provided are SDI-search documentation, SDI-search; bibliographic search, English equivalent search, family search, assisted search, on-line search, patent copy supply, foreign patents, etc.

PIS has an exhaustive collection of patent documents stored as hard copies, microfilms and CD-ROMs. The details of its holdings are as follows:

Full text of patent documents

Country	Code	Media	Year
USA	US	Microfilm	1951–1992
		CD-ROM	1994 onwards
UK	GB	Microfilm	1952–1992
		CD-ROM	1990 onwards

Continues

Continued

European Patent Office (16 European countries as members)	EP	Microfilm CD-ROM	1978–1984 1994 onwards
Patent Cooperation Treaty (53 countries as members)	WO	CD-ROM	1990 onwards
Australia	AU	Paper Microfiche	1964–1974 1975 onwards
India	IN	Paper	1912 onwards

Databases available

Database	Medium	Information retrieval	Year (till 1994)
INPADOC (VIENNA)	Microfiche	Bibliographic, including data title of patents from more than 55 countries	1968
APS/CAPS	CD-ROM	Bibliographic data and abstracts of US patents	1969
CASSIS-BIB	CD-ROM	Bibliographic data of US patents	1969
ESPACE/ ACCESS	CD-ROM	Bibliographic data and abstracts of EPO patents	1978
		Bibliographic data of PCT applications	1988
BREF	CD-ROM	Bibliographic data and abstracts of French patents	1989
INDIAN PATENTS DATA	Magnetic tape* CD-ROM* Hard Copies	Bibliographic data and abstract claim	1975 1993

* These will be developed during the modernization project.

6. *IPR cell in Department of Electronics,*
   R & D Policy and Coordinate Division (DoE),
   Department of Electronics,
   6, CGO *Complex, New Delhi 110 003.*
   e-mail : rct@xm.doe.ernet.in

The DoE has recently created an IPR cell. This cell deals with IPR related issues, especially electronics, computer and integrated circuits. Acting as a resource centre, DoE strives to provide patent information services such as search and analysis using CD-ROMs, on-line databases and internet.

Subject specific Technology Alert Patent Search (TAPS) system has now been made feasible at low cost. DoE has already set up this system which can be replicated at a low cost. TAPS can also be linked up to national facilities dealing with patent information through e-mail and can have access to on-line patent databases and internet.

International databases

Scientific & Technical Information Network (STN) International from American Chemical Society, DIALOG and DATASTAR services offer comprehensive and global information on intellectual property. DIALOG covers USA and international patents from a number of sources and full texts. It also has an extensive collection of trademarks and US copyrights as an on-line facility.

They have a large number of files which they term as Smart Tool for intellectual property. DIALOG and DATASTAR have structured retrievable information on patent application, patent references, patent citations and industry-specific information from patent literature which covers class codes, family data, abstracts, claims, legal status, citations from patents, subject classifications, etc.

The patent citation covers author-cited literature, author-cited patents, examiner-cited literature, examiner-cited patents.

The industry-specific patented technology information files contain bibliographic information in industries classified as agriculture and food science, chemistry and chemical industry, energy, medical and biosciences, science and technology, and engineering.

Some of the widely used databases are :

Chemical Abstracts The Chemical Abstracts database covers all areas of biochemistry and chemical engineering. Sources of information include over 9000 journals, 28 patent issuing authorities and conference proceedings. It contains more than 13 million records.

MARPAT	The Chemical Abstracts Markush Search Service database contains the Markush structures for chemical molecules discussed in patents. Because a typical Markush structure represents several hypothesized substances, the probability of locating all relevant patents based on the "paper chemistry" approach is very high. This is a unique feature of the database and hence for most new molecules, scientists search this database to verify if it is patented.
Derwent	This database covers over 3 million inventions in more than 7 million patent documents from 39 patent-issuing authorities around the world. Pharmaceutical patents are covered from 1963 to the present, agricultural, chemical patents from 1965; polymers from 1966; chemicals from 1970; and all other patents from 1974. Produced by Derwent Publications Ltd., London, UK, this database is updated every week.
INPADOC	This is the world's most comprehensive source of information about patent documents and their legal status. Produced by International Patent Documentation Centre, Vienna, this database covers nearly 25 million patents issued by 66 leading countries, including India. The legal status of patents is also available for 11 countries. INPADOC lists patents in all areas of technology and every week brings together all published documents related to a specific invention into one patent family.
IFI Patent Database	All US utility, reissued, design patents and defence publications from 1950

onwards are covered. The patent records include front page information, covering abstracts and all claims listed from 1971 onwards. Produced by IFI/Plenum Data Corporation USA, this database is updated monthly.

JAPIO Proceedings of the Japanese Patent Office. Over 4 million unexamined patent applications with the Japanese Patent Office are available. All citations and abstracts are in English and cover all type of patents including mechanical, electrical, chemical and physical patents. Companies all over the world seek patent protection in Japan, so the file lets you monitor patent and new product activity on a global scale.

IMS World Patents International (DRUGFAT) This database provides an analysis on the product patent position of more than 1,000 commercially significant drugs either marketed or in active R&D. Each record includes an evaluated entry for all international patents and estimated patent expiry dates country by country. This unique database links patent data with drug name or trade name or Chemical Abstract Service (CAS) registry number or therapeutic group.

A judicious use of these tools helps obtain targeted information on patents collated from a wide number of sources. These databases are "user friendly" but best results are obtained when the searches are planned by the information experts and the client as a team and executed by the information retrieval experts.

The user is expected to list out the information requirements as clearly as possible. One should also consider all the alternative words, expressions dealing with related subjects. It is also important to decide what one is *not* looking for. The team of users and the information expert can then arrive at the appropriate search strategy before going "on-line". Corrections mid-course during the searches are also possible. The searches can be most productive if the user is present during the search. However, with a well-designed search strategy adopted in consultation with the user, the information expert can obtain the desired information.

(A few examples of patent information obtained from such targeted searches are given in Appendix V.)

CASE STUDY

Search 1: Identifying patents in Kevlar

This search is directed at identifying patents on Kevlar—a high speciality construction material used in the space industry. This is a tradename of the polymer. The focus is on its application in rockets, satellites, shuttles, etc. It also looks at alternatives or substitutes either as such or as laminates or fibres.

A judicious combination of the search terms helps arrive at the relevant records. For example, the group S8 combines Kevlar with laminate or fibre to arrive at three hits whose assignees are ranked in the order of their filing numbers. It is also possible to get an on-line patent assignee's report with the patent titles, basic patent date, and IPC code. This can be used to get to the specific patent for further details.

The full report not only gives all the relevant details of the patent but also lists the various polymer fragment codes, plasdoc key serials, plasdoc coding, Derwent Class, etc., which can be used to get targeted information on this subject.

However, a proper search exploiting all the potential of this tool is best done through an information search trained expert.

CASE STUDY

Search 2: Patents in computing and control

This search looks at patents in the file of computing and control as applied to computing.

At first consider the number of patents in the field of computing from 1990–96 — initially during the entire period and then in shorter time spans such as between 1995 and 1996, only in 1996 and finally on a weekly basis. This illustrates how a search can be designed to get patent information for a targeted time-frame. It also searches the period 1990–96 for the number of patents in a few fields such as digital computers, analog and hybrid systems, computer data entry, road signals, etc. In the field of counting, checking, vending, ATM and POS systems the search is ranked in terms of the assignees as a function of the number of patents against their names. The patents in the field of road-signalling computer systems is ranked in terms of the assignees, and for a few assignees even the entire range of subjects (as per the International Classification) on which these assignees have patents is listed. A few sample patent abstracts also can be downloaded to show the type of information available in these databases.

A sample questionnaire for a search request

A typical search request to an information expert can have the following features:

- Title of the project
- Objective of the project
- Topic — Full description should include possible keywords, expressions, alternate words or expressions representing the topic and closely related areas. Also, words or expressions closely related but to be avoided in the searches should be indicated.
- Objective of the search — Is it a search :
  - for priority documents ?
  - to identify various researchers in the field ?
  - to monitor the number and type of patents filed by other researchers/ competitors ?
  - for mapping technologies, etc. ?
- Period of coverage required
- Countries to cover
- International Patent Classification codes if known.

An information expert can prepare a search strategy based on the above information and discussions with the users. A mock search is usually conducted and a few titles with abstracts are downloaded.

After consulting the users on the appropriateness of the results of the mock search, the "search strategy" is refined before embarking on the final search. Based on the titles and abstracts one can order the full text from any of the patent information centres in the country. The internet has now opened new avenues to search for patent information. All the international databases can be accessed through the internet. There are a number of databases that can be accessed free of cost and downloaded from the internet. US patents with their abstracts and claims can be accessed and downladed from the IBM patent server at http//patent. womplex.ibm.com/ibm.html. The availability of CD-ROM databases has revolutionized the patent retrieval system.

15

Harmonization of patent systems

With the emergence of the WTO, there is a major initiative towards harmonization of IPR. This has a number of implications. Various regional cooperation treaties deal with the issue of international priority right of patent protection. Efforts to harmonize intellectual property protection began with the Paris Convention of 1883.

Paris Convention and World Intellectual Property Organization (WIPO)

The Paris Convention has been revised several times (the last one in 1967 in Stockholm and amended in 1979), and now has over 150 members. The Convention handles all forms of intellectual property, including protection against unfair competition. It has three main substantive provisions: (i) national treatment; (ii) right of priority; and (iii) common rules. Though the convention has framed a set of common rules on various ways of dealing with issues related to intellectual property, it also offers freedom to the members to legislate their own laws within the broad framework provided by it. India is not a member of the Paris Convention.

The international body called the WIPO, set up in Geneva, organizes and administers all international activity related to intellectual property.

The most important points of the international conventions are the so-called "national treatment" and the "international priority right" relating to the special rights for the first inventor to file the patent. The priority right gives the inventor the option to file an application in one member country and wait for a year before deciding whether and where to file in other countries without endangering his priority in such countries. Thus the novelty of the invention is preserved irrespective of the publications, irrespective of the invention being made public in any form in these countries during those twelve months. (See Box 15.1.)

Box 15.1 Priority

- Convention countries as defined through Gazette notification of the Government of India.
- Priority date valid up to 12 months from the date of filing in any one of these countries.
- Paris Convention countries priority date valid up to 12 months from the date of filing in any one of the member countries.

European Patent Convention (EPC)

One of the most comprehensive international treaties is the European Patent Convention (EPC), which has one Patent Office, designated as the European Patent Office, in Munich. This performs the functions of centralized filing, examination and granting procedure for its 17 member States. This is also the platform which harmonizes many points of substantive patent law which determine the "after grant protection" of a European patent. However, these patents are still subject to the prevailing national laws in the member states.

Patent Cooperation Treaty (PCT)

The Patent Cooperation Treaty (PCT), covering at present 83 member states, is another attempt towards harmonization of patent systems at the international level. India is not yet a member of this convention. It provides for centralized filing and a common preliminary examination procedure. Thereafter, the application enters the so-called "national" phase in which the examination is completed and the patent granted or refused by the various national offices.

By filing only one application with any of the receiving offices, the PCT applicant can obtain the effect of regular national filings in any PCT State without initially having to furnish a translation of the application or to pay national fees. The national patent granting procedures and the related high expenses are thus postponed.

The patent application filed under the PCT is usually termed an "international" application. However, this application, at best, can lead to grant of patents in the 83 member countries. It does not create a world patent. The patent application has to specify the member countries where the inventor wishes to patent his/her inventions. The receiving office sends the application to an International Search Authority, which undertakes the initial steps in examining the application, including about 16 months from the priority date, which is the date of submitting the application with the receiving office. The application and the search report are published by the International Bureau of the PCT 18 months after the priority date. The application is then transmitted to designated offices and to the applicant.

Within two months of the transmission, an applicant may decide to file the application at the national patent offices of the designated countries. While filing the application at these offices, various fees for patent filing, translation if any, and other official charges of the different countries will have to be paid. From that moment onwards, the patent application is treated just like a normal application filed directly in that country. The applicant has thus avoided expenditure towards these costs for 18 months and the applicant can reconsider whether the protection is now required in all the designated countries or not.

If the applicant so requests, the applications can be examined to see whether it satisfies the criteria of novelty, inventive step and industrial applicability. The report is received by the applicant about 28 months from the priority date. He is now in a much better position to decide whether it is worthwhile to protect the invention in all the designated countries.

A PCT application can even claim the benefit of the priority date of an earlier national patent application under the Paris Convention. If an application can be filed in country 'X' for a national patent, it is possible to seek protection later on in a number of foreign countries using the PCT route by filing a PCT application within 12 months of filing the application in country 'X'. The PCT application can be backdated to the priority date in country 'X'.

Organization Africaine de la Propriete Industrielle (OAPI) and African Regional Industrial Property Organization (ARIPO)

In Africa it is possible to file patent applications through Organization Africaine de la Propriete Industrielle (OAPI) and African Regional Industrial Property Organization (ARIPO). OAPI consists of 14 member countries, namely, Benin, Burkina Faso, Cameroon, Central African Republic, Chad, Congo, Gabon, Guinea, Ivory Coast, Mali, Mauritania, Niger, Senegal and Togo. These countries share a common registry application. ARIPO has 11 member states, namely, Botswana, Gambia, Ghana, Kenya, Lesotho, Malawi, Sudan, Swaziland, Uganda, Zambia and Zimbabwe. ARIPO applications can be filed in any member state. However, all the applications are examined by the ARIPO Industrial Property Office in Harare, Zimbabwe for the granting of patents. Countries where protection is required have to be mentioned and the cost is directly proportional to the number of countries one has selected.

The most recent push to further harmonization has come from the so-called TRIPS part of the GATT. This prescribes minimum standards for protection of "intellectual property". Countries which have not yet met these standards have been given a period of five years to readapt their laws, extendable for the least developed third world countries by another five years. As India is a GATT member, it is obliged to adapt its patent laws within the prescribed time limit.

Other Conventions

Harmonization has been attempted through conventions in other fields of IPR too, for example, the Berne Convention on copyrights and the Madrid Convention on trademarks.

The Madrid Convention

The Madrid Agreement concerns the international filing of trademarks-registration applications. It enables registration of trademarks in WIPO's International Bureau in Geneva, in much the same way as the PCT provides for international filing of patent applications. The WIPO acts as the administering agency for actions taken under the Paris Convention and the registered trademark is protected in each member country. However, the protection obtained is governed by the national laws of individual member countries and is limited by national laws. Signatories to the Madrid Agreement and other countries are negotiating a new agreement referred to as the **Madrid Protocol**. The Madrid Protocol aims at obtaining protection for trademarks through international recognition, and is to be policed by the WIPO, which will maintain records of all applications. It is proposed that each registration will be effective for ten years, although this period would be indefinitely extendable on request for additional ten-year terms.

The North American Free Trade Agreement (NAFTA)

NAFTA is a general trade agreement between Canada, Mexico and USA. It lists general requirements for both domestic and international treatment and enforcement of IPR. The agreement recognizes the need, at a minimum, to accede and give effect to the main international conventions relating to intellectual property, i.e. the Paris Convention (intellectual property), the Berne Convention (copyrights), the Geneva Convention (protection of phonograms or audio works), and the Union for the Protection of New Varieties of Plants (UPOV).

The Budapest Treaty

The Budapest Treaty, consisting of 35 contracting states, was signed on 28 April, 1977 and amended on 26 September, 1980. It deals with the subject of deposition of micro-organisms with institutions recognized as "depository institutions" for biological materials. A list of these institutions is given in Appendix VII.

The 35 contracting states are Australia, Austria, Belgium, Bulgaria, China, Cuba, Czechoslovakia, Denmark, Finland, France, Germany, Greece, Hungary, Holland, Iceland, Italy, Japan, Latvia, Liechtenstein, Norway, Philippines, Poland, Republic of Korea, Republic of Moldova, Russia, Singapore, Slovakia, Spain, Sweden, Switzerland, Tajikistan, Trinidad and Tobago, UK, USA and Yugoslavia.

The approved collection centres are called International Depository Authority (IDA). There are 26 such IDAs spread over the above countries. Evidently, all the countries do not have IDAs. Some of the IDAs are: Australian government analytical laboratories, Australia; Belgian coordinated collections of micro-organisms, Belgium; China Centre for Type Culture Collection and China General Microbiological Culture Centre, China; Collection Espanola do Cultivos, Spain; Culture Collection of Yeasts, Slovakia; Czech Collection of Micro-organisms, Czechoslovakia; Korean Cell Line

Research Foundation, Korean Culture Centre of micro-organisms and Korean Research Institute of Bioscience and Biotechnology, Korea; and so on. There are four centres in the UK, two in the USA and three in Russia. A small country like South Korea has three such centres. A large variety of micro-organisms, such as algae, animal embryos, animal viruses, cell culture, bacteria, fungi, moulds, hybridomas, oncogenes, yeasts, plasimids, protozoa, RNA, seeds, etc., are handled by these centres.

An IDA must store a deposited micro-organism for at least five years after the most recent request for a sample and for at least thirty years from the original date of deposit. While applying for patents, an applicant must deposit the micro-organism no later than the patent application. A person may obtain a culture sample from a centre but cannot pass on the sample to anyone till the patent application is pending in the Patent Office or so long as the essential patent lasts. While the application is pending, the person obtaining the sample undertakes to use the culture for experimental purposes only. Both these conditions will only apply if the patent is denied or the application is withdrawn by the applicant.

To become a member of the Budapest Treaty, the country must be a member of the Paris Convention. India is not a member of the Paris Convention and as a consequence does not qualify to be a member of the Budapest Treaty.

The GATT

The General Agreement on Tariff and Trade (GATT) was an international platform established in 1947 to evolve a framework for enhancement of global trade in "goods". The first seven rounds of the discussions till 1979 addressed issues related to the goods sector and aimed at establishing non-tariff barriers across the nations.

However, the well-known Uruguay round of multilateral trade negotiations initiated in September, 1986, made a major deviation from the traditional goods sector to include three new areas, namely investments, services and IPR. In addition, the traditional goods sector also broadened its scope to bring in issues related to textiles and agriculture.

This entire package generated varied views from the different nations as the GATT umbrella would strongly influence the domestic socio-economic policies to meet the requirements of GATT. This created a virtual split among the member states, resulting in what may broadly be termed as a "North–South Debate".

In December 1991, the GATT Director-General Mr Arthur Dunkel proposed some "compromise solutions" which were tabled as the "Dunkel Draft". This document aimed at establishing the WTO with a commitment from its "member states" to implement the agreed-upon "interrelated features" of GATT, such as the Trade Related Investment Measures (TRIMS), the General Agreement on Trade Services (GATS), the agreement on TRIPS and the agreement on establishing the WTO.

The "Dunkel Draft" has been one of the most publicized international documents which has raised a wide range of controversies in India within all sections of the society; including politicians, government, bureaucrats, trade, industry, farmers, academicians, scientists, technologists, trade unions, students, etc. The response was dependent on one's perception of the issues involved, either in "isolation" or in a "cross-related" manner.

With specific reference to TRIPS it was feared in many quarters that the signing of the GATT would force India to change her Patents Act of 1970, in a direction not favourable to her socio-economic interests. The arguments in favour were that a stronger and more harmonized IPR regime in India would enhance industrial and economic progress through higher Foreign Direct Investments (FDI), access to world-class productive technologies in all sectors, including agriculture, create a thrust for internationally competitive research and development activities in the national institutions, etc.

Even though India finally signed the GATT, she is yet to arrive at a consensus on the exact changes to be introduced in the Indian Patents Act, 1970, the Indian Designs Act, 1911 and the Indian Trade & Merchandise Act, 1958.

Box 15.2 GATT highlights

- In addition to the traditional goods sector, three new areas — investment, IPR and services — were added.
- TRIPS is a part of the GATT.
- Technology is becoming a valuable commercial and tradeable asset.

Continues

Continued

- Knowledge-based industries and intellectual goods are on the rise.
- Huge loss to world markets due to piracy of intellectual property in pharmaceutical, chemical, film and computer software industries.

  TRIPS covers copyrights, trademarks, geographical indications, industrial designs patents, integrated circuits and trade secrets.

The major implication of the GATT and the establishing of the WTO is the harmonization of IPR across the borders, leading to easier trade and business practices (see Box 15.2). In the present Indian Patents Act, 1970, no product patents are allowed for pharmaceuticals, food products and agrochemicals. However, on a complete review of the present Act in the light of India's signing the GATT, a number of changes may be forthcoming: (i) Product patents to be allowed in all fields of technology without exception. (ii) All patents to have a uniform duration of 20 years. (iii) Under the current patent law, Government of India has powers to grant compulsory licenses in public interest without consulting the patent holder. In future, compulsory licenses may have to be given only on merit of each case

Box 15.3 Present Patents Act and suggested modifications

CURRENT PATENTS ACT IS TO BE MODIFIED AS A RESULT OF THE GATT

Present Act	Modification
• No product patent allowed for pharmaceuticals, food products and agrochemicals; only process patents.	• Product patents to be allowed in all fields of technology without exception.
• Duration : 14 years for all except for patents in pharmaceutials, food products and	• Uniform duration of 20 years.

Continues

Continued

agrochemicals, where it is seven years.	
• Government has powers to grant compulsory licenses.	• Compulsory licenses to be given only on merits of each case. Patent holder will be given an opportunity to be heard.
• Importation does not amount to working of patent.	• No discrimination between imported and domestic products.
• For process patents, in case of infringement, burden of proof on plaintiff.	• The burden of proof will rest on the infringer (reversal of burden of proof).

and the patent holder will have to be given an opportunity to be heard. (iv) Non-production of the patented item in India and mere importation amounts to non-working of patent under the present Act. In the modified form, no discrimination may be made between imported and domestic products on the issue of working of patents. (v) In case of infringement of a process patent the burden of proof is on the plaintiff and not the alleged infringer as per the prevailing law. The burden of proof in future will have to shift onto the alleged infringer under the terms of the GATT. In TRIPS' parlance this is called the "reversal of burden of proof".

The implication of these modifications will be that firms in India have to strengthen their innovation system and take a more proactive approach towards patents. (See Boxes 15.3 and 15.4.)

Box 15.4 Transition period

- General transition period of five years to developing countries.
- Also an additional transition period of five years to those developing countries which presently do not provide for

Continues

Continued

accepted as from the date of the GATT. If those products have already been granted patents and marketing approval in any other country, and the patent owner desires to introduce those products in the Indian market, he should be given exclusive rights for five years or till the pending application in India is approved or rejected, whichever is earlier. This is also called the pipeline protection.

WTO excludes the following from patentability

Under the WTO agreements, member countries, if they so desire, are given a choice of excluding some items from patentability. These items are spelt out in Section 5, Article 27 of the agreement on TRIPS:

- Members may exclude from patentability such inventions, the prevention, within their territory, of commercial exploitation of which is necessary to protect public order or morality, including the protection of human, animal or plant life or health or to avoid serious prejudice to the environment, provided that such exclusion is not made merely because the exploitation is prohibited by their law.
- Members may also exclude from patentability:
  - — diagnostic, therapeutic and surgical methods for the treatment of humans and animals;
  - — plants, animals other than micro-organisms, essentially biological processes for the production of plants or animals; non-biological and microbiological processes are patentable. However, members shall provide for the protection of plant varieties either by patents or by an effective *sui generis* system or by any combination thereof. The provisions of this sub-paragraph shall be renewed four years after the date of entry into the WTO agreement.

Each country has freedom to frame its patent laws within the broad framework defined in the WTO agreement to protect national interests.

Patents Amendment Bill 1999 — It's Implications

1. *January 1st 1995*: India signed the GATT, became a member of the WTO and was obliged to meet the provisions of the Trade Related Intellectual Property Rights (TRIPs). The Indian Patent Act (IPA) of 1970 was amended to satisfy articles 64, 70.8 to 70.9

of TRIPS, comprising (i) setting up a mailbox facility to file patents for drugs, pharmaceuticals and agro-chemicals. (ii) providing opptions to obtain 'Exclusive Marketing Rights' (EMR) in the above 3 fields. (iii) and setting up an Expert Group, suggested by the Govt. of India, so that amendments were implemented

2. *December 31st 1994*: The President of India promulgated the Patent Ordinance (PO) No. 13, 1994, which became effective on 1st January 1995.
3. *March 1995*: The Patent Amendments Bill (PAB) was passed by the Lok Sabha, but was rejected by the Rajya Sabha. It was presented to a select Committee which gave its report on 10 May '96. Meanwhile, the PAB lapsed in 1995 with the dissolution of the 10th Lok Sabha.
4. *January 1st 1995 – 15th February 1997*: 1,339 application for patents. U.S. companies filed a total of 363 applications.
5. *December 1998*: The PAB was passed by the Rajya Sabha. This was followed by the Patents Ordinance (No. 3 of 1999), published in the Gazette of India, Part II Section I, dated Jan 8, 1999.

The essential features of the Ordinance are

General Aspects applicable to any invention in any field

i) Omission of Section 39 of the Indian Patents Act 1970. All sections in the Patent Act connected with Section 39 (e.g. Section 40, part of 64, 118 which are penalties for not adhering to Section 39 of the Patents Act) were removed as well. This implies that persons resident in India can make the first filings of their patents anywhere in the world.
ii) Government of India retains the right not to disclose any information relating to patentable inventions, and the power to take action, including revocation of any patent in the interest of the security of India. For eg:
    - fissionable materials, traffic in arms, ammunition
    - and in times of war or other emergencies

Aspects applicable only to Drugs, Pharmaceuticals, Agroc-hemicals

Filing of product Patents

Section 5 subsection (a) and (b) of the Patents Act 1970 does not allow grant of Product Patents for foods, drugs, medicines or even to substances prepared or produced by chemical processes including alloys, optical glass, semiconductors and inter–metallic compounds. Only Process Patents are allowed in these areas.

This ordinance removes this restriction for inventions related to drugs and medicines only. The restrictions for foods and other chemically prepared products remain.

However, Patent Applications for drugs and medicines would not be examined until 31st December 2004 or until the New Indian Patent Act is passed and comes into force, whichever is earlier.

The term "Medicines or Drugs" includes: medicines, insecticides and fungicides, and chemical substances used in the preparation of medicines.

It will, therefore, be seen that this ordinance allows filing of applications for Product Patents in the area of Pharmaceuticals, Agro-chemicals and intermediaries which are used in the manufacture of medicinal and allied substances.

The Ordinance & Exclusive Marketing Rights (EMR)

A major change is the inclusion of a pipeline protection of five years for drugs and medicines after filing a Product Patent application on or after 01.01.95. These products can qualify for the granting of Exclusive Marketing Rights (EMR) provided certain conditions were fulfilled.

The controller would not refer all applications made under this ordinance to an examiner until December 31,2004. Only inventions which do not fall within the preview of Section 3 and Section 4 (IPA 1970) (i.e. satisfy the criteria or patentable invention) would qualify for consideration of EMR in India.

A special provision in the ordinance states that any substance or article based on the System of Indian Medicine as defined in clause (e) of sub-section (1) of Section 2 of the Indian Medicine Council Act 1970 and such substance or article already in the public domain will not qualify for the granting of EMR in India.

To obtain EMR (pipeline protection) for products application, for which patents are filed in India, exclusively in the areas of Drugs, Pharmaceuticals and Agrochemicals, the applicant would have to meet the following requirements:

a) Inventions made in India or in a country other than India
   The applicant must have filed an application for a patent in any convention country for an identical invention on or after 01.01.95.

The patent approval is based on tests conducted on or after January 1, 1999, or after the date of making the patent application in India.

b) Inventions made in India
The applicant must have filed a patent application in India for the process relating to the identical product on or after 01.01.95.

c) He/she must have received the approval to sell or distribute the article or substance from the authority specified by the Government of India.

The term of the exclusive marketing rights will be for five years on or from the date of approval till the date of grant of the patent or the date of rejection of application for the grant of patent, whichever is earlier.

If the invention has been recorded in a document or the invention has been tried or used before or the article has been sold by a person before the claim for a patent of that invention is made in India or in a convention country, then the sale or distribution of the article or substance by such a person after the claim referred to in the patent application shall not be deemed to be an infringement of EMR.

Before granting EMR, the controller will have to ascertain
- that the application for the product patent is a "patentable invention under the sections 3 & 4 of the Indian Patents Act 1970
- conduct other investigation he deems necessary
- ensure that all the other conditions outlined in the ordinance are satisfied.

Other Issues in the Ordinance

They are:

1) Selling and distribution of the article in India would be considered as working of the invention.
2) Clause (d) and (c) under Section 90 dealing with importation and working of patent were deleted. This implied that importation would be considered as working of the invention in India.
3) In the public interest the Government had reserved the right to intervene while granting EMR and issuing Compulsory Licenses and to decide on the pricing of articles covered under the EMR.
4) All suits relating to infringement of an EMR would be dealt with in the same manner as suits concerning infringement of patents under Chapter 18 of the Patents Act 1970.

The PAB of 1999 brings in continuity with respect to all actions taken under the ordinance of 1994 as if this ordinance is operative from January 1, 1995.

16

Debatable issues

The rapid advances in science and technology and growing concern for protection of innovations makes it obvious that patents influence the research process significantly as they touch every aspect of science and technology. A few selected titles for further reading are listed in Appendix IX. It is relevant to consider whether the patent system provides a platform for protecting innovations without witholding the progress of knowledge or, more importantly, without "cornering knowledge". Global debates on various issues linked to the commercial world of gene hunting and control of genetic data, and private banks of "expressed sequence tags" (ESTs) remain unresolved.

Various private companies are already setting up collaborative gene banks with the help of research institutions. An example of this is, the Institute of Genomic Research and Human Genome Sciences Inc. founded by Smithkline Beecham. To use information from such private databanks, one will have to agree on appropriate legal arrangements especially with respect to the ownership of any intellectual property generated from research using the data.

On the technical aspects, patentability tests in terms of "prior art", " non-obviousness", differences between "true inventiveness" versus "extensions of discoveries", stating of exact boundary of claims, deciding on the issues of "first to invent" versus "first to file", enforcement of patents, especially interpreting claims while dealing with infringements, etc. pose tricky and sensitive problems. Moral and ethical issues, including "research exemption", which may have a direct impact on the "research process", "protection of living forms and gene sequences" are increasingly being debated. Many of the advances in information technology and biotechnology today have a very broad scope for future utilization. Aspects related to the "utility factor" are also troubling the patenting process in biotechnology and software. New questions are being raised: "How much of utility has to be demonstrated to make generic claims on such inventions?"

The point in question is: "Has the pendulum in patenting moved to the extreme edge where the laws are beginning to hinder free creative thinking and progress that the patent system is actually supposed to encourage?" The number of patent litigations in biotechnology is obviously raising such concerns.

According to some schools of thought, the patenting system is propagating "cornering of knowledge" and we are progressing towards non-sharing of the products of the human intellect. A contrasting view is that this act of protecting knowledge will encourage concerted team effort by cross-utilization of global expertise via mutually acceptable "cross-licensing" arrangements. These will be facilitated by the powerful emerging tools of information technology, leading to the formation of effective cooperative networks.

Biodiversity, exploitation of traditional knowledge available with tribes held by the tribal settlements by researchers for development of new products, and use of geographical indicators have become emotional subjects which have generated a lot of political interest. This chapter attempts to highlight some of these aspects.

Research exemption

Patent information is easily accessible from various sources. In this growing "information-protection" driven society, a major fear haunting researchers in the field of biotechnology, computer software, etc., is the question: Should scientists be allowed to carry out research using a patented process without either a license or the permission of the patent holder?" Will such use amount to infringement? Some of the glaring confusions while defining "research exemption" are highlighted in Box 16.1.

Box 16.1 Research exemption

- In principle, the use of information from patented inventions in "pure research" is exempt from infringement liability.

Continues

Continued

- However, problems arise when what constitutes pure research has to be defined. How "pure" should "pure research" be to qualify for this exemption? This is particularly relevant to research in biotechnology/software, and high speciality materials.
- Patents are also being obtained on research tools!

Issue

Can such patented research tools be used in "competitive research"?

Answers to these questions are not clear at this stage.

CASE STUDY

Roche vs Bolar (1984)

This case highlights issues related to the use of patented information for the development of drugs prior to the expiry of the patent for that particular drug.

Denying defence to a generic drug manufacturer who used a patented drug during the patent term in order to conduct clinical tests so that they would be able to get approval from the Food and Drug Administration to market the drug as soon as the patent expired. The US Supreme Court (1990) gave a more liberal interpretation and upheld the amendment to Patent Statute 271(e), which permits the use of patented inventions for the purpose of developing and submitting information under laws regulating manufacture, use or sale of drugs.

(*Source* : Rebecca Eisenberg, *ABSP working series in Intellectual Property Rights*, 11–14 July 1994, Washington, USA.)

The matter has been compounded due to the ambiguities in the current judicial interpretations on this question when applied to inventions related to biotechnology and software. The research community needs to be made sensitive and aware of the possible pitfalls as they "carry out research" using information drawn from patents.

The dispute between Promega and Hoffman-La Roche on the use of thermostable Taq polymerase for research purposes in various laboratories and the case of Murex Diagnostic Limited and Organon Teknika Limited vs Chiron related to the making and selling of test kits for Hepatitis-C virus highlight the dilemma.

(*Source*: Simon Cohen, *Nature*, **376**: 17 August, 1995, and references therein.)

As Murex was involved in the development of an assay for serotyping the Hepatitis-C virus, Chiron successfully sued Murex for patent infringement. Murex had to reach an agreement with Chiron while awaiting the hearing of its appeal. Similarly, Roche identified scientists as having "infringed" its patent on the enzyme Taq by using an unauthorized Taq produced by Promega for experiments using polymerase chain reaction (PCR) technique. (*Nature* **375**, 348, 1995). This case highlights the need to be aware of patent-related issues even while using materials and techniques.

Disclosures and record maintenance

In most countries, the principle of "first to file" is recognized while deciding on priority. However, in USA, priority is awarded on the "first to invent" principle. Until recently, this protection was given only to inventions made in USA. However, since the formation of the WTO, USA has changed its patent laws. The protection under "first to invent" rule is now extended to all members of the WTO. To take advantage of this feature, researchers are required to maintain their research records in a prescribed way for them to be considered valid in the US courts. (This has been elaborated in Chapter 8, Box 8.2.)

One of the weaknesses in the Indian research institutions has been the lack of systematic documentation of research results and their disclosure in conferences, meetings, etc. Systems will have to be put in place in the Indian institutions for proper maintenance of their research records for recognition by US courts, if necessary.

CASE STUDY

Case of "backing storage"

Summary: This involves a software technique which provides multiple programs with Windows. Helps to temporarily/partially save contents of Window in an off-screen memory.

MIT scientists and AT&T were working on this simultaneously. MIT considered the invention obvious, though AT&T believed it to be patentable.

AT&T applied for a patent about a week before MIT published a programmers' manual for their "LISP" machine.

AT&T was granted US Patent No. 4555775 and the MIT manual was not considered prior art:

All computer companies and many users who accepted the software from MIT on the understanding that it was free are facing possible law suits.

The only way MIT can escape is if, through documentary evidence they can prove that they were the first to invent.

Trade secret law

With rapid growth and diversification of industry and increased competition, alternate employment opportunities are opening up. Trade secret law addresses the issue of "employee's freedom to accept a new position which may be subject to the restriction that trade secrets of the former employer be protected". This feature is specially important while deciding on employee's service contracts, material-transfer agreements and research collaborations. This coupled with the discipline of research records maintenance and controlled/ institutionalized disclosures will ensure proper protection of institutional intellectual property.

"Trade secret" means information, including a formula, pattern, compilation, program, device, method, technique or process, that

- derives independent economic value, actual or potential by
  - — not being generally known (to persons who can use and obtain economic value from its disclosure or use); and
  - — not being readily ascertainable by proper means by other persons who can use, obtain economic value from its disclosure or use;
- is the subject of efforts that are reasonable under the circumstances to maintain its secrecy.

An example of a trade secret litigation is given below.

CASE STUDY

Case of US Patent No. 5082813

A laboratory assistant P. Taborsky was awarded the USPatent No. 5082813 for a process to obtain a "clay-form" useful for sewage treatment.

In 1987, Taborsky was working on a day-testing research project in a university's engineering laboratory. This research project was sponsored by a subsidiary of the Florida Progress Corporation. Taborsky had signed a routine confidentiality agreement as part of his job application. According to Taborsky, his professor gave him permission to experiment with leftovers after the three-month project ended. Taborsky invented a new way to heat the substance beyond 850°F (i.e. 454°C) without destroying it. This clay form found application in sewage treatment plants. His professor Robert Camahan claimed that the invention belonged to the University as it grew out of the original project.

Taborsky was arrested and charged with theft. He accused Taborsky of having stolen two research notebooks from a locked laboratory. This act was a violation of the confidentiality agreement with the University.

Professor Robert Camahan and Taborsky had submitted two independent patent applications to the US Patent Office for the process of heating the clay to achieve it in the "specific form" prior to the case.

In 1990, Taborsky was convicted of "grand theft" and "theft of trade secrets" and was sentenced to one year's house arrest and 15 year's probation.

On examination of the applications side by side, the US Patent Office granted three US patents to Taborsky. Robert Camahan's application was rejected. In 1992, the judge found Taborsky guilty of violating probation for using the disputed notebooks. Taborsky was sentenced to three years in the state prison when he refused to assign the patent to the University.

The University has challenged the ownership of the other two patents and civil law suits are pending.

(*Source: Pioneer*, June 20, 1996.)

This highlights a very important point regarding classification of information and information security arrangements in any organization. There must be a formal definition of "confidential", "private", "public" information in an organization which is made known to all associated or dealing with the organization. Without this it may not be possible to defend an institutional case especially in disputes related to ownership and use of information.

Software protection

Growing importance of software in our information technology driven society, calls for effective legal systems for its protection. In

1995–96 the software industry in India had grown by 61% with a turnover of $ 734 million. With this galloping growth rate, by the year 2000 the Indian software industry is expected to command a dominant position in the world market. To retain the competitive edge it is imperative that Indian software professionals are sensitized and made aware of the avenues available to them for protecting the software they create. Likewise, they must be made aware of the pitfalls and legal constraints while using the available knowledge, thereby avoiding possible infringement of others' rights. The issue becomes even more complex when one considers software developments via "off-shore services" — a common feature in today's world. Box 16.2 highlights the major aspects of software protection.

Box 16.2 Software protection: Major aspects

The debate is: what is the best mode of protection for software — copyright or patent ?

- Historically, software has been considered as:
  - — more art than process;
  - — more idea than device;
  - — therefore would fall under copyright.
- However, it has also been considered for patenting in USA.
- More than 3,500 software patents have been approved in USA and the rate is accelerating.

Issues

- Poses problems while differentiating from prior art.
- Using patent information for further developments.
- Commonly used software techniques do not appear in scientific literature for they are :
  - — either too obvious to be published or too general, or even open secrets;
  - — there are varied interpretations by courts on validity.

Copyright: A means

TRIPS recognizes copyright as the main modality for protection of computer programs. Article 10, Part II of TRIPS suggests that computer programs, whether in source or object code, be protected as literary works under the Berne Convention (1971). Even though most countries, including India, have adopted the Berne Convention, there are a number of features in their national copyright laws which provide avenues for varied interpretation and continue to be intensely debated.

For instance, though Article 10 applies to computer programs "in source or object code", it is silent with respect to cases where they are embedded in micro-electronic devices. In the same way, no specific rule exists in connection with reverse engineering, an aspect which is most common and yet controversial in the software field. The TRIPS agreement also introduces exclusive "rental rights" for computer programs. Further, there is non-clarity on "authorship", especially when it comes to deciding "authorship in computer generated works" and "artificial intelligence" (see Box 16.3). In certain cases it creates problems in exactly identifying the elements of human contribution *vis-à-vis* the job "preformed" by the machine. Software being a rapidly developing field with a very short lifespan in the innovation cycle, the relevance of such long-term protection (60 years) provided through copyrights is questionable. There are no international standards or directives dealing with the applicability of "moral rights" to authors of computer programs and the legitimacy of its reproduction by users for private use. A host of questions arise. For example: What constitutes infringement? How many copies can legally be made and for what purposes? What is the scope of the right to adapt a program for use on a specific hardware or with a different computing language? What governs the admissibility of decompilation and reverse engineering, interfacing of programs, etc.?

However, there are a few issues whose interpretations are clear. These include: (i) making of copies or adaptation of a computer program by a lawful possessor of a copy, or making back-up copies purely as a temporary protection against loss, destruction or damage in order to utilize the computer program for the purposes for which it was supplied. This would not amount to infringement of a computer program. (ii) Compilations of data or other material, whether in machine readable or other form, which either because of their selection or arrangement of the contents constitute intellectual creations and are protectable as copyrights. However, such protection is not extended to the data itself.

The inclusion of databases as protectable under copyrights raises further questions on their lawful "usage", "conditions of infringement", etc. The problem gets compounded in today's cyberworld with "virtual libraries", "on-line database access", "electronic data transfer", etc.

Box 16.3 Definition of "computer", "computer program" and "author" in the Indian Copyright Act, 1957

- "Computer" includes any electronic or similar device having information processing capabilities.
- "Computer program" means a set of instructions expressed in words, codes, schemes or in any other form, including a machine readable medium, capable of causing a computer to perform a particular task or achieve a particular result.
- "Author" is the person who causes the work to be recorded would be the author. The expression "computer generated" has not been defined in the Act.

The Indian Copyright (amendment) Act, 1994 which was brought into effect on 10 May, 1995 included provisions for "protection of computer software" (by considering them as literary works) and "computer generated works". Computer software as "literary work" included computer programs and computer databases.

This definition suffers from a few drawbacks:

- The words, "codes, schemes or any other form," cannot by themselves cause a computer to perform a particular task unless it is incorporated in a machine readable medium.
- A machine readable medium alone, without the set of instructions expressed in words, etc., being incorporated in it, cannot cause a computer to perform. The Indian definition misses the essential element of incorporation in a medium and therefore creates problems in implementing unless suitably amended.
- Use of the expression "computer generated" in the definition of "author" signifies that if any work literary, artistic, musical, etc., is computer generated, the author will be the person who causes the work to be recorded. The expression "computer generated" has not been explicitly defined in the Act.

The Copyright, Designs and Patents Act, 1986 of UK is the first national law to include provisions on computer generated work. According to Section 178 of the UK Act of 1988, *"computer generated" in relation to a work, means that the work is generated by the computer in circumstances such that there is no human author of the work.* There have also been divergent opinions on whether there can be an artificial computer intelligence which can really create work without any human creative contribution.

If such computer "creations" are possible, the results of such creations being covered by the Berne Convention, which is based on the notion of intellectual creations by human beings, is questionable.

These are only a few debatable aspects of this evolving field.

Patenting software

Computer programs, including algorithms under certain conditions, are also protectable as trade secrets or even patents in countries like USA.

Initially, computer programs with mathematical algorithms were not considered patentable because they were equated with laws of nature. However, after the historic judgment in 1991 in Diamond vs Diehr, the US Supreme Court allowed for a process in which the claims were broader than just software.

After this judgement the standards were modified as follows:

- A mathematical algorithm is not patentable in and of itself, but may be part of a larger patentable process or machine.
- Inclusion of a mathematical algorithm, or the implementation or use of a programmable digital computer will not in itself render an invention unpatentable.

Thus a patent may be available for technical effects produced by the operation of a computer program, but such a patent does not extend any protection to the computer program itself.

For example the US Patent No. 926591 describes an apparatus and method for setting and maintaining the set points of a plurality of product variables for a glass product on a production line. A programmed computer establishes and maintains the set points in response to feedback signals representing the actual values of the product variables. This helps optimize operations in the production line.

Similarly, the US Patent No. 504579 discloses a method and device for automatically controlling the time-period of photographic development for each specific combination of a photographic developer and a photosensitive material for the purpose of obtaining a substantially identical or optimum photographic development at various temperatures. These patents based on computer programs were allowed because technical effects were produced by the operation of the programs.

In a case where no technical effect is produced, a patent will not be available in respect of the computer program. This is well illustrated in the case of Wang Laboratories International's application of 21 March, 1990 published in December, 1991. In this case, a computer was so programmed that an expert could store his knowledge in a hierarchical form (a computer system shell), from which, expert advice could be obtained. Both the computer system shell and the expert system were claimed in the patent. Hardware was conventional as there was no change in the way it functioned. The application was rejected on the ground that it was a mere computer program performing a mental act.

Typical examples of software patents

- Application software—spell checks, translations
- Parts of operating systems/compilers
- User interfaces—data entry screen and Apple mouse
- Business methods employing computers/data processing systems
- Computer-controlled machines

Advantages of protecting software through patents

There are many advantages of protecting software through patents. They include the following:

- provide strong protection;
- exclude all use, even independent creation;
- cover ideas implemented in the invention, as well as their expression;
- do not require the owner to prove copying in an infringement suit;
- provide broad remedies;
- allow one to disclose the invention without fear of proprietorship loss.

The possible disadvantages, if any, are:

- the software must satisfy strict novelty requirement;
- there must be a disclosure of invention in the patent application; in view of this, the software developer is always at a loss to decide whether to patent or to keep the innovation a secret.

The validity of a patent can always be challenged; thus one runs the risk of the patent or even some claim being declared invalid after a lengthy and expensive litigation process. Under such circumstances, enforcement of the patent could be problematic.

Borderline cases in the computer software area which may be protectable under copyrights or patents, need to be scanned with special professional care. In such cases, it is always advisable to apply for a patent because, even if the patent fails on the grounds that the invention relates to a computer program, the subject will still automatically be protected by the copyright law. The inventor does not stand to lose in making a patent application for such inventions, but a decision, when in doubt, not to file a patent could be fatal because no patent can be applied for once the invention is made public by use or publication.

Generic Drugs

For product patents to be allowed under TRIPS, drug houses will have to intensify their R&D efforts to create new molecules which will finally qualify as safe drugs for commercialization. To retain competitiveness one will have to conceive of a number of "forms" of the "same" or structurally similar molecules which have the potential of acting as a drug, and protect them through a judicious set of broad claims in a number of patents. The recent dispute between Novopharma and Glaxo illustrates this need most effectively.

CASE STUDY

Novopharma vs Glaxo — 1996

- Glaxo patented the ulcer drug molecule in form 1 (which expired in July, 1997) and also registered it via trademark Zantac.
- Subsequetly Glaxo also patented a form 2 which will expire by 2002.
- Novopharma USA Inc. developed a generic version of form 1 of the drug and planned to produce the same on a commercial scale. But Glaxo filed a patent infringement suit in a US District Court in California against Novopharma USA in 1994.
- The judge decided that Novopharma's form 1 does not infringe on the patent for form 2 held by Glaxo.

What is a generic drug?

A generic drug is a formulation containing the same active compound as an earlier approved drug.

For the purposes of the Food, Drug and Cosmetic Act (FDC) USA, a new drug may be described as:

- a novel chemical compound;
- a known chemical or substance, but not previously used in medicine;
- a newly proposed use or dosage of a known drug; or
- a drug which, although recognized as safe and effective, has not been used to a material extent or for a material time.

Normally, a new drug is patented by the inventors. When the approval is obtained under the FDA in USA, the patented information on the approved drug is published in the "*Orange Book*".

In the case of generic drugs, one can request for an expedited Food and Drugs Authority (FDA) approval by filing an Abbreviated New Drug Application (ANDA).

This application must include one of the following statements :

- Such patent information has not been filed.
- Such patent has expired.
- Such patent will expire on a particular date.
- Such patent is invalid or will not be infringed by manufacture, use or sale of the drug for which approval is being sought.

The patent holder of the original drug is notified of such an ANDA application.

If the patent holder files an infringement suit within 45 days on receiving the ANDA notification, then the FDA puts the approval on hold for 30 months or till the court gives a ruling on the same.

The patent law in the USA has changed and the term of patents is now 20 years. As a transitional provision, all patents in force on 08-06-95 will have a term of 20 years from the date of issue, whichever is longer. As per this provision, a few patents will receive an extension of their term.

This extension period is called the "delta" period. Assuming that some companies would have made substantial investments with the hope of exploiting patents which are due to expire (as per the 17-year period), they could find themselves running into a problem. Accordingly, the new law provides for a "safety net" or "safe harbour" which gives protection to those who fall in this category by legislating that the patent owner cannot obtain an injunction against the infringing competitor. However, the competitor must pay the patent owner a "fair amount".

Interestingly when the patent term was modified by inclusion of a safe harbour provision, no amendment was made in the FDA Act. This has resulted in confusion on the approval process for generic drugs. Litigations on infringement issues have already surfaced in the US courts.

Drug manufacturers are therefore advised to consult experts in the field before taking business decisions on generic drugs. This is especially important for Indian companies involved in development, manufacture and export of generic drugs.

CASE STUDY

Bristol-Myers Squibb (BMS) — and the patent for Captopril

The BMS patent was due to expire on 8 August, 1995. The amended US Act provided as extension of its term to 13 February, 1996.

DuPont Merck Pharmaceutical Co., Endo Labs, LLC., Mylan Pharmaceuticals Inc. served BMS for a declatory judgment. They claimed that during the delta period they could sell, make, use Captopril without being considered as infringers of the BMS patent. They also sought an injunction to compel BMS to waive the FDA's 45 day notice period for filing suit.

Court verdict: Federal Circuit Court of appeals ruled against the generic drug manufacture.

CASE STUDY

Bristol-Myers Squibb (BMS) vs Royce Laboratory Inc.

- BMS sued Royce Laboratory Inc. for patent infringement after Royce amended its Captopril ANDA from an expiry certification to a non-infringement certification.
- BMS asked FDA to put the approval on hold.
- The District Court considered that the actual sale of Royce's Captopril drug during the delta period would not infringe the BMS patent because of safe harbour provision.
- On appeal, the Federal Circuit Court reversed the District Court's decision in favour of BMS.

  (*Source*: Newspaper reports and M.R. Buscher, A.G. Minsk, *Chemtech*, January 1996, pp. 54–57.)

Many of the drug companies in India are looking at ways to service the "bulk generics" market in the USA which is expected to grow to $ 3 billion over the next five years. With the introduction of the Supplementary Protection Certificate (SPC) in Europe, the drug manufacturers in Europe will also have to submit an equivalent of ANDA (as in the USA) to drug authorities. Samples of the "drug" together with the ANDA will have to be submitted at least "four years" before the drug "goes off patent". This requirement automatically chokes the new US generic drug market for European producers, especially in Italy and Spain. Many of the Indian producers of "bulk generics" are already "eyeing" the US market through the establishment of joint ventures, alliances, etc.

Indian industries engaging in the manufacture and sale (especially export to USA and Europe) of generic drugs must be aware of the actual patent status of such drugs in various countries, including USA.

Protection of living forms

Any living form that has existed in nature does not qualify for a patent. However, anything created by human ingenuity and application of human intellect, if "new" and "non-obvious," is in principle patentable. Though this appears fairly simple, the issue has multifaceted dimensions and inhibits single-track interpretations.

Biotechnology

The last two decades have experienced remarkable progress in biotechnology. Subjects which were popularly classified as "fiction" and "fantasy" have rapidly been converted into "working reality". This has been due to our enhanced understanding of the various processes, and structural–functional relationships in basic genetic entities, aided by sophistication in instrumental and manipulation techniques. Reproducible "transgenic organisms / plants" with unique features and functions have also emerged. These advances have become possible due to major efforts by cross-functional teams in biology, physics, chemistry, engineering, computers, etc. Concepts and techniques across all disciplines have got so intimately integrated that their interdependence cannot be easily separated.

Such innovations developed by large inputs of manpower and money have become active items for protection through patents. However, our legal systems have also to undergo an appropriate metamorphosis to deal with such rapid changes which, in addition to technological complexities, have ethical undertones of considerable gravity.

The phase lag between the biotechnological advances and the evolution of an appropriate legal framework to deal with them has already erupted into a number of litigations. Interestingly, the varied judgments on many identical/similar cases only highlight the prevailing inadequacies in the patent laws in various countries, including those in USA and Europe.

Ethical and moral issues have also been subjects of intense debate in our rapidly advancing society. A key question has been: Should anyone be allowed to own patents on the human DNA sequence? (See Table 16.1.)

Many innovations for therapeutic diagnostic tools till date have satisfied the existing conditions of patentability. The concentration of such "ownership" appears to be localized in USA and Japan, who hold the rights for their exploitation.

Currently, there have been a number of debates on what the appropriate legal system should be to ensure:

- farmers' rights;
- researchers' rights;
- extent of protection to hybrid and high-yielding seeds;
- transgenic plants and microbes;
- plants containing patented genes;
- extent of protection to gene sequence.

Clear directives are still to emerge.

Table 16.1 Human DNA sequence patents granted worldwide

Private	Country of origin	No.	Public	Country of origin	No.
Ashai	Japan	15	Green Cross	Japan	15
Takeda	Japan	63	US department of Health and Human Service	USA	28
Genentech	USA	41	University of California	USA	13
Immunex	USA	23	National Institute of Health	USA	11
Roche	Switzerland	18	University of Washington	USA	11
Ciba-Geigy	Switzerland	16	Universtiy of Texas	USA	7

Continues

Table 16.1 *Continued*

Private	Country of origin	No.	Public	Country of origin	No.
Suntory	Japan	18	Japan Foundation for Cancer Res.	Japan	6
Sumitomo	Japan	16	NY State University	USA	6
Cetus	USA	15	Agency of Industrial Science and Tech.	Japan	5
EliLilly	USA	15	Salk Institute	USA	5

Includes all the human DNA sequence patents granted worldwide

Source: *Nature*, 380, 4 April, 1996, p. 387.

It was recently reported that the DNA sequence containing the breast cancer susceptibility gene BRCA2 was put on the internet by Sanger Centre at Cambridge, England, and the University of Washington, St. Louis. They did so with the aim of sharing knowledge and supporting research in this area.

What followed rapidly was that the US company Myriad Genetics located the gene and filed a patent for all diagnostic and therapeutic applications. This is an excellent example where the appropriate combination of inventiveness and utility can lead to a patentable invention.

To summarize the major issues with regard to patentability in biotechnology:

Patent scope: How broad a patent is the applicant entitled to? Many biotechnology inventions will still "work" even after a competitor partially modifies them from what is patented, e.g. minor changes in the DNA sequence, amino acid sequence of a protein, use of a different recombinant vector or host organism.

Similarly, the question of demonstrating the utility of a biotechnologcal invention must be addressed. One of the grey areas is the extent of effectiveness of "new" drugs to be demonstrated to satisfy the criteria of patentability. There are no clear guidelines or thumbrules, though EPO has relaxed the conditions on utility.

On a number of occasions arguments on utility have been derived such as:

Relating to a novel process for making a known steroid. Arguments:

- Steroids are useful. Therefore the steroid of the researcher's invention is inherently useful.
- Method of making these compounds was patentable even if the compounds had no known or explained use.

A number of recent articles in the journals have discussed these issues in some depth. (The readers are advised to refer to the following articles *Nature*, Vol. **374**, p. 398, 1995, Vol. **375**, p. 348, 1995, Vol. **376**, pp. 541, 622, 1995, *Biotechnology*, Vol. **13**, pp. 640–644, 656–657, 1995, *Current Science*, Vol. **60**, No. 2, pp. 85–86, 1995, *Tibtech*, Vol. **13**, pp. 162–164, May 1995.)

The following case studies illustrate the complexities while dealing with matters on infringement and validity of patents in the field of biotechnology.

CASE STUDY

Scripps vs Genentech

Both Scripps and Genentech were interested in making Factor VIII: C — a protein involved in the clotting of blood through recombinant DNA technology.

The first step was that the protein had to be sufficiently purified to be able to characterize it.

Scripps developed a process for purifying Factor VIII: C from blood plasma using monoclonal antibodies. They obtained a patent with claims for both the process of purifying the protein and the purified protein itself.

Genentech cloned the gene for Factor VIII: C and produced the protein in a recombinant organism.

The District Court construed Scripps' patent claims as covering:

"Any Factor VIII: C preparation, regardless of how it was produced, having the same material, structural and functional characteristics as the plasma derived preparation."

The court found that Genentech's recombinant protein infringed the Scripps patent.

The Federal Court rejected Genentech's view that product claims should be construed as limited to plasma-derived Factor VIII: C. However Genentech suggested that one may apply the "reverse doctrine of equivalence".

Genentech argued that its recombinant product was substantially different from the Scripps' plasma-derived product in both specific activity and purity, and that the "reverse doctrine of equivalence" should apply.

The final decision after 10 years of litigation was in favour of Scripps.

Source: 18 US PQ2d p. 1896; 18 US PQ2d pp. 1001–1016; Rebecca Eisenberg, op. cit.

CASE STUDY

Amgen
vs
Chugai and Genetics Institute

The patent rights in this instance revolved around erythroprotein which stimulates production of red blood cells. Different teams working competitively in the same area reached different goals at different points in time.

Parties involved: Amgen, Genetics Institute and Chugai Pharmaceuticals of Japan

Issues

- Patent infringement action in the US District Court
- Interference or priority contest in the US Patent Office
- A tariff proceeding before the US International Trade Commission.

The Genetics Institute applied for a patent on a method for purifying EPO protein and for the purified protein. The Institute's patent for the purified protein was held invalid by the Federal Court for lack of an enabling disclosure.

Amgen applied for a patent on starting materials to make recombinant EPO, including a purified and isolated DNA sequence for EPO, and recombinant vectors and host cells transformed with that sequence. Its patent on DNA sequence included broad, generic claims attempting to cover all possible DNA sequences.

Angen held the US patent rights only in the recombinant starting materials to make recombinant erythroproteins — "not on the end-product" or the process.

Chugai used the recombinant materials covered in the patent and made the recombinant EPO in Japan. But it never made/used/sold the recombinant materials in USA.

Thus Chugai remained unaffected as Amgen did not have a process patent but a patent covering starting materials used in an unpatented process.

Result: Amgen won the battle against Genetics Institute getting $ 14 million by way of compensation in 1993.

(*Source*: *Patent Wars*, pp. 214–224, Rebecca Eisenberg, op. cit.)

CASE STUDY

Genentech
vs
Wellcome Foundation

Genentech held several TPA patents, including a patent directed to the natural protein extracted from human cells and a patent directed to the starting materials needed to make protein recombinantly.

Wellcome and Genetics Institute, both used recombinant DNA technology to produce proteins that were structurally distinct from natural TPA.

Wellcome and Genetics Institute were charged with infringing Genentech's patent.

The major question which arose out of this debate was: Do patent rights cover products with structural differences that have some similar biological activity?

The federal Circuit Court submitted to the jury to decide whether Wellcome and Genetics Institute's TPA variant infringed any of the patent claims under the doctrine of equivalence.

The Court's view was that:

- TPA was identified by its structure and not by its function.
- The molecule made by the Genetics Institute was not an allelic variant on the natural TPA molecule disclosed by Genentech.
- The specific activity of the molecule of the Genetics Institute was well below that of the natural TPA and within the range found in the prior art.
- Genetics Institute's TPA had half the binding affinity of the natural TPA and considerably longer half-life in the human body.
- The product was independently invented and not copied from Genentech

Thus Wellcome and Genetics Institute were not considered as infringing Genentech's patent.

CASE STUDY

Ownership of BRCA1 patent

The Search for BRCA1—a cancer susceptibility gene—was conducted by a team from the University of Utah, Myriad, Mc Gill University and the National Institute of Environmental Health Services (NIEHs)

The University of Utah filed the patent for this gene, but National Institute of Health was not named co-inventor.

The problem was further compounded by the following :

- The University of Utah agreed to license commercial use of the patent exclusively to Myriad. Myriad sublicensed rights to EliLilly and a subsidiary of EliLilly, Hybritech of San Diego.
- Myriad funded 45 people who co-authored the BRCA1 article. Six were funded by EliLilly. NIH funded six in the NIEHS team and also provided some grants to the University of Utah. However, major funds came from Myriad and EliLilly.
- NIEHS investigators had no agreement such as a Research & Development Agreement (CRADA) with Myriad. However they did have a co-signed document detailing the order of authorship in the "unlikly event" that they isolated BRCA1. Negotiations are in progress.

  Source : *Nature*, **373**, November 1994, p. 118 and *Nature*, **373**, February 1995, p. 469.

Ownership issues and contracts

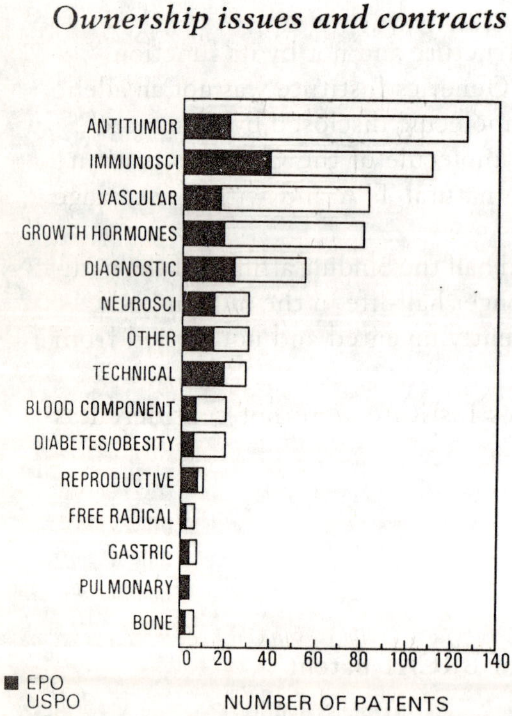

Fig. 16.1 Classification of Human Genome Patents
Source : *Nature*, **380**, 4 April, 1996, p. 387

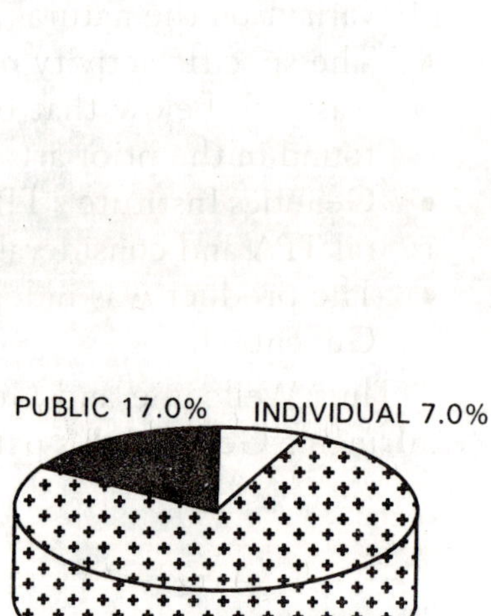

Fig. 16.2 Ownership of Human DNA sequence patents

Classification and ownership of patents for human genome are shown in Figs. 16.1 and 16.2.

Protection of new varieties of plants

Though the GATT has excluded certain items from patentability, it has also included a clause binding all members to "provide for protection of plant varieties either by patents or by any effective *sui generis* system or any combination thereof".

Over the years there has been considerable effort by farmers, plant breeders, and seed producers to enhance the productivity of agricultural produce by developing new plant varieties with special traits. It is natural that these innovators would seek some protection of their products and processes through an appropriate legal system. There is much confusion among professionals about the system under which such innovations can be protected.

New plant seeds and varieties in most countries are not protected by patents but by separate national/international legal systems. India is not yet a part of any such global legal system. It is yet to arrive at an appropriate and nationally relevant *sui generis* system.

The Union for Protection of new Varieties of Plants (UPOV)

The UPOV which was formed in 1961 has undergone revisions in 1972, 1978, and 1991. As on March, 1993, it had 22 member states.

Two internationally well-known national laws are the Plant Variety Protection Act of USA and Plant Varieties and Seeds Act of UK.

Under the UPOV, breeder rights give the holder exclusive rights to produce for sale; and to sell or offer for sale the reproductive material of the protected variety. The term of protection is 15 years. Production by a farmer for his own use or his saving of the seed for planting does not constitute an infringement of the plant variety right.

The word "variety" applies to any cultivar, clone, line, stock or hybrid which is capable of cultivation and satisfies the following provisions:

- The new variety must be sufficiently homogenous, having regard to the particular features of its sexual reproduction or vegetative propagation.
- The new variety should be stable in its essential characteristics, i.e., its characteristics remain unchanged on repeated reproduction or propagation.

A breeder is required to choose a specific name for each protected variety and to use the name in its marketing. The owner may initiate legal action against anyone who uses the name or a confusingly similar name for selling any other variety belonging to the species of the same class.

However, patents afford much broader protection than plant breeders rights. For example, the process for developing a new plant or plant material and the variety itself may be protected by patents, but the process cannot be protected under plant breeder rights which only facilitate protection of the variety.

Biodiversity

In India, there is a growing pressure from agricultural and environmental experts urging the government to take immediate steps to patent the country's rich biodiversity, consisting of over 45,000 plant and 75,000 animal species, and set up an independent Biodiversity Commission to determine the country's genetic wealth and bring it under intellectual property control.

Worldwide, there is a mad rush to file patents on plant and animal wealth. At least 32 US patents have been granted to date on the various properties of *neem*. Another 385 US patents have been granted on non-American food crop species.

Considerable debate has taken place on the controversial issue of protecting the rights of farmers in conserving and protecting plant genetic resources. At the Fourth International Conference on Plant Genetic Resources at Leipzig in Germany, the Developing Countries managed to ensure inclusion of a proposal calling for countries to take legislative measures for protecting the traditional rights of farmers.

India's efforts to protect the farmers rights in a proposed legislation awaits Cabinet clearance. If this is cleared, then the farmer's traditional right to keep a part of the harvest for the next sowing will no longer be threatened. Nor can the seed companies restrain farmers from sharing or bartering crop seeds among themselves.

All signatories of the global plan of action on plant genetic resources adopted at the Leipzig Conference are committed to a just share of benefits derived from the use of plant biodiversity which they have developed, maintained and made available for commercial use.

Although the proposed Plant Varieties Protection Act (PVPA) in India envisages returning a share of the royalties on seed sales to a fund for strengthening farmers' plant genetic resource activities, the implementation of farmers' rights to be truly meaningful requires international action. At the same time, the global action plan formulated at the end of the Leipzig Conference now provides an alternate route to framing national seed laws. These laws now need not be defined within the parameters set by the International UPOV.

The proposed Indian legislation, modelled on the UPOV 1978 pattern, allows for the rights of plant-breeders and farmers. But the 1991 version of UPOV, does not permit both. However, the FAO has already succeeded in getting a global endorsement for farmers' rights.

Main features of the convention on biological diversity

This international Convention ratified by over 30 countries became legally binding on its members on 29 December, 1993. The main objectives of the Convention are: the conservation of biological diversity, the sustainable use of biological resources, and the fair and equitable sharing of resulting benefits. It also recognizes the interdependency of nations.

It prescribes certain codes of conduct among those utilizing genetic resources for research or commercial purposes, provides recommendations for interaction between national governments and their agencies for the handling of biotechnology and the distribution of its benefits. It also addresses the administrative, financial and legal issues that may arise from the Convention. Although it was specifically stated that "no reservations may be made to this Convention" (Article 37), several interpretative statements and reservations have been included in the ratifying legislation by many countries.

The essential features of this Convention are as follows:

- It gives recognition to the sovereign right of source countries over their genetic resources—their right to exploit such resources in accordance with the nation's own environmental policies, and the responsibility to ensure that activities within their area of jurisdiction and control do not cause damage to the environment of other nations.
- It encourages cooperation between the parties to the Convention, directly or through competent international organizations, to help in the conservation and sustainable use of biological diversity, especially as it relates to areas outside individual national jurisdictions.
- It outlines measures and strategies expected of nation states to promote conservation.

- It deals with issues pertaining to species identification, classification and monitoring.
- It gives guidance on measures to be used for both *in situ* and *ex situ* conservation.
- It provides recommendations for the sustainable use of the components of biological diversity. It specifically encourages the integration of conservation and sustainability into national policy frameworks. National governments are also requested to encourage the participation of the private sector in developing methods for the sustainable use of biological resources.
- It calls for economic and social incentives that promote its objectives.
- It deals with research and training, and requires the contracting parties to recognize the special needs of developing nations in scientific and technical education. The provisions under this Article can provide a more beneficial method of compensation to source countries than the over-rated royalty sharing arrangements.
- It stresses the need for public education and awareness of biodiversity conservation.
- It speaks of the need for impact assessment and the need to minimize adverse impact on the environment from development projects.
- It reaffirms the sovereign rights of states over their natural resources and recognizes the authority of national governments to grant access to their genetic resources. It also encourages the contracting parties to endeavour to create conditions that would facilitate access to genetic resources for environmentally sound use by others.
- It provides for access to, and transfer of, technology. It calls on each contracting party to provide, and/or facilitate, access to, and transfer of, other contracting parties' technologies that are relevant to conservation.
- It encourages the exchange of information relevant to conservation and sustainable use of biological diversity, "taking into account the special needs of developing countries".
- It promotes technical and scientific cooperation among nations, and emphasizes the need for training and education in the source country. It requires that "... special attention should be given to the development and strengthening of national capabilities by means of human resources", so as to establish a clearing house to promote and facilitate technical and scientific cooperation.

IPR audit

IPR will play an increasingly important role in all features of business management with a significant contribution from R&D to maintain its competitive edge and business leadership. Integrating IPR and information security into the organizational system is imperative. Monitoring of institutional information and intellectual assets and those of competitors are the emerging tools for establishing business dominance.

In the era of mergers and acquisitions, establishing joint ventures, acquiring technologies and globalization of businesses it is becoming increasingly important to understand the IPR strengths and weaknesses of partners as these would significantly influence a number of issues related to the operational aspects of the business.

Such an institutional audit should cover a review of all relevant documents related to employee contracts, copyrights, trademarks, patents, design registrations, all contracts dealing with research and project funding, licenses and licensing agreements, rights towards further development of the technology to be acquired, interactions with contractors, customers, etc.

This must also include a cost-benefit analysis of the IPR assets. On an on-going basis most organizations with business operations in many countries need to evaluate their IPR in all the geographical locations to determine whether they require continued protection in all the places. In consultation with the various busines groups or profit centres in the organization, they must audit the intellectual assets and decide on continuation of renewal fees for their patents in those countries. This helps the organization to take decisions with regard to acquiring or purchasing technology from others, or even licensing/transferring technology, maintaining the appropriate product /service portfolios, etc. Such a knowledge of the competitors also enables one to be aware of their strengths and weaknesses, identify the possible products to be launched in the market at various geographical locations and to prepare one's responses to events in the short, medium and long terms.

US Patent No. 54015404 was granted to two researchers of the University of Mississippi by the US Patent and Trademark Office (USPTO) for the use of turmeric powder (*haldi*) as a wound healing agent on March 28, 1995. This was opposed on October 20, 1996 by the Council of Scientific and Industrial Research (CSIR), India, on the basis that it does not satisfy the essential criteria of patentability in terms of novelty as the use of turmeric powder as a wound healing agent has been well known in India over the centuries. Thirty-two references about the wealth of India, citations from the **Journal of the Indian Medical Association** and ancient treatises on home remedies were submitted to the US patent office in support of this opposition. The USPTO unequivocally rejected all the six claims of this patent on August 13, 1997.

This case highlights the significance of systematic documentation of traditional knowledge and how appropriate prior art can be used to effectively oppose patents.

Source : *Business Line* 24-08-97

The issues discussed above will have an impact on the research process and will influence the course of science, technology and business in the future. IPR management will be an integral part of the research and business strategy of institutions.

17

Patenting as a strategic tool

This chapter briefly looks at the process of technology mapping to arrive at broad conclusions on business focus, research and patenting policies through an analysis of patent information available in international databases. Patenting is a result of the business needs of an organization, its technology focus, research concentration, and proactive and reactive response to its competitors (see Fig. 17.1). Appropriate, timely patenting and an effective patent portfolio protect innovations to create and maintain a competitive lead in the marketplace. Thus monitoring and analyzing the patent portfolio and its dynamics in any organization could help in understanding the evolving scenario and planning one's business strategy.

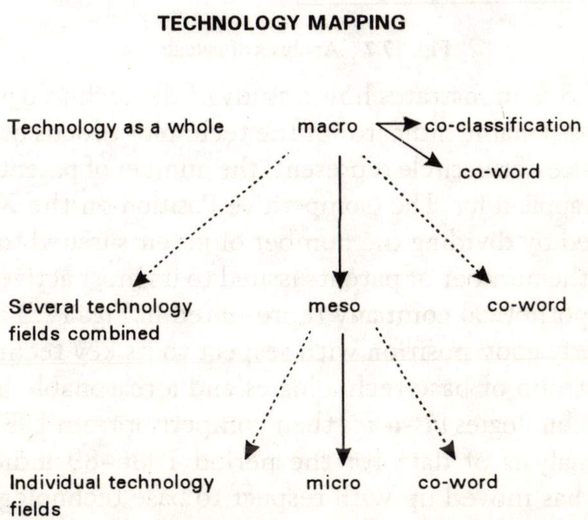

Fig. 17.1 Hierarchical levels of the different mapping approaches

A patent document is well structured; vital details such as the title, inventors, assignees, date of the patents, references cited, countries where they are filed, their legal status in various countries where they are still in force, abstracts, full text, etc., are indexed. This facilitates easy electronic retrieval. Patents are classified under various technological groups and sub-groups identified by an internationally accepted system of classification known as the International Patent Classification (IPC). The unique codes help to identify specific technologies, processes, groups of compounds, activities, formulation, techniques, functionalities, etc. The IPC coupled with appropriate bibliometric techniques serves as a tool for effective technology mapping from a macro to meso and further, to the micro level with respect to organizations, time periods, and other relevant parameters (see Fig. 17.2).

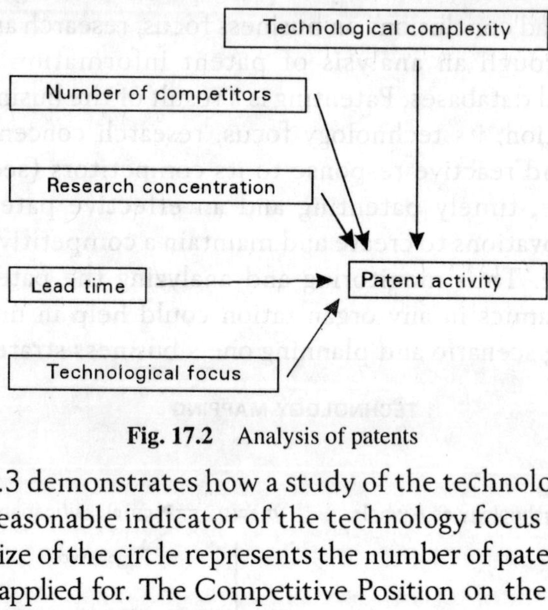

Fig. 17.2 Analysis of patents

Figure 17.3 demonstrates how a study of the technology portfolio becomes a reasonable indicator of the technology focus of an organization. The size of the circle represents the number of patents the organization has applied for. The Competitive Position on the X-axis may be calculated by dividing the number of patents issued to the organization by the number of patents issued to its most active competitor. The hypothetical company represented in Fig. 17.3 appears to occupy a fairly good position with respect to its key technologies, a healthy portfolio of base technologies and a reasonable position in emerging technologies *vis-à-vis* their competitor from 1982 to 1985. A similar analysis of data for the period 1986–89 indicates that its position has moved up with respect to base technologies, but it has lost its dominance in key technologies and has marginally improved in emerging technologies. Such a study in conjunction with

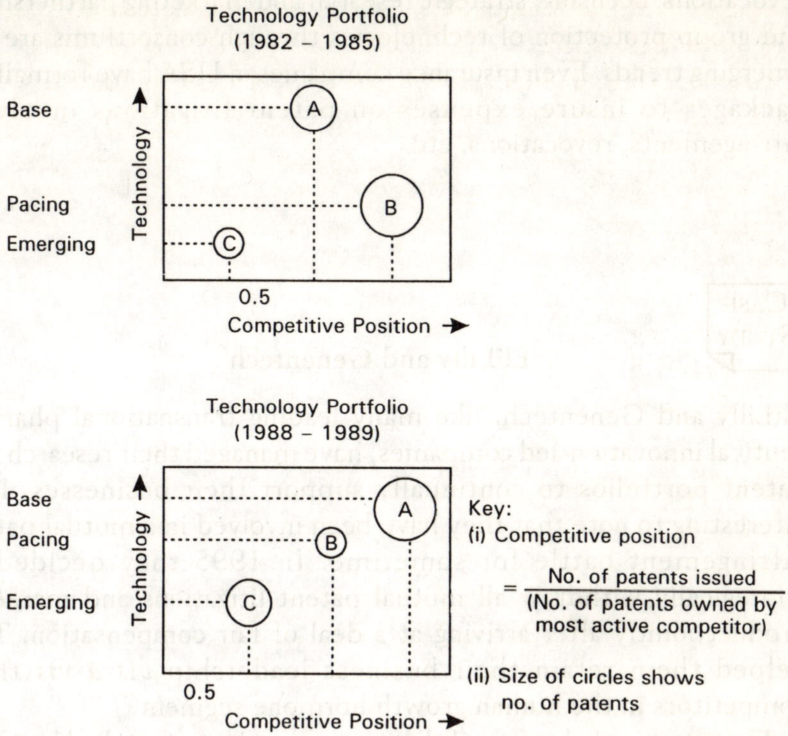

Fig. 17.3 Technology Focus

information on other business related parameters serves as a highly useful input to the planning of corporate business strategy.

Effective knowledge sharing with "appropriate credits", innovative partnerships assisted by techno-legal "support", facilitated by all the modern information technology tools to achieve cost effectiveness in R&D, technology generation and utilization of global expertise are some of the approaches likely to dominate the future. Symbiotic relationships without losing "organizational character" is an emerging concept in creating and retaining dominance and business leadership. Patents and all forms of IPR will be some of the tools aiding this process. A few Case Studies outlined below illustrate these features.

Biotechnology is an area which has experienced unprecedented activity in the last couple of decades. The rate of innovations in this area has been higher and their conversion to useful technologies has been rapid. This has made the field fiercely competitive, and protecting these innovations through patents has been a significant activity in most innovation-led companies. Infringements, litigations, revocations, licensing, strategic research and marketing partnerships, and group protection of technologies through consortiums are the emerging trends. Even insurance companies in USA have formalized packages to insure expenses on patent litigations involving infringements, revocations, etc.

CASE STUDY

EliLilly and Genentech

EliLilly and Genentech, like many leading transnational pharmaceutical innovation-led companies, have managed their research and patent portfolios to continually support their businesses. It is interesting to note that they have been involved in a mutual patent infringement battle for sometime. In 1995 they decided to strategically withdraw all mutual patent litigations and market a product jointly after arriving at a deal of fair compensation. This helped them retain their business leadership *vis-à-vis* their competitors in the human growth hormone segment.

The patenting behaviour of the two companies was studied based on information retrieved from the international business and patent databases. This was used to arrive at their probable business strategies.

Box 17.1 Mapping of technology strengths

(a) **Genentech**

—International classification based search
1992 —102 records

Items	IPC codes
38	A61K-037/02
27	C07K-013/00
24	C12N-005/10

(b) **EliLilly**

Search example:
1994 — 362 records

Items	IPC Codes
114	A61K-031/445
113	A61K-031/40
87	A61K-031/38

Continues

Continued

24	C12P-021/02	63	A61K-031/55
21	A61K-039/395	55	A61K-000/00
21	C12P-021/08	52	C07D-333/56
18	C12N-015/09	47	A61K-031/44

Source : On-line search results from Derwent Databases

Derwent databases were scanned during the period 1992–96 to identify the patents filed by EliLilly and Genentech. These patents were sorted out and ranked according to the IPC codes. Dialogue Rank Command was used to rank the top eight IPC codes. Box 17.1 illustrates the filings for the year 1994 in the case of EliLilly and for 1992 in the case of Genentech. This process was repeated every year individually from 1992–96 and the patenting profile for this period for EliLilly and Genentech was drawn.

Box 17.1 may be interpreted with the help of the IPC codes. For example, "A61K" refers to preparations for medical, dental or toilet purposes. A further sub-classification "037" and "031" within "A61K" would indicate pharmaceutical preparations characterized by active ingredients and organic active ingredients. It is possible to go a step further into targeted information. For example, "045" within the sub-class "031" refers to Hydroxy compounds, e.g. alcohols, salts and thereof. Thus decoding A61K-031/445 would help to identify the subject matter of the patent. Similarly C07K-013/00 would refer to pharmaceutical preparations involving proteins having a fully defined sequence of aminoacids and their derivatives. Thus, using the IPC codes one can classify the patents into their specific subjects which can be used as an effective tool to plot or monitor subjects of R&D in various organizations or of research groups.

Figures 17.4 and 17.5 present the results of such an analysis for EliLilly and Genentech.

Observations on EliLilly

The following observations can be made about EliLilly:

- The strategy has been to concentrate on a few areas of research in drugs, involving nitrogen and sulphur heterocyclics. They are also concerned with concentrated hypoglycemic agents,

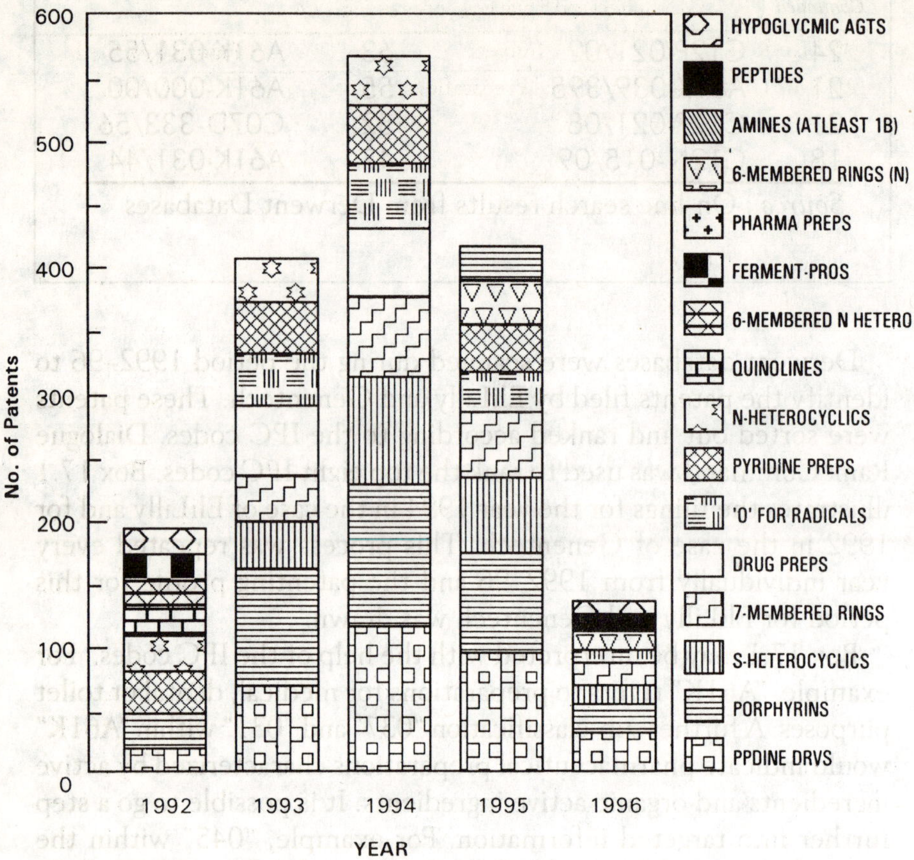

Fig. 17.4 Patenting profile of EliLilly

chemistry of peptides, and porphyrins. Expertise in radical chemistry has also been used for anti-tumour research. Pharmaceutical preparations containing active organic heterocyclics, for treatment of neuro-disorders, post-menopausal syndrome, osteoporosis, cardiovascular problems, diabetes, etc., have been patented. Fermentation for targeted synthesis and products based on human insulin analogues and anti-thrombosis agents and development of drugs have been key areas of strength.

- They have selectively added as well as dropped a few areas of research during the period 1992–96, indicating that R&D was refocused to meet the changing business needs.
- The business focus of EliLilly has been on central nervous system products, endocrine diseases, infectious diseases, cardiovascular disorders and cancer.

Table 17.1 IPC codes, subject and figure key codes of Fig. 17.4

IPC Code	Subject	Figure Key Codes
A61K-031/	Pharmaceutical Preparations with organic active ingredients.	PHARMA PREPS
/445	Piperidine and derivatives.	PPDINE DRVS
/40	Having 5-membered ring with one nitrogenation as the only hetero atom	PORPHYRINS
/38	Having sulphur as the hetero atom.	S-HETEROCYCLICS
/55	Having 7-membered rings.	7-MEMBERED RINGS
/44	Pyridine and derivatives.	PYRIDINE PREPS
/395	Having nitrogen as a ring hetero atom.	N-HETERO CYCLICS
/47	Quinolines and Isoquinolines.	QUINOLINES
/435	Having 6-membered rings with one nitrogen as the only ring hetero atom.	6-MEMBERED RINGS (N)
/535	Having 6-membered rings with at least one nitrogen and one oxygen as the hetero atom.	6-MEMBERED N HETERO
/135	Having benzene rings.	AMINES (AT LEAST
A61K-000-/00	Drugs/other biological compositions capable of preventing, alleviating, treating or curing abnormal or pathological conditions.	1B) DRUG PREPS
A61K 037/02	Medicinal preparations containing proteinaceous materials, lipids, or derivatives thereof proteins; peptides; peptones (ergot alkaloids of the cyclic peptide type 31/48).	
A61K-038/00	Pharmaceutical preparations having hypoglycemic activity.	HYPOGLYCEMIC
CO7D-333/56	Preparation of heterocyclic compounds containing rings with less than 5 members having 1 sulphur atom as the only hetero atom and radicals substituted by oxygen atoms.	'O' FOR RADICALS
CO7K-014/00	Preparation of heterocyclic compounds such as peptides.	PEPTIDES
C12P-021/02	Fermentation or enzymes using process to synthesize proteins or peptides having a known sequence of two or more amino acids.	FERMENT-PROS

- Business databases reveal an annual revenue of $ 6.76 billion. Their products in the pipeline are expected to add $ 1 billion to the bottomline.

It may be generally concluded that EliLilly has a strong research base with a patent portfolio in heterocyclic chemistry and related areas of biotechnology, including formulation of drugs, and is ready to feed new products continually into the market. It is not a company with major strengths in a wide range of genetic engineering techniques, in which they may look for collaborations/alliances/ licensing arrangements, etc. See Table 17.1.

Observations on Genentech

The business reports indicate the following about Genentech:

- Revenue: $ 917,845,000. Product sales: $ 635,263,000.
  Royalties: $ 190,811,000. Markets: 5 of its own products. Sales of Protropin and Nutropin: $ 219.5M.
  1995 R&D spending: $ 363.0 million.
- Leader in genetic engineering techniques, growth hormones and selected areas of biotechnology applications.

The patenting profile of Genentech (see Fig. 17.5) shows that over the years they have developed expertise in a wide range of genetic engineering techniques, fermentation processes, antibody chemistry, cellular chemistry, etc. See Table 17.2.

The technology strengths based on the patents are:

- Chemistry of heterocyclics, proteins, peptides, sequencing, manipulation of micro-organisms using genetic engineering techniques, human, animal and plant cell lines, tissue culture, recombinant DNA technology, genes encoding animation processes, DNA sequences coding for human proteins, fermentation techniques for targeted synthesis, monoclonal antibodies, etc.
- Pharmaceutical preparations involving antibodies, heterocyclic organic active compounds.
- The strategy of Genentech appears to be one of being leaders in genetic engineering with a few products of their own, but earning substantially through royalties from other companies who have had to take licenses from Genentech to use their techniques or have infringed Genentech's processes or intermediate products during the course of their research and development activities.

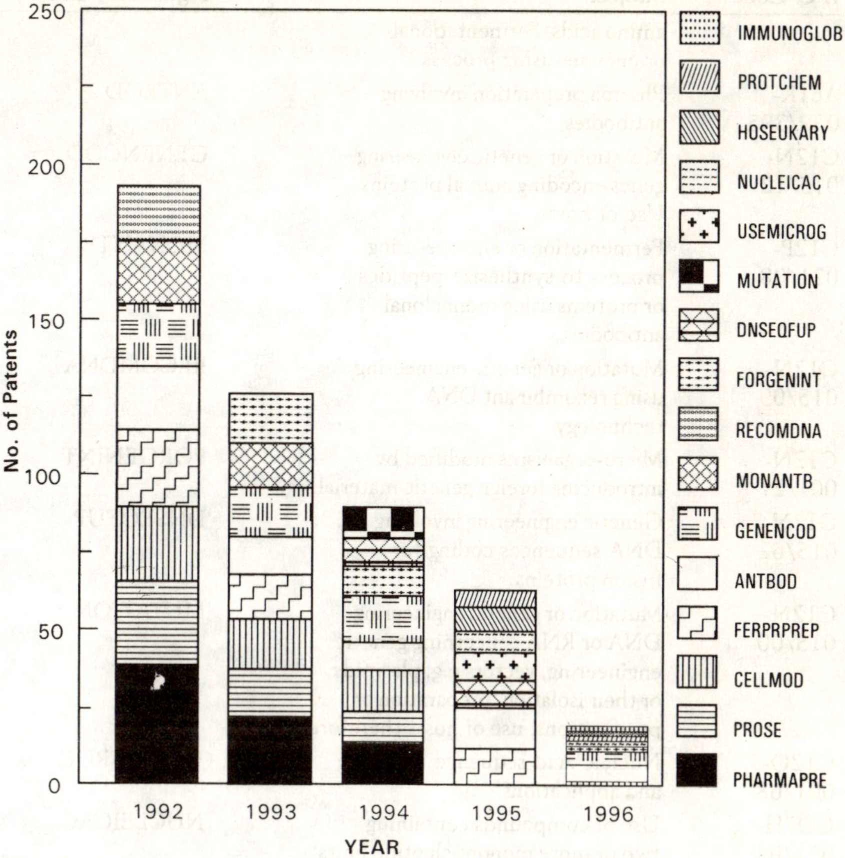

Fig. 17.5 Patenting Profile of Genentech

Table 17.2 IPC codes, subject and figure key codes of Fig. 17.5

IPC Code	Subject	Figure Key Code
A61K 073/02	Medical preparations containing proteinaceous materials, lipids, or derivatives thereof proteins, peptides, peptones (ergot alkaloids of the cyclics peptide type 31/48)	PHARMAPRE
C07K -013/00	Proteins having fully defined sequence of amino acids	PROSE
C12N-005/10	Undifferentiated cells, tissues modified by introduction of foreign genetic material.	CELLMOD
C12P-021/02	Preparation of protiens having a known sequence of two or more	FERPRPREP

Continues

Table 17.2 *Continued*

IPC Code	Subject	Figure Key Code
	amino acids. Fermentational- or enzyme-using process.	
A61K-039/395	Pharma preparation involving antibodies	ANTBOD
C12N-015/12	Mutation or genetic engineering genes encoding animal proteins. Use of hosts.	GENENCOD
C12P-021/08	Fermentation or enzyme-using process to synthesize peptides or proteins using monoclonal antibodies.	MONANTB
C12N-015/09	Mutation or genetic engineering using recombinant DNA technology.	RECOMDNA
C12N-001/21	Micro-organisms modified by introducing foreign genetic material.	FORGENINT
C12N-015/62	Genetic engineering involving DNA sequences coding for fusion proteins.	DNSEQFUP
C12N-015/00	Mutation or genetic engineering DNA or RNA concerning genetic engineering, vectors e.g. plasmids or their isolation, preparation or purifications; use of hosts therefore.	MUTATION
C12Q-001/68	Nucleic acid sequence encoding and applications.	USEMICROG
CO7H-021/04	Use of compounds containing two or more mononucleotide units having separate phosphate or polyphosphate groups linked by deoxyribosyl as saccharide radical.	NUCLEICAC
C12N-015/85	Mutation or genetic engineering with use of eukaryotes as hosts for animal cells.	HOSEUKARY
C12N-015/13	Mutation or genetic engineering, vectors, or their isolation, preparation or purification, use of hosts thereof (involves immunoglobulins).	IMMUNOGLOB

They appear to have an effective patent policing system to detect possible infringement of their patents by others and have used it to establish dominance by creating strategic entry barriers for their competitors.

Genentech has been very active in patent litigations and striking symbiotic partnerships to retain leadership. Infringement suits filed by it illustrates this feature. Genentech filed patent infringement suits against Nordisk (norditropin), Biogen (biotropin) and EliLilly (humatropin). Injunctions in favour of Genentech did not allow the competitors to market their product in USA.

The above injunctions gave Genentech an opportunity to evaluate the most effective partner to strike a strategic settlement on this issue to jointly introduce a product in the market. In January 1995, a settlement with EliLilly on humatropin was made following the end of law suits and a breach of contract, and settlement of related claims between the two companies. The product was marketed by EliLilly and a mutually agreeable compensation package was worked out by Genentech and EliLilly.

As part of the settlement, EliLilly agreed to pay Genentech about $ 145 million and make future payments contingent on product sales.

The arrangement gave Genentech an initial $ 25 million payment and 16 quarterly payments of about $ 7.5 million that began in March, 1995. Each company agreed to dismiss litigation against the other for infringement of patented technology.

CASE STUDY

DNX Corporation

This case illustrates how enhanced core competence and targeted research supported by effective patenting can yield tangible results in terms of royalties.

DNX's foundation has a basic US microinjection patent for inserting human genes into animals—microinjection being the process most commonly used for developing transgenic animals.

Other research groups can use the method only under license from DNX. Already some 25 license agreements are in place (with Merck & Co, EliLilly, Pfizer, Monsanto, Bristol–Myers Squibb, Glaxo–Wellcome and Genentech amongst others).

This patent is a considerable source of revenue for the company, at present bringing in about $ 500,000 annually.

CASE STUDY

Digital Video Display Consortium

An example of "Borderless Consortiums".

This consortium consists of Sony, Phillips, Hitachi, Matsushita, Mitsubishi, Pioneer, Thomson Multimedia, Time Warner and Toshiba, Victory Company of Japan.

The effort has been to pool the patents of all the members and evolve a one-step license system which can be offered to other hardware and hard disk manufacturers. The royalty structure and licensing procedure to be arrived at will have to be fair and undiscriminatory. The details of such a partnership are being worked out. This is an example of emerging trends in cooperative leadership in high technology areas supported by patents.

Appendix I

An example of a complete specification

Government of India, The Patent Office,
214, Acharya Jagadish Bose Road, Calcutta 700 017

Complete Specification No. 171359 dated 24-08-1987
Application No. 741/DEL/87 dated 24-08-1987
Acceptance of the complete specification advertised on 19th September, 1992

Index at acceptance – 32F 3b, 32F 3 C IX (1)
International Classification – C 07 C 31/22, 53/00, C 11 C 1/04.

Title: A process for the production of fatty acids and glycerol

Applicant : COLGATE–PALMOLIVE COMPANY,
a corporation organized under the Laws of the
State of Delaware, United States of America,
300 Park Avenue, New York,
New York 10022, United States of America.

Inventors : EDWARD ALBERT TAVSS, EDWARD EIGEN.

The following specification particularly describes and ascertains the nature of this invention and the manner in which it is to be performed:

Background of the invention and prior art

This invention relates to the process of converting high-melting fats, such as high-grade beef tallow, into a high yield of fatty acids and glycerol, comprising the hydrolysis of beef tallow in the presence of a minor amount of coconut oil by means of the castor bean lipase enzyme, at low temperatures, of about 25 to 50°C, and preferably about 37°C, for use in the production of soap. The high yield of fatty acids (98% conversion to fatty acids and glycerol), and the utilization of low temperatures in this process is accomplished by the addition of a minor amount of coconut oil or other vegetable oil, which permits the emulsification of the beef tallow at lower temperatures (37°C). This process eliminates undesirable thermal products and provides a saving in energy without resorting to undesirable additives. The fatty acid and glycerol mixture is free of undesirable extraneous materials, because the coconut oil additive also hydrolyses into fatty acids and glycerol.

Soap manufacturing is usually accomplished by saponification of high-grade beef tallow with lye. This is a high temperature reaction which has become expensive in recent years due to the sharp rise in fuel costs. Hence, a low temperature reaction was sought, and enzymatic hydrolysis with lipase was investigated, as a substitute for the lye process.

The optimum condition of lipase reactions is usually as an emulsion at 37°C. Unfortunately, the problem is that fats such as high-grade beef tallow, do not start melting until at least 41 to 50°C. Therefore, they do not form emulsions at 37°C in water without additives. It is apparently for this reason that in systems containing only beef tallow and a lipase preparation, the yields of fatty acids are always low or not reported. [Moskowitz *et al.*, *J. Agric. Food Chem.*, **25**, 1146 (1977); Constantin *et al.*, *Biochim. Biophys. Acta*, **43**, 103 (1960); Ralston, *Fatty Acids and Their Derivatives*, pp. 274–279, Wiley (1948); Haley *et al.*, *J. Am. Chem. Soc.*, **43**, 2664 (1921)].

Raising the temperature of the lipase reaction did not solve this problem, because of the rapid loss of stability of lipase at elevated temperatures. For example, pancreatic lipase loses 36% of its activity after 10 minutes at 50°C because enzymes are denatured at raised temperatures.

In an attempt to overcome this problem, the reaction system was modified by the addition of metallic additives such as calcium and magnesium salts, which did give higher yields, as disclosed in Constantin *et al.*; Altschul *et al.*, Federation Proc., **18**, 180 (1959); Kokusho *et al.*, Jpn Kokai Tokyo Koho **79**, 95, 607 (1979); Benzonana *et al.*, *Biochim. Biophys. Acta*, **164**, 47 (1968). However, the metal soaps formed in this reaction are hard soaps which provide unsatisfactory foaming and cleansing action. Haley *et al.* added petroleum ether as a fat solvent in order to get better physical contact between enzyme and substrate (beef tallow) to increase or accelerate hydrolysis. This process however is one of considerable danger due to the high explosion potential of the solvent.

Since solid fats are very difficult to emulsify, a study on the selection of emulsifiers of natural (solid) fats was made by Lobreva *et al.*, [*Micro-biologiya*, **48**, 53 (1979)] in an attempt to increase lipolytic activity on fats. The emulsifying agents, disclosed herein for the lipolysis of animal fats such as lard, beef and lamb fats are : Triton X-305, egg albumen, gelatin, gum arabic, lecithin and Tween-60. Not all of these agents were successful in emulsifying beef tallow. This lipolytic reaction did not give a high yield of fatty acids and glycerol. Furthermore, these emulsifying agents have the disadvantage of providing undesirable materials to the hydrolysis mixture.

The use of the castor bean lipase in the hydrolysis of fats, and its preparation, are well known in the art, as disclosed in US Patent No. 2485779, wherein a solvent-extracted ground castor bean meal, prepared at a temperature not exceeding 120°F is used in the partial hydrolysis of fish oil. Diethyl ether-extracted ground castor seed kernels have been used in the hydrolysis of low quality industrial fats, as disclosed in Trosko *et al.*, Maslo–Zhir, Prom–st., **27**, (1977); and in the hydrolysis of sunflower oil, as disclosed in Meerow *et al.*, *Prikl. Biokhem. Microbiol.*, **12**, 934 (1976). Castor bean lipase prepared by centrifuging a homogenate of the kernels into a fatty layer which is extracted by ether in the presence of a saturated salt solution has been used in the hydrolysis of cottonseed oil, mono- and diolein, castor oil and a cottonseed oil emulsion, as disclosed in Altschul *et al.* (supra). Haley *et al.* (supra) discloses a method of preparing a castor bean lipase by extracting the hull-free kernels with petroleum ether hydrolysis of fats and oil . Ralston, *Fatty Acids and Their Derivatives*, Wiley, p. 276 (1948) discloses variations in the method of preparing an active lipase from castor beans for use in the hydrolysis of fat containing 40 to 50% water, and in the presence of a small amount of acetic acid or an activating salt such as manganese sulfate. The general method includes grinding the dehulled seeds in water, filtering the solids, and centrifuging to form an emulsion. One variation thereof is grinding the dry seeds in cottonseed oil and centrifuging the mixture. Another method includes extracting the macerated beans with petroleum ether, drying, pulverizing and sifting the product, which retains its original activity, over a period of ten years.

However, there is no disclosure of the low temperature hydrolysis of high-melting point fats such as beef tallow with a non-stereospecific animal or vegetable lipase, particularly the castor bean lipase, in the presence of a vegetable oil emulsifying agent such as coconut oil at an acidic pH and a low temperature under 50°C.

Summary of the invention

It has been now found that the low temperature enzymatic hydrolysis of high-melting fats such as beef tallow, utilizing a non-stereospecific animal or vegetable lipase enzyme, such as castor bean lipase, and a vegetable oil emulsifying agent such as coconut oil provides the almost quantitative hydrolysis of the mixture of said beef tallow and coconut oil into fatty acids and glycerol free of undesirable materials. Neutralization with sodium hydroxide forms a high-grade soap (i.e. free of contaminants).

Accordingly, it is an object of the present invention to provide a process of hydrolysing high-melting fats, such as high-grade beef tallow, into a high yield of fatty acids and glycerol, at a low temperature, with a non-stereospecific lipase such as castor bean lipase, in the presence of a vegetable oil emulsifying agent.

Another object of this invention is to provide a process of converting high-melting beef tallow into fatty acids and glycerol, in high yield, at low temperatures by hydrolysing a mixture of beef tallow and a minor amount of coconut oil with the castor bean lipase enzyme.

Still another object of this invention is to provide an enzymatic hydrolysis process of converting a mixture of a high-melting fat and a low-melting vegetable oil into a reaction mixture of fatty acids and glycerol free of undesirable minerals, i.e., thermal products and additives.

Another object of this invention is to provide an enzyme system to hydrolyse beef tallow and coconut oil into fatty acids (and glycerol) and neutralizing said fatty acids with sodium hydroxide (NaOH), sodium carbonate (Na_2CO_3) or sodium bicarbonate ($NaHCO_3$) to form soap.

Additional objects and advantages will be apparent from a consideration of the following description and in part will become apparent to those skilled in the art upon examination of the following or may be learned by practice of the invention. The objects and advantages of the invention may be realized and attained by means of the instrumentalities and combinations particularly pointed out in the appended claims.

To achieve the foregoing and other objects and in accordance with the present invention, as embodied and broadly described herein, the process of this invention of converting high-melting fats into fatty acids and glycerol comprises hydrolysing an emulsified mixture of a high-melting beef tallow and about 10 to 25% by weight of the mixture of a vegetable oil, preferably coconut oil, in an aqueous medium, with a non-stereospecific animal or vegetable lipase enzyme, at a temperature of about 25 to 50°C, preferably 37°C, and at a pH of about 4 to 5.5, and recovering a final reaction mixture consisting of fatty acids, glycerol and lipase. The mixture is agitated for a sufficient period of time, about 2 to 48 hours, to obtain substantially complete hydrolysis into fatty acids and glycerol. The final reaction mixture is free of undesirable materials, and consists of three layers, a fatty acid top layer, a lipase mixture middle layer and an aqueous glycerine (sweet water) bottom layer. The layers may be separated; the fatty acid layer is skimmed off, neutralized with NaOH, Na_2CO_3, or $NaHCO_3$, and the resulting soap purified in the usual manner of soap manufacturers skilled in the art. The bottom layer is separated, and the glycerine removed. The middle layer, containing more than 50% of the original lipase still being active, is reused after adding a lesser quantity of fresh lipase.

The present invention also relates to a process of producing a high-grade soap, free of undesirable additives, which comprises hydrolysing an emulsified mixture of a high-melting fat and about 10 to 25% by weight of a vegetable oil in an aqueous medium, with a non-stereospecific animal or vegetable lipase at a temperature of about 25 to 50°C and at a pH of about 4 to 5.5, agitating the mixture for a period of time to obtain substantially complete hydrolysis into fatty acids and glycerol separating the fatty acids from the glycerol and neutralizing.

Accordingly, the present invention provides a process for the production of fatty acids and glycerol from high-melting fats such as beef tallow, the said process comprising hydrolysis of an emulsified mixture of said high-melting beef tallow and a vegetable oil of the kind such as herein described, said beef tallow being present in the weight ratio of 75 to 90%, and said vegetable oil in the weight ratio of 25 to 10%, said hydrolysis being conducted in an aqueous medium and in the presence of a non-stereospecific animal or vegetable lipase enzyme at a temperature in the range of 25 to 50°C, and at a pH of 4 to 5.5 to produce fatty acids and glycerol.

ing an emulsified mixture of a high-melting fat and about 10 to 25% by weight of a vegetable oil in an aqueous medium, with a non-stereospecific animal or vegetable lipase at a temperature of about 25 to 50°C and at a pH of about 4 to 5.5, agitating the mixture for a period of time to obtain substantially complete hydrolysis into fatty acids and glycerol separating the fatty acids from the glycerol, and neutralizing said fatty acids with an alkaline material to form a soap, free of undesirable additives. More specifically, the final reaction mixture consists of three layers, a fatty acid top layer, a lipase mixture middle layer and an aqueous glycerine bottom layer, and the process includes separating the top layer of fatty acids from the final reaction mixture, and neutralizing said fatty acids with an alkaline material selected from the group consisting of NaOH, Na_2CO_3 and $NaHCO_3$ to form a sodium soap substantially free of contaminants. The resulting soap and glycerine are much lighter in color than the corresponding sulfuric acid hydrolysis of fats or the high temperature NaOH saponification of fats.

More specifically, the present invention relates to a process of hydrolysing a high-melting fat into a high yield of fatty acids for use in the production of a soap free of undesirable additives, which comprises reacting a mixture of about 90 to 75% of a high-melting beef tallow and about 10 to 25% of coconut oil, with castor bean lipase, in about 20 to 50% water acidified to a pH of about 4 to 5.5 with a weak acid such as acetic acid, phosphoric acid, phosphorous acid or carbonic acid, and at a temperature of about 37°C, agitating the reaction mixture for about 3 to 48 hours, to obtain a final reaction mixture consisting of three layers: a fatty acid top layer, a lipase mixture in the middle layer and an aqueous glycerine bottom layer, separating the layers and neutralizing said fatty acids to form soap. The middle layer, which contains active castor bean lipase, is reused in the hydrolyzation process.

The lipase enzyme used as a catalyst in the present hydrolysis process may be any animal or vegetable lipase which is non-stereospecific, i.e., the lipase must split the *beta*–(middle carboxyl linkage) glyceride linkage at about the same rate as splitting the *alpha*–(outer carboxyl) linkages. Suitable examples of non-stereospecific lipase enzymes are derived from the castor bean, *Candida cylindracea*, *Propionibacterium acnes*, *Rhizopus arrhizus*, *Staphylococcus aureus*, *Aspergillus flavus* and *Geotrichum candidum*. Most lipases are stereospecific and therefore are ineffective, e.g., porcine pancreatic lipase. Normally, the extent of the hydrolysis with these enzymes does not exceed 70%, whereas the non-stereospecific enzymes affect substantially complete hydrolysis.

The preferred lipase enzyme utilized herein is the castor bean lipase (*Ricinus communis*). It is insoluble in water, and its activity is materially reduced by contact with water. The enzyme is stabilized by the presence of fats. It is rapidly inactivated by alkalis and functions only in a neutral or slightly acidic medium. This enzyme is activated by the presence of acids, preferably weak acids, such as acetic acid, phosphoric acid, phosphorous acid, carbonic acid, etc., which exerts the greatest accelerating effect. Accordingly, the optimum temperature for ricinus lipase action is about 37°C and is inactivated at temperatures above about 50°C. The amount of lipase used in the hydrolysis process is about 3 to 15% of the substrate (fat and oil) by weight, if the lipase activity (LA) is unknown. If the LA is known, approximately one LA unit is used for every 10 microequivalents of potential acid. [See N. Pelch and M.C. Kranz, *Anal. Biochem.*, **112**, 219–222, (1981) for a procedure for determination of lipase activity.]

An additional advantage in the use of the castor bean lipase in the hydrolysis reaction is the ability to recover (separate) the said lipase from the final reaction mixture and recycle it for use with a fresh substrate (fat and oil). This capability results from the natural immobilization property of castor bean lipase.

The castor bean lipase cannot be obtained commercially, but can be prepared as disclosed in the prior art previously discussed. The castor bean lipase utilized herein is prepared by dehulling castor beans, extracting the endogenous oils by grinding the dehulled beans in the presence of low-boiling petroleum ether, filtering the ground bean pomace and discarding the filtrate, i.e., ether layer containing endogenous oils, repeating the extraction and filtration steps two more times, air-drying the filtered pomace and recovering a lipase preparation in the form of the pomace. Another method of preparing the castor bean lipase enzyme without allergen may also be used. This method of preparation should be considered because of the presence of a potent allergen in the bean. The dehulled bean is macerated in water, rather than petroleum ether and then centrifuged. The fat layer is separated from the aqueous layer, and the aqueous layer is discarded. Since the lipase is in the spherosomes along with the endogenous oil, it will remain in the fat layer. The fat layer is extracted with petroleum ether and saturated NaCl solution. The petroleum ether contains the endogenous oil, and is discarded. The saturated NaCl solution contains the lipase in particulate matter.

The optimum conditions for activity of castor bean lipase is about 25 to 50°C and preferably about 37°C and a pH of 4 to 5.5. A dilute acid such as 0.1N acetic acid, or other weak acids may be added to bring the pH to approximately 5.0. The amount of the castor bean lipase enzyme used in the present hydrolysis process should be sufficient to effect a substantial degree of conversion of the beef tallow–coconut oil mixture into fatty acids and glycerol.

An amount of about 3 to 15% and preferably about 10% by weight of the triglyceride substrate mixture is used. It has unexpectedly been found that the addition of a vegetable oil such as coconut, corn, soybean, linseed, olive and palm oil, to the high-melting point beef tallow enables the beef tallow to emulsify at a lower tem-perature, about 37°C. The lipase enzyme hydrolyses the emulsified tallow–vegetable oil mixture almost quantitatively at the lower temperature with a resultant saving in energy.

The vegetable oil such as coconut oil also hydrolyses into fatty acids and glycerol. Thus, no undesirable extraneous materials are present in the reaction mixture, thereby yielding a substantially pure soap upon neutralization of the fatty acids with NaOH, Na_2CO_3 or $NaHCO_3$. The coconut oil constitutes a lesser amount by weight than the beef tallow in a mixture thereof. The weight ratio of beef tallow to vegetable oil is about 75 to 90% to about 25 to 10% vegetable oil.

Table AI.1 Extent of castor bean lipase hydrolysis of fats and oils

	Lit. SV *	Observed enzyme hydrolysis
Value		
Olive oil (control)	186–196	185
83:17 Tallow:Coconut	203–213	203

*Saponification Value is the weight (mg) of KOH required to saponify 1 g of fat, and is indicative of the extent of hydrolysis of the fats and oils.

The data in Table AI.1 show that a mixture of high-grade edible beef tallow and coconut oil, at the same ratio as may be used in soaps, was hydrolysed approximately 98% into fatty acids under the described conditions. This is in clear contrast to results reported in the literature (Haley *et. al.*), in which beef tallow was reacted with castor bean lipase but was only hydrolysed about 3% (Table AI.2). In the latter case, coconut oil was absent. The combined results clearly show that the addition of coconut oil unexpectedly yields a high conversion of the high-melting beef tallow into fatty acids. It is believed that the clearly show that the addition of coconut oil unexpectedly yields a high conversion of the high-melting beef tallow into fatty acids. It is believed that the coconut oil lowered the melting point of the beef tallow enough so that it would form an emulsion at 37°C.

Table AI.2 Hydrolysis of beef tallow by castor bean lipase

Duration of experiment (hrs)	Extent of hydrolysis (%)
24	2.8
48	2.8
72	2.8

The saponification value is determined by conventional methods described in the literature, M. Applewhite, Kirk-Othmr, *Encycl. Chem. Tech.*, 3rd Ed., 9, 795 (1980). The saponification procedure utilized herein comprises adding 30 ml of absolute ethanol to a 2 to 3 g sample in a covered flask, warming on a steam bath (50 to 60°C), adding 50 ml standardized 0.5N alcoholic KOHsolution and boiling for one hour, adding phenophthalein indicator solution and titrating with standardized 0.5N HCl to the disappearance of the pink color, and the saponification value is determined.

Saponification of fats and oils in the absence of lipase, to determine the maximum yield of soap available from fats and oils was conducted on four substrates. Triolein and olive oil are standards used in literature. Beef tallow and coconut oil are components of the soaps prepared herein. The data in Table AI.3 show that the observed results are in fairly good agreement with the literature values for the two standards and coconut oil, but low for beef tallow.

Table AI.3 Saponification Values (SV)

	Lit.	Obs.
Triolein	189 (calc)	190
Olive oil	186–196	182
Beef tallow	193–202	173
Coconut oil	250–264	253

The advantages of the enzymatic hydrolysis process of the present invention are multifaceted. Higher yields of fatty acids and glycerol are obtained, about 98% conversion. The use of lower temperatures resulted in considerable cost savings. The use of vegetable oil such as coconut oil which also hydrolyses into fatty acids and glycerol yields fatty acids and glycerol free of undesirable additives. Said fatty acids yield a pure soap upon neutralization with NaOH, Na_2CO_3 or $NaHCO_3$. This low temperature hydrolysis reaction requires less utilization of energy, and therefore, less atmospheric pollution is produced. The use of a low reaction temperature in this process yields fewer undesirable thermal products, and a lighter color.

Detailed description of the invention

The following examples are merely illustrative of the invention and are not to be construed as limiting thereof.

Example I

Preparation of enzyme

Dehull 60 g of castor bean. Grind the dehulled beans in a blender in the presence of 600ml of low-boiling (30 to 60°C) petroleum ether. The ether extracts endogenous oils from the beans. Filter and discard filtrate. Repeat extraction and filtration two or more times. Air-dry the crude lipase preparation.

Enzymatic hydrolysis of tallow–coconut mixture

Mix 1.67 g of the lipase preparation and 16.7 g of an 83:17 mixture of high-grade beef tallow and coconut oil, and 10 ml of 0.1N acetic acid. Stir for approximately 24 hours at 37°C. The final mixture consists of three layers: fatty acid on the top, lipase mixture in the middle, and sweet water (aqueous glycerine) at the bottom. The fatty acid layer is skimmed off, neutralized with NaOH, Na_2CO_3 or $NaHCO_3$, and the resulting soap purified in the usual manner of soap manufacturers skilled in the art. The bottom layer is separated, and the glycerine removed. The middle layer, containing more than 50% of the original lipase, still being active, is reused after adding a lesser quantity of fresh lipase.

Analysis of the extent of hydrolysis is determined by adding 3.4 g of reaction mixture to 100 ml absolute alcohol, and titrating to pH 9.5 with 0.1N alcoholic KOH.

Results: 98% conversion to fatty acids and glycerol.

Example 2

Preparation of castor bean lipase

60 g of dehulled castor beans are macerated in water and centrifuged. The fat layer is separated from the aqueous layer, which is discarded. The fat layer is extracted with 600 ml low-boiling petroleum ether (30 to 60°C) and saturated NaCl solution. The petroleum ether is discarded, and the NaCl solution contains the lipase in particulate form. 1.67 g of this particulate lipase is used in the hydrolysis of the tallow–coconut oil mixture in accordance with the process of Example 1. Substantially complete hydrolysis into fatty acids and glycerol is obtained.

Example 3

The high-melting beef tallow is melted at a temperature of about 42°C until it is liquified. The liquified tallow is mixed with the coconut oil in the weight ratio of 80:20 tallow : coconut oil. 1.67 g of the lipase preparation of Example 1 is mixed with 16.7 g of the liquified fat and oil mixture, and 10ml of 0.1N acetic acid for about 25 hours at 37°C. Substantially complete hydrolysis into fatty acids and glycerol is obtained.

Other weak acids may be substituted for the acetic acid in the examples, such as phosphoric, phosphorous or carbonic acid. Lower melting point fats such as sheep tallow, industrial quality beef tallow, lard and butter may be used in the present lipase hydrolysis process.

Also, other vegetable oils such as corn, soybean, linseed, olive and palm oil may be substituted for the coconut oil in the examples. It is understood that the foregoing detailed description is given merely by way of illustration and that variations may be made therein without departing from the spirit of the invention. The "Abstract" given above is merely for the convenience of technical searchers and is not to be given any weight with respect to the scope of the invention.

We claim

1. A process for the production of fatty acids and glycerol from high-melting fats such as beef tallow, said process comprising hydrolysing an emulsified mixture of said high-melting beef tallow and a vegetable oil of the kind such as herein described, said beef tallow being present in the weight ratio of 75 to 90% and said vegetable oil in the weight ratio of 25 to 10%, said hydrolysis being conducted in an aqueous medium and in the presençe of a non-stereospecific animal or vegetable lipase enzyme at a temperature in the range of 25 to 50°C, and at a pH of 4 to 5.5, to produce fatty acids and glycerol.
2. A process as claimed in Claim 1, wherein said mixture is agitated for a sufficient period of time in the range of 3 to 48 hours to obtain substantially complete hydrolysis into fatty acids and glycerol.
3. A process, as claimed in Claim 2, wherein said vegetable oil is coconut oil.
4. A process, as claimed in Claim 3, wherein said mixture of beef tallow and coconut oil is in the weight ratio of 83:17.
5. A process, as claimed in Claim 2, wherein said lipase enzyme constitutes about 3 to 15% of the weight of said tallow and vegetable oil mixture.
6. A process, as claimed in Claim 2, wherein said lipase enzyme is derived, from castor bean, *Candida cylindracea*, *Propionibacterium acnes*, *Rhizopus arrhizus*, *Staphylococcus aureus*, *Aspergillus flavus* and *Geotrichum candidum*.
7. A process for the production of fatty acids and glycerol substantially as herein described with reference to the foregoing examples.

Dated this 24th day of August, 1987

Appendix II

An example of a selection patent

Ethyl Corporation (Cook's) Patents M.10, pp. 227–233

A Summary

Specification No. 949268 to Ethyl Corporation	Related prior art in 941742
Claim 1	**Claim 1**
Antiknock composition comprising • tetramethyl lead • ethylene dibromide and/or propylene dibromide and • one more hydrocarbon (90 to 150°C B.P.) which are alkanes and mononuclear aromatics containing only aromatic unsaturation — ethylene and/or propylene dibromide: tetramethyl lead is 1:1 — hydrocarbon content 10 to 30% by weight of composition	Antiknock concentrate comprising • tetramethyl lead • a hydrocarbon liquid (100 to 120°C B.P.) — hydrocarbon content 10 to 15% by wt. of tetramethyl lead

Continues

Continued

Claim 2	**Claim 2**
The composition according to Claim 1, wherein content of the said hydrocarbon range is 10 to 15% by weight based on total weight of the composition.	Concentrate according to Claim 1 and further comprising a halohydrocarbon scavenger.
Claim 3	**Claim 3**
The composition according to Claim 1 wherein the said hydrocarbon is a liquid.	An antiknock concentrate according to Claim 1 or 2 wherein the liquid hydrocarbon is an aromatic hydrocarbon.
Claim 4	**Claim 4**
The composition according to Claim 1 wherein the hydrocarbon is toluene. The specification in the text mentioned "The most outstanding results from a cost and effectiveness standpoint are achieved with hydrocarbon ranging from 10 to 15% by weight, and, therefore, this constitutes a preferred embodiment of this invention not only from the cost and effectiveness standpoint but from the standpoint of optimum shipping characteristics in a composition as above defined wherein the hydrocarbon content is present in the mixture in amount such that it is equivalent on a weight basis to substantially 20% of the total weight of tetramethyl lead and the hydrocarobon."	An antiknock concentrate according to Claim 3 wherein the hydrocarbon liquid is toluene. This specification also explicitly gave a composition for the improved antiknock which comprises 48.8% tetramethyl lead, 34.6% ethylene dibromide concentrations and 16.6% toluene ethylene bromide-tetramethyl lead mole ratio of 1:1 represents a proportion of 70% by weight of dibromide based on tetramethyl lead.

While deciding on this application, the tribunal observed :

1. Claims 1, 3 and 4 of the applicant's Specification No. 949268 are in effect merely reclaiming part of the range previously claimed in the prior document No. 941742.
2. However, with respect to Claim 2 of Specification No. 949268, it was stated that in the range of 10 to 15% of the use of the hydrocarbon has a great advantage over anything disclosed in Specification No. 941742.The specification broadly discloses in the examples, a working range of 25 to 40%. This was allowed to go through a selection patent.

However, the earlier patentee also disclosed an example with the use of hydrocarbon as low as 16.6%, but it is fair to say that no emphasis was placed on the figure as giving the cost and effectiveness advantage alleged by the Application No.949268 in which they claimed a slightly lower range of 10 to 15%. They further observed:

"...the earlier patentee clearly did not appreciate that here was a range between 10 and 15%, where the cost and effectiveness advantages were outstanding and that if he had appreciated it, he could not have failed to have mentioned it and given an example within that range".

Details of the case

In the Appeal Tribunal
***Before*: Mr Justice Graham**
2nd and 24th February, 1970
Ethyl Corporation (Cook's) Patent

Patent — opposition — prior claiming — claimed range fell within range claimed in earlier patent — selection situation — objection not made out — appeal dismissed — objection made out in Patent Office against other claims which specified use of substance referred to in body of prior specification.

In opposition proceedings, the superintending examiner upheld a prior claiming objection against certain claims relating to a tetramethyl lead antiknock composition comprising, inter alia, ethylene (or propylene) dibromide, the position being that ethylene dibromide was referred to in the body of the cited patent specification concerning similar compositions. The superintending examiner held, however, that the objection was not made out against a claim for such a composition which included hydrocarbons in a limited range of 10 to 15% by weight, this range falling within the range claimed in the earlier patent. On an appeal by the opponents to the Appeal Tribunal against the latter finding, the applicants contended that it was clearly alleged in their specification that their range had a great advantage over anything disclosed in the cited specification, and that they could (had the earlier patent been a prior publication) have framed their specification in the form of a selection patent.

Held, dismissing the appeal (1) that if the true position in a prior claiming case was that, had the prior document been published, the later inventor would have been able to frame his specification in the form of a selection patent and would have been able to claim specific advantages for his later and narrower claim, then there was no reason why he should not also in effect be in that position in a prior claiming case, in which event there would be no prior claim. If, however, he was merely reclaiming a small portion of the field already claimed without being, as it were, in the selection position so far as the prior invention was concerned, then the decision should be the opposite; (2) that in the present case the applicants should be given the benefit of any doubt and ought to be allowed thereafter to allege and prove if they could that their invention was really in essence different from that of the prior document.

Mr Walton: Ethyl Corporation (Cook's) Patent

This was an appeal by the opponents, Chevron Research Company, from a decision of the superintending examiner, Mr H.S.Walton, dated 17th March, 1969, whereby he found, inter alia, that a prior claiming objection was not made out against Claim 2 of Patent Application No. 949268 of Ethyl Corporation. The facts of the case appear from the following decision.

In the Patent Office, John Whitford, Q.C., instructed by Stevens, Hewlett and Perkins, appeared for the applicants. A. Kynric Lewis, instructed by Haseltine, Lake and Co., appeared for the opponents.

Walton — The application relates to antiknock compositions and is opposed on the following grounds:

1. Prior claiming of the invention, so far as claimed in at least Claims 1, 2, 3 and 4, in Claims 2, 3 (as appendant to Claim 2) and 4 of Specification No.941742.
2. Insufficient and unfair description.

Claims 1, 2, 3 and 4 of Application No.949268, against which prior (concurrent) claiming is alleged, is as follows:

1. An antiknock composition comprising tetramethyl lead, ethylene dibromide and/or propylene dibromide and one or more hydrocarbons which boil at 90 to 150°C, the said hydrocarbons being alkanes and mononuclear aromatics containing only aromatic unsaturation: the ethylene dibromide and/or propylene dibromide content being such that there is substantially one mole thereof per mole of tetramethyl lead; the hydrocarbon content being such that there is from 10 to 30 % by weight thereof based on the total weight of the composition.
2. The composition, according to Claim 1, wherein the content of said hydrocarbon ranges from 10 to 15% by weight, based on the total weight of the composition.
3. The composition, according to Claim 1, wherein said hydrocarbon is a liquid hydrocarbon.
4. The composition, according to Claim 1, wherein said hydrocarbon is toluene.

The first four Claims of Specification No. 941742, of which Claims 2, 3 (as appendant to Claim 2) and 4 are alleged to prior Claim, the applicants' invention, are as follows:

1. An antiknock concentrate comprising tetramethyl lead and a hydrocarbon liquid boiling in the range of 100 to 120°C, the hydrocarbon liquid content of the concentrate being in the range of 10 to 15% by weight of the tetramethyl lead.
2. An antiknock concentrate, according to Claim 1, and further comprising a halohydrocarbon scavenger.
3. An antiknock concentrate, according to Claim 1 or 2, wherein the hydrocarbon liquid is an aromatic hydrocarbon.
4. An antiknock concentrate, according to Claim 3, wherein the hydrocarbon liquid is toluene.

Below the Table on page 4 of Specification No. 941742 is to be found set out a composition (c) which, at lines 10 and 11 on page 5, is described as being "the improved antiknock concentrate according to the invention". Composition (c) comprises, 48.8% tetramethyl lead, 34.6% ethylene dibromide, 16.6% toluene. Ethylene dibromide being a halohydrocarbon scavenger, the use of which in the concentrate is claimed in Claim 2, and toluene being a hydrocarbon liquid boiling in the range of 100 to 120°C, the use of which in the concentrate is claimed in Claim 1, to which, Claim 2 is appendant. Toluene is specified as the hydrocarbon liquid in appendant Claim 4. Composition (c), in which the specified percentage proportions can without doubt, in my view, be taken to be by weight, lies clearly within the ambit of Claims 1, 3 and 4 of the applicants' Specification No. 949268. In this respect, I must observe that, in accordance with the applicants' specification at lines 27 to 32 on page 1, an ethylene dibromide-tetramethyl lead mole ratio of 1:1 represents a proportion of 70% by weight of the dibromide based on the tetramethyl lead and the latter percentage proportion is substantially that obtained with respect to the dibromide and tetramethyl lead contents of the composition (c) set out above.

To assist me in determining whether prior claiming has been established, I turn to the decision in the matter of Merck and Co.(Macek's) Patent (1967) RPC 157, and particularly the passage from lines 18 to 22 on page 163 where the Patents Appeal Tribunal, after consideration of how the phrase "the invention so far as claimed in any claim" should be construed and concluding that there would appear to be no ground for construing the phrase in different senses in the sub-divisions of Section 14(1), observed

"......if the cited prior claim on its fair construction can be seen to grant as a manner of manufacture that which the later claim on its fair construction would re-monopolize, the objection of prior claiming is established and this despite the inclusion in the later claim of variants of the manner of manufacture to which no objection can properly be raised".

Turning now to Claim 2 of Specification No. 941742 and considering it in conjunction with the composition designated (c) on page 4 of the specification and in accordance with the dictum expressed in the preceding paragraph, I am of the opinion that this claim, on its fair construction—that is to say, a construction which must necessarily be inclusive of any specific exemplification in the specification of the antiknock concentrate forming the subject of the invention set out in the claim—can be seen to grant as a manner of manufacture not merely an antiknock concentrate consisting of tetramethyl lead, ethylene dibromide and toluene in which the latter compound is present in a proportion of 10 to 15% by weight of the tetramethyl lead, but one in which an ethylene dibromide-tetramethyl lead mole ratio of 1:1 obtains when the proportion of toluene in the composition is 16.6% by weight, the latter figure lying within the range of 10 to 30% by weight, specified in Claim 1 of the applicants' specification for the hydrocarbon content of the antiknock composition claimed therein. On fair construction, Claims 1, 3 and 4 of the applicants' specification clearly seek to re-monopolize this particular concentrate, and accordingly I find the opponents' plea of prior (concurrent) claiming to be established in respect of these three claims, but not, I must observe, in respect of Claim 2.

On grounds of insufficiency the opponents have alleged that the applicants' invention cannot be performed without substantial risk of infringement of at least Claims 1, 2 and 3 of the cited Specification (Patent) No. 941742. Mr Whitford in fact conceded that there was a risk of infringement with respect to these claims but referred to the documentary evidence with a view to challenging their validity on the ground that a substantial number of compositions within the scope of Claim 1, or of Claims 3 and 4 dependent thereon, of Specification No. 941742 are not useful in the sense promised by the said specification. Mr Lewis, on the other hand, was able to satisfy me that the validity of Claim 2 of the citation had not been challenged. Accordingly I hereby direct that the applicants' complete specification bear a reference to Patent No. 941742 in the form prescribed by Rule 34 of the Patent Rules 1968.

With reference to my finding the prior (concurrent) claiming has been established. I prescribe a period of six weeks from the date of this decision for the applicants to submit proposals for amendment of the complete specification said proposals by way of, and being stated in writing to be by way of, disclaimer, and being shown in red on a printed copy of the specification. A further printed copy, similarly amended, should at the same time be transmitted to the opponents, who, within a period of four weeks from the date of receipt thereof, are at liberty to submit any comments they may wish to make upon the proposals.

Thereafter I shall determine the course to be taken.

I defer the question of costs pending the issue of a final decision.

On appeal to the Patents Appeal Tribunal, Ralph Lunzer, instructed by Stevens, Hewlett and Perkins, appeared for the applicants (respondents). A. Kynric Lewis, instructed by Haseltine, Lake and Co., appeared for the opponents (appellants).

Graham — This case raises an important and interesting question in relation to prior claim. The objection of prior claim, or prior grant, is of course the modern statutory equivalent of the same objection to validity made in days gone by the writ of *scire facias*. The objection in its then more general form is set out in Coke 4 Institute, page 88, as the first ground on which *scire facias* lies to repeat letters patent in the following words: "When the King doth grant by several letters patent one and the self-same thing to several persons, the first patentee shall have a *scire facias* to repeal the second patent".

The "general rules" respecting patents, which include the recitation of the passage quoted above from the Institute, are conveniently set out in R.V. Mussary, 1 WPC 41.

The development of the modern practice of a series of detailed and specific claims and the reduction of the prior claim objection into statutory form, represented at present by Sections 8, 14(b) and 32(a) of the Patents Act 1949, has resulted over the years in specialization of the objection. There are by this date a large number of cases on the subject, some of which, as a result, have for some time caused more or less difficulty to the court and practitioners. It is, however, not necessary for present purposes to review these cases and I certainly do not propose to do so on this occasion. They have recently been well reviewed in Merck and Co., (Macek's) Patent (1967) RPC 157, and the reasoning of Lloyd–Jacob, J. generally and in particular from page 162, line 44 to page 168, line 26 should be noted. This shows that, just as in cases of anticipation and obviousness, a claim by analogy if a later claim includes something already claimed in an earlier claim it is *prima facie* bad until amended.

It may, however, perhaps be useful to note that the practice of having claims in the modern form has, speaking quite generally, resulted in three typical instances where conflict arises. First, using the spatial analogy, where the earlier claim lies wholly within the area of the later claim; secondly, where the areas of the earlier and later claims are not coterminous but overlap; and thirdly, where the earlier claim is broader than, and includes within it, the area covered by the later claim.

The first two cases can usually and should, in my judgment, continue to be dealt with in the way they are normally dealt with, namely, by amendment. The area covered by the later claim which includes or overlaps the area of the earlier claim should be excluded from it by amendment. There is then no conflict between the two claims and objection to double grant *ex hypothesi* no longer lies.

It is the third case which is liable to give rise to difficulties in practice and the present appeal is an instance of such a case. Here again, however, experience shows that there are mainly two alternative situations which arise — first, where the earlier and later inventors are really concerned with the same problem and provide the same solution but claim their respective inventions in words which result in the later claim being smaller in area than the earlier, and, secondly, where the two inventors can on the proper construction of their specifications and claims be seen fairly to have been addressing their minds to different problems or different aspects of the same general problem, and to have provided different or sometimes more specific solutions. Of course, the situations envisaged are seldom absolutely clear-cut and questions of degree are bound to arise. Solutions provided are not likely to be exactly the same nor likely to be wholly different when two inventors address their minds to solving essentially the same or closely related problems. Thus, difficult cases for decision will certainly arise, but neither the court nor the Controller shrinks from deciding questions of degree and it should always be possible to come to a conclusion as to on which side of the line any particular case lies. In such circumstances it is unwise, if not impossible, to lay down specific guidelines which will always be of general application, and the conclusion must be reached after a full study of the specifications and other relevant circumstances in each case.

There is, however, one test which in my judgment is of assistance in all prior claim cases of this third type because it is of general application. This test is derived by analogy from the position of a so-called "selection" patent. In a "selection" case the position is that there is a narrower later claim which falls wholly within the broader area of the disclosure of an earlier published prior document. In such a case there will be anticipation unless the patentee of the later invention can show that he has selected an area from the prior broad disclosure which gives advantages beyond or different from those disclosed by the prior document. Provided the strict rules for validity laid down in I.G.Farbenindustrie's Patents (1930) 47 RPC 289, and other cases are observed, there is no reason why the claim in the later selection patent should not be valid. The patentee must of course frame his specification in proper form and the court must be satisfied that there are real advantages in fact in his selection, but provided that this be so there is no reason why he should not have such a claim and why, if it is fought, such a claim should not be upheld. By analogy it seems to me that, if the true position in a prior claiming case, where of course the prior document has been published, the later inventor would have been able to frame his specification in the form of a selection patent and would have been able to claim specific advantages for his later and narrower claim, then there is no reason why he should not also in effect be in that position in a prior claiming case. If the proper conclusion is that he is in such a position, then in my judgment the right decision is that there is no prior claim. On the other hand, if the conclusion is that he is merely reclaiming again a small portion of that field already claimed in the prior document without being, as it were, in the selection position so far as the prior invention is concerned, then the decision should be the opposite. In the present case the superintending examiner, Mr Walton, has decided that Claims 1, 3 and 4 of the applicants' specification are in effect merely reclaiming part of the range previously claimed in the prior document. He took the opposite view, however, in respect of Claim 2, though he does not give any reasons as to why he did so. In my judgment there are good reasons why his decision is right in respect of Claim 2 and it may be useful in deference to the argument before me that I should very shortly set these out.

Mr Lunzer, on behalf of the applicants, says that the range claimed in Claim 2, namely, a composition according to Claim 1 wherein the content of the hydrocarbon ranges from 10 to 15% based on the total weight of the composition, when that claim is read in the light of the advantages which are stated to be obtained by that range on page 1 of the specification, line 66 onwards, would have enabled the inventor to claim that his invention was in the nature of a selection from the invention of No. 941742, if that specification had been published before the priority date of No. 949268. The passage at page 1 in question reads as follows:

Now, it must be understood that the figure of 20% just quoted in fact means a figure of 12.5 %, when the composition is as claimed in Claim 2, which is expressed to be according to Claim 1, i.e. where there is not only present tetramethyl lead but also a substance such as ethylene dibromide in the molar proportions of 1:1. The 20% example is, therefore, in that event in fact an example half-way between the 10% and 15% range which has just been mentioned at line 69.

Now, it is said on behalf of the applicants that it is clearly alleged in the specification that this range of 10 to 15% has a great advantage over anything disclosed by the prior patentee in his Specification No. 941742. That specification broadly discloses in the examples a working range of 25 to 40% in Table 1. Example (c) of Table 2 which was relied upon is not, strictly speaking, set out as an example of working in accordance with the invention but as a test of explosibility characteristics. Nevertheless, as the figure of 16.6% for toluene is within the range claimed in Claim 1, it must be taken also to be such of hydrocarbon as low as 16.6% but it is fair to say that no emphasis was placed on the figure as giving the cost and effectiveness advantage alleged by the present applicant to be found in his slightly lower range of 10 to 15%.

With regard to the layout of the whole prior specification and to all the figures it contains, it is contended on behalf of the applicants that the earlier patentee clearly did not appreciate that there was a range between 10 and 15% where the cost and effective-ness advantages were outstanding and that, if he had appreciated it, he could not have failed to have mentioned it and given an example within that range. There seems to me to be reasonable justification for this contention and there is, of course, at this stage no evidence to the contrary. I am concerned as to whether the claim should be allowed to go forward on the basis of the documents alone and of the allegation in the specification, which is not as yet denied by the opponents, that outstanding results are obtained by using a hydro-carbon concentration within the range in question. If this is right, and I cannot see that in the life of the patent the court can assume that it is not, then the applicant ought to be given any benefit of doubt if such be there, and ought to be allowed thereafter to allege and prove if he can that this invention is really in essence different from that of the prior document. On the assumptions I have made here, he can justifiably allege that, had the prior document been a publication, he could have framed his specification in the form of a selection patent and there is, at present no reason for thinking that it would not have been a good one. At any rate, there is no reason for thinking that it would not have been allowed to go forward, if properly drafted, as an application for a selection patent.

For these reasons, I agree with the conclusion of Mr Walton and I therefore dismiss the appeal. I award the applicants 35 guineas costs and direct that this sum be paid to them by the opponents.

Appendix IIIa

An example of a main patent

Government of India, The Patent Office,
214, Acharya Jagadish Bose Road, Calcutta 700 017

Complete Specification No. 170499 dated 18-06-1990
Application No. 157/BOM/90 dated 18-06-1990
Postdated/Antedated to date
Acceptance of the complete specification advertised on 4th April 1992

Index at acceptance - 89 [XLI (6)]
International Classification - G 01 N - 3/42, 3/52

Title : An improved composite indentation hardness tester with built-in base for rubber, and the like substances such as soft or hard plastics and textile-wound packages

Applicant : KUMAR BALRAM BHATIA, an Indian national 408-A, Poonam Apartments, Dr Annie Besant Road, Worli, Mumbai 400018, Maharashtra, India.

The following specification particularly describes and ascertains the nature of this invention and the manner in which it is to be performed:

This invention relates to an improved composite indentation hardness tester with built-in base for rubber and like substances such as soft or hard plastics, foam, polymeric substances and textile-wound packages.

In the prior art for testing, the hardness of rubber or like substances, a separate stand is required for mounting the hardness tester thereon.

The indentation hardness tester and the stand having a stem and a testing table, are made separately. While testing the hardness of rubber or like substances, the tester is fixed on the stem of the stand and the specimen is fixed on the testing table of the stand and a constant perpendicular pressure is applied between the tester and the specimen/sample, which is about 2 kg in Shore-A and about 3 kg in Shore-D principle. The accuracy of the hardness of the rubber or like substances obtained by the tester very much depends on the perpendicularity of this load application i.e. the constant pressure applied between the tester and the specimen should be perfectly perpendicular for getting accurate hardness.

The main drawbacks of the existing hardness tester for rubber and like substances are:

1. The indentor tip protrudes out of the pressure foot of the tester which makes a point contact with the specimen while testing, thereby perpendicularity of the load application is not possible and thus accurate hardness reading is not possible.
2. A separate stand is required for testing the hardness with same accuracy.
3. The tester and the stand being two different units increase the weight of the combined tester involving extra cost and the units are carried separately in their respective boxes thereby occupying extra space and increasing the transport cost.
4. For carrying out the test, the tester is to be fixed on the stem of the stand properly, which is cumbersome, time consuming and requires some skill, which ultimately increases the cost of testing.
5. The space available for specimen, in between the indentor of the tester and the testing table of the stand, is limited because the tester is to be fixed on the stem of the stand and the specimen is to be fixed on the testing table of the stand; therefore samples of bigger size such as a finished product like a tyre, cannot be tested.
6. After some use, due to repeated fixing and removing of the tester from the stand, constant perpendicularity of load application cannot be achieved, thereby accuracy of testing the hardness cannot be ensured.

The main object of this invention is to obviate the above-mentioned drawbacks of the existing tester and to provide an improved composite indentation hardness tester with a built-in base for rubber or the like substances, thereby making the whole tester in a single composite unit which is light in weight, more economical and which can easily be carried in a single case like a small handbag for on-the-spot testing, and which is more accurate by ensuring constant perpendicularity of the load application onto the specimen surface for correct results.

Another object of this invention is to provide an improved composite indentation hardness tester with built-in base in which there is no limitation of the space between the indentor and the specimen, thereby making it possible to test all specimens on the spot, without any difficulty.

The invention will be clear from the following description with reference to the accompanying drawings wherein :

Figure AIIIa.1 shows part-sectional elevation of the improved composite hardness tester with built-in base according to this invention.

Figure AIIIa.2 shows another embodiment of the invention shown in Fig. AIIIa.1.

Figure AIIIa.3 shows part-sectional elevation of the existing hardness tester.

Referring to Fig. AIIIa.3, the existing hardness tester for rubber consists of a main block (20) provided with a locking knob (21), a dial block (22), a foot (23), an indentor (24) protruding out of the foot, a calibrating spring (25) and fixing pin (26) for fixing the dial block to the main block. While testing hardness the indentor makes a point contact with the specimen. A separate stand is required for ensuring perpendicularity of load application. The stand (27) is separately made and comprises a stem (28) over which the main block of the tester is slidably mounted with the help of the knob. A table (29) is mounted above a base (30) for supporting the specimen. As described earlier, the existing tester is not suitable for large size products due to limited space between table and indentor. It is complicated in construction and the testing process is cumbersome; besides, very accurate readings are not possible due to non-perpendicularity of load application.

Referring to Figs. AIIIa.1 and AIIIa.2, the improved hardness tester, according to this invention, comprises a base (5) having a stepped presser foot (4) at its bottom, the dimensions of which are kept strictly according to international standards. The base is provided with two slots (13) diametrically opposite each other in which two pins (8) for slidably holding a container cover (7) over the base move up and down. A stopper means such as a setting nut (6) having a

Kumar Balram Bhatia
Application No. 157/BOM/1990

Total sheets 3
Sheet no. 1

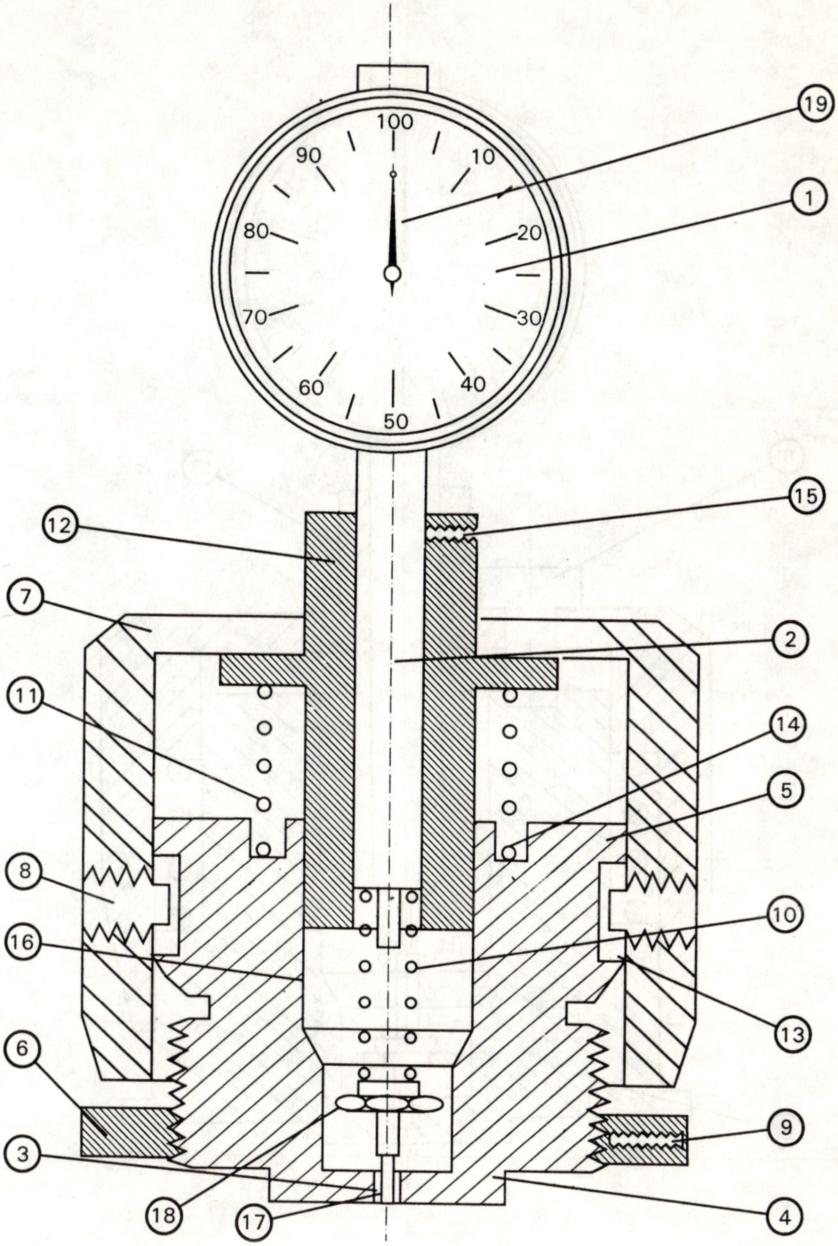

(Kumar Balram Bhatia)

Fig. AIIIa. 1 The improved hardness tester

Kumar Balram Bhatia
Application No. 157/BOM/1990

Total sheets 3
Sheet no. 2

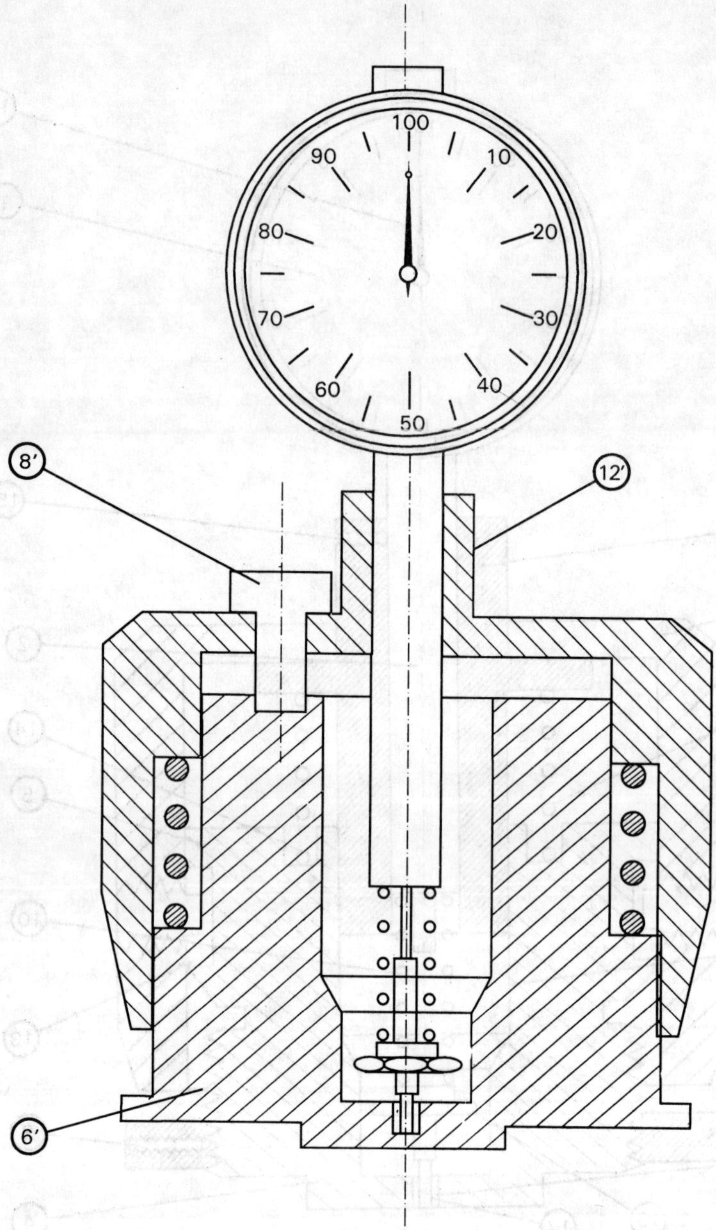

(Kumar Balram Bhatia)

Fig. AIIIa. 2 Another embodiment of the improved hardness tester

Kumar Balram Bhatia
Application No. 157/BOM/1990

Total sheets 3
Sheet no. 3

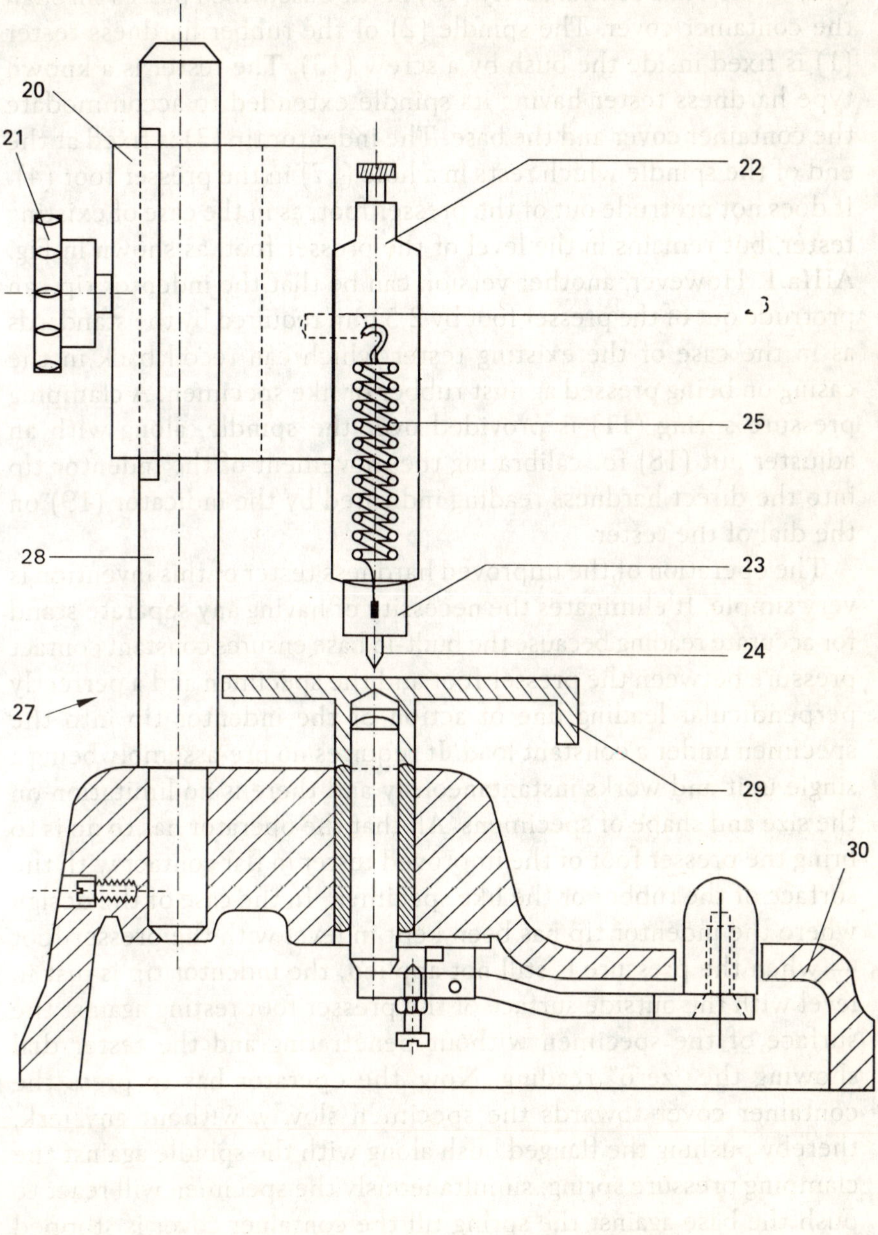

(Kumar Balram Bhatia)

Fig. AIIIa. 3 The existing hardness tester

locking screw (9) is threaded over the base below the container cover for setting the movement of base and the container cover which should be 2.5 mm as per international standards. A flanged bush (12) is fixed in a central cavity (16) in the base which passes through the container cover. The spindle (2) of the rubber hardness tester (1) is fixed inside the bush by a screw (13). The tester is a known type hardness tester having its spindle extended to accommodate the container cover and the base. The indentor tip (3) is fixed at the end of the spindle which rests in a hole (17) in the presser foot (4). It does not protrude out of the presser foot, as in the case of existing tester, but remains in the level of the presser foot, as shown in Fig. AIIIa.1. However, another version can be that the indentor tip can protrude out of the presser foot by 2.5 mm required by the standards as in the case of the existing tester which can recoil back in the casing on being pressed against rubber or like specimen. A clamping pressure spring (11) is provided over the spindle, along with an adjuster nut (18) for calibrating the movement of the indentor tip into the direct hardness reading indicated by the indicator (19) on the dial of the tester.

The operation of the improved hardness tester of this invention is very simple. It eliminates the necessity of having any separate stand for accurate reading because the built-in base ensures constant contact pressure between the presser foot and the specimen and a perfectly perpendicular leading line of action of the indentor tip into the specimen under a constant load. It requires no pre-assembly being a single unit and works instantaneously and there is no limitation on the size and shape of specimens. All that the operator has to do is to bring the presser foot of the improved tester in flat contact with the surface of the rubber or the like specimen. In the case of the design where the indentor tip has been kept in level with the presser foot — when the pressure is still not applied, the indentor tip is just in level with the outside surface of the presser foot resting against the surface of the specimen without penetrating and the tester dial showing the "zero" reading. Now, the operator has to press the container cover towards the specimen slowly, without any jerk, thereby pushing the flanged bush along with the spindle against the clamping pressure spring; simultaneously the specimen will react to push the base against the spring till the container cover is stopped by the setting nut, which determines that had there been no resistance of the specimen on the indentor tip, the indentor tip would have been protruding out of the presser foot by 2.5 mm, the standard gap between the container cover and the setting nut. But because of the resistance of the specimen, the indentor tip will be lifted up proportionally to that resistance, thereby lifting the spindle into the hardness tester, which is calibrated properly by the calibrating spring (10) to show exact hardness of the specimen in standard shore units. In the case of the design where the indentor tip is made to protrude out of the presser foot already by 2.5 mm as per the standards — when the pressure is still not applied, the indentor tip will just touch the specimen surface and the presser foot is away from the surface of the rubber specimen. Now, when the operator applies pressure on the container cover first, the indentor tip is moved up against the calibrating spring which is softer than the clamping pressure spring — thereby, the presser foot starts coming closer to the specimen surface till it is just in contact with the specimen surface. But, the required constant perpendicular pressure of about 2 kg in Shore-A principle and about 3 kg in Shore-D principle is not achieved and therefore the reading shown by the dial of the hardness tester is not final. When the operator applies further pressure on the container cover towards the specimen slowly, without any jerk, thereby compressing the clamping pressure spring, he is guaranteeing the required constant perpendicular pressure of about 2 kg in Shore-A principle and about 3 kg in Shore-D principle between the presser foot and the specimen surface. At the same time, the indentor tip is being forced into the specimen surface by the precalibrated load of the calibrating spring as per the standard. Depending on the hardness of the specimen, the indentor tip is partially penetrated into the specimen and is partially lifted up into the dial of the tester. Since the calibrating spring is properly calibrated as per the requirements of the standards to the extent to reach the indentor tip, the spindle is lifted up into the hardness tester above exact hardness of the specimen in standard shore units.

The above description is only to understand the invention rather than limiting its scope, as various modifications are possible within the ambit and scope of this invention. Such as, the base and container cover can be modified as shown in Fig. AIIIa.2. The setting nut from Fig.AIIIa.1 is replaced in Fig. AIIIa.2 by an extended flange (6′) as an integral extended part of the base, and flanged bush (12) of Fig. AIIIa.1 is replaced by a collar (12′) in Fig. AIIIa.2, which is integrally made with the container cover as in Fig. AIIIa.1. Holding pins (8) of Fig. AIIIa.1 are being replaced by a single stepped pin (8′) in Fig. AIIIa.2, which holds the container cover over the base and prevents any rotary action between the two. The clamping pressure spring is placed between the stepped flanges formed in the container cover and the base in Fig. AIIIa.2.

The calibrating spring can be placed inside the tester, as shown in Fig. AIIIa.3, to make it possible to use any conventional rubber tester with its indentor tip protruding out of the presser foot, whether having dial gauge, using rack and pinion or slot and pin sliding arrangement as well as whether analog type meters or digital indicating hardness testers, using mechanical systems or electronic systems.

Claims

1. An improved composite indentation hardness tester with built-in base for rubber and the like substances comprising a base having a stepped presser foot at its bottom, a hole provided in the presser foot, a central cavity (16) provided in the base, a container cover slidably held over the said base, a stopper means provided on the said base and the said container cover, a clamping pressure spring provided inside the said container cover over the said base, a rubber hardness tester of the known type, with its extended spindle passing through the said container cover into the central cavity of the said spindle passing through the hole in the said presser foot and a calibrating spring provided over the said spindle inside the said central cavity in the base.
2. An improved hardness tester as claimed in Claim 1 wherein the said indentor tip protrudes out of the presser foot by 2.5 mm as per international standards.
3. An improved hardness tester, as claimed in Claim 1 or 2, wherein the said stopper means is a setting nut threaded over the base below the container cover for setting a desired standard movement of the said base and the container cover.
4. An improved hardness tester, as claimed in Claim 3, wherein a locking screw is provided in the said setting nut for locking it over the said base in a set position.
5. An improved hardness tester, as claimed in Claim 1, wherein the said stopper means is a flange integrally made in the said base.
6. An improved hardness tester, as claimed in Claims 1 to 5, wherein the said container cover is provided with a pair of pins sliding inside a pair of slots in the said base for slidably holding the said container cover over the said base.
7. An improved hardness tester, as claimed in Claims 1 to 5, wherein a stepped pin is provided for slidably holding the said container cover over the said base.

8. An improved hardness tester, as claimed in Claims 1 to 7, wherein a flanged bush is provided in the central cavity of the base and projecting out of the said container cover for supporting the extended spindle of the tester.
9. An improved hardness tester, as claimed in Claims 1 to 7, wherein a collar is made integrally with the said container cover for supporting the extended spindle of the tester.
10. An improved hardness tester, as claimed in Claims 1 to 9, wherein the said calibrating spring is provided inside the tester so as to make use of any of the conventional rubber hardness testers.
11. An improved composite indentation hardness tester with built in base for rubber and the like substances, as claimed in Claim 1 and substantially as herein described and illustrated in Figs. AIIIa.1 and AIIIa.2 of the drawings accompanying this specification.

Dated this 14th day of June,1990
(KUMAR BALRAM BHATIA)

Appendix IIIb

An example of a patent of addition

The Patent Office, 2nd M.B.O. Building 234/A,
Acharya Jagadish Chandra Bose Road, Calcutta 700 020

Indian Patent Specification 172840

(B1) Ind. Cl : 2 01 N 3/42, 3/52 (11) Document No. : 172840
Date of Document : 10-11-91
(B2) Ind Cl : 89 (42) Date of Publication : 11-12-92

(21) Application No : 354/BOM/91
(71) Applicant: KUMAR BALRAM BHATIA, an Indian citizen, 408A, Poonam Chambers, Dr Annie Besant Road, Worli, Mumbai 400018, Maharashtra, India.
(22) Date of filing : 29-11-91.
(61) Addition to : 157/BOM/90(170499) (72) Inventor : IDEM of 18-06-90.
(74) Agent : KUMAR BALRAM BHATIA
Claims : 2
Text : 4 Pages : Drgs. 1 Sheet.

(54) Title: An improved composite indentation hardness tester with built-in base for rubber, and the like substances, such as soft or hard plastics and textile-wound packages

(57) Abstract : An improved composite indentation hardness tester with built-in base for rubber and the like substances as claimed in my main Patent No. 170499 dated 18-06-90 the improvement/

modification being in replacing the single clamping pressure spring (11), working in compression, by two or more spiral springs (14), provided vertically — in between the top of base (5) and the flange of the bush (12), to give constant load of buckling, at all the stages of pressure, thereby assuring an absolute constant clamping load on the specimen.

This invention relates to an improvement in or modification of my main Patent No. 170499 dated 18-06-90. The invention described in my main Patent No. 170499 dated 18-06-90 relates to an improved composite indentation hardness tester with built-in-base for rubber and the like substances comprising a base having a stepper presser foot (4) at its bottom, a hole (17) provided in the presser foot, a central cavity (16) provided in the base, a container cover (7) slidably held over the said base, a stepper means (6) provided in the said base for achieving a standard desired movement of the said base and said container cover, a clamping pressure spring provided inside the said container cover over the said base, a rubber hardness tester of the known type, with its extended spindle (2) passing through the said container cover into the central cavity of the said base, an indentor tip (3) fixed at the bottom end of the said spindle passing through the hole in the said presser foot and a calibrating spring (10) provided over the said spindle inside the said central cavity in the base.

In my main patent application, described above, only one spiral spring is provided inside the container, over the base, which has been termed as clamping pressure spring, and works in compression only. It is now observed that absolute constant clamping load on the specimen is not possible in the arrangement described above, as the load goes on increasing with the increase in compression of the spring and to achieve the desired load of a fixed value, (i.e. about 2 kg in Shore-A and about 3 kg in Shore-D) a mechanical stopper such as the setting nut is to be used. This makes the hardness tester cumbersome and costly as well as creates a calibration problem. Further, the mechanical stopper/the setting nut is adjusted at the time of manufacturing and if the user tampers with the setting nut then the desired load changes, which gives a defective clamping pressure resulting in the wrong hardness values of the specimen.

To overcome the above-described problems, according to this invention, the improvement in or modification of my main invention lies in modifying the clamping pressure spring only. Two or more spiral springs are used vertically to give constant load by buckling at all the stages of pressure, thereby assuring an absolute constant clamping load on the specimen.

The improvement/modification, according to this invention will be clear from the following description when read along with my main invention in the Patent No. 170499. In the drawing accompanying this specification, all the features in common with the main invention have been given the same reference numerals. Only the modified features have been indicated by separate numerals. Figure AIIIb.1 shows a part-sectional elevation of the modified composite hardness tester with a built-in base according to this invention.

Referring to Fig. A IIIb. 1, the modified hardness tester with built-in base according to this invention, comprises a base having stepped presser foot at its bottom. This base has two slots (13) in which two pins (8) for slidably holding a container cover over the base are provided. A flanged bush is fixed in a central cavity in the base. A spindle of the rubber hardness tester(1) is fixed inside the bush by a screw (15)which extends into the base. An indentor tip is fixed at the end of the spindle. A calibrating spring is provided over the spindle along with an adjuster nut (18) for calibrating the movement of the indentor tip into the direct hardness reading indicated by the indicator (19) on the dial of the tester. Modification of the main invention lies in replacing the clamping pressure spring, working in compression, by two or more spiral springs, in between the top of base and the flange of the bush. These springs work as clamping pressure springs and are provided vertically, to give constant load by buckling at all the stages of pressure, thereby assuring an absolute constant clamping load on the specimen. This arrangement also eliminates the need of the stopper setting nut used in the main invention. Thus the tester becomes cheap, and there is no possibility of tampering with the calibration.

Working of the modified tester is the same as described in the main patent application. In this case two or more clamping pressure springs used vertically give constant load by buckling at all stages of pressure thereby assuring an absolute constant clamping load on the specimen, thereby giving perfect values of hardness of the specimen.

Claims

1. An improved composite indentation hardness tester with built-in base for rubber and the like substances are claimed in my main Patent No. 170499 dated 18-06-90, the improvement/

Kumar Balram Bhatia
Application No. 354/BOM/1991

Total sheets 1
Sheet no. 1

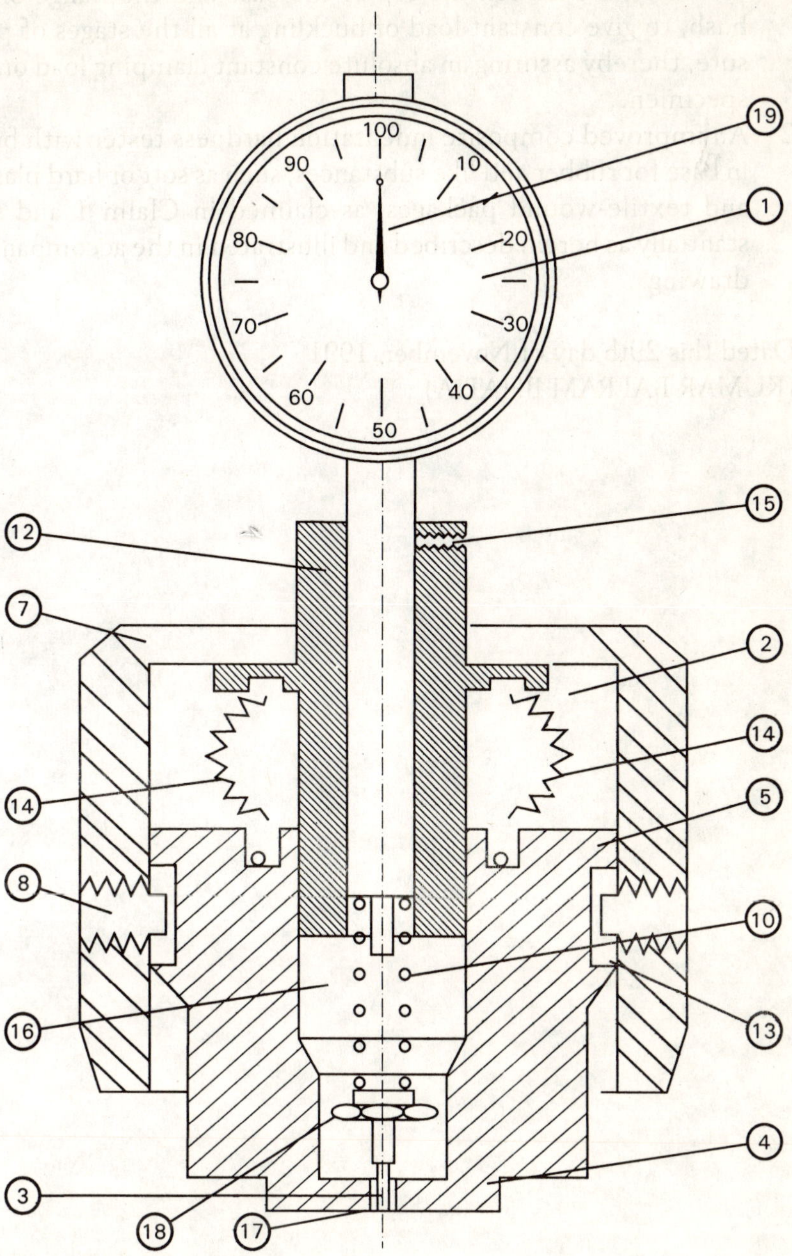

(Kumar Balram Bhatia)

Fig. A IIIb. 1 The modified hardness tester

modification being in replacing the single clamping pressure spring working in compression, by two or more spiral springs provided vertically in between the top of the base and the flange of the bush, to give constant load of buckling at all the stages of pressure, thereby assuring an absolute constant clamping load on the specimen.

2. An improved composite indentation hardness tester with built-in base for rubber and like substances, such as soft or hard plastics and textile-wound packages, as claimed in Claim 1 and substantially as herein described and illustrated in the accompanying drawing.

Dated this 29th day of November, 1991
(KUMAR BALRAM BHATIA)

Appendix IV

The Gazette of India

भारत का राजपत्र

The Gazette of India

प्राधिकार से प्रकाशित

PUBLISHED BY AUTHORITY

PART III SECTION 2

The Gazette of India, No. 51, December 21, 1996, (Agrahayana 30, 1918), pp. 1033–35

[Notifications and Notices Issued by the Patent Office relating to Patents and Designs]

THE PATENT OFFICE

PATENTS AND DESIGNS

Calcutta, 21st December, 1996

Address and jurisdiction of the offices of the Patent Office

The Patent Office has its Head Office at Calcutta and Branch Offices at Mumbai, Delhi and Chennai having territorial jurisdicton on a zonal basis as shown below:

Patent Office Branch, Todi Estates,
IIIrd Floor, Lower Parel (West),
Mumbai 400 013.

The States of Gujarat,
Maharashtra, Madhya Pradesh,
Goa and the Union Territories of
Daman and Diu and Dadra and
Nagar Haveli.
Telegraphic address "PATOFFICE"

Patent Office Branch,
Unit No. 401 to 405, IIIrd Floor,
Municipal Market Building,
Saraswati Marg, Karol Bagh,
New Delhi 110 005.

The States of Haryana,
Himachal Pradesh, Jammu and Kashmir,
Punjab, Rajasthan, Uttar Pradesh, Delhi
and the Union Territory of Chandigarh.
Telegraphic address "PATENTOFIS"

Patent Office Branch, 61,
Wallajah Road, Chennai 600 002.

The States of Andhra Pradesh,
Karnataka, Kerala, Tamil Nadu,
Pondicherry and the Union Territories
of Laccadeive, Minicoy and
Aminidivi Islands.
Telegraphic address : "PATENTOFIC"

Patent Office, (Head Office),
Nizam Palace, 2nd M.S.O.
Building, 5th, 6th and 7th Floor,
234/4, Acharya Jagadish Bose Road,
Calcutta 700 020.

Rest of India.
Telegraphic address "PATENTS"

All applications, notices, statements or other documents or any fees required by the Patents Act, 1970 or the Patent Rules, 1972 will be received only at the appropriate Office of the Patent Office.

Fees: — The fees may either be paid in cash or may be sent by Money Order or payable to the Controller at the appropriate Offices or by bank draft or cheque payable to the Controller drawn on a scheduled bank at the place where the appropriate office is situated.

Applications for patents filed at the Head Office, 234/4, Acharya Jagadish Bose Road, Calcutta 20

The dates shown in the cresent brackets are the dates claimed under Section 135, of the Patents Act, 1970.

09-09-96

1597/Cal/96 Tai-Her Yang. "The combined power system using a co-generative type rotation speed and torque difference detector or device for proportional control."

1598/Cal/96 Krone Aktiengesellschaft. "Termination device for the telecommunication and data technique" (Convention No. 19537528.9 on 29-09-95 in Germany).

1599/Cal/96 Siemens Aktiengesellschaft. "A method for the removal of graphite from a surface region of a workpiece, and also a corresponding workpiece" (Convention No. 19536569.0 on 29-09-95 in Germany).

1600/Cal/96 Armco Inc. "Method for direct use of chromite ore in the production of stainless steel" (Convention No. 08/573, 316 on 14-12-95 in USA).

1601/Cal/96 Hakkert. "Display device."

1602/Cal/96 (1) Nihon Parkerizing Co. Ltd. (2) Kawasaki Steel Corporation. "A method for treating sludge precipitated in a plating bath containing haloid ions and an equipment therefore" (Convention No. 7218883 on 28-08-95 in Japan).

10-09-96

1603/Cal/96 Montell North America Inc. "Stretch blow-molding process for the preparation of polypropylene containers." (Convention No. 95/A 001931 on 15-09-95 in Italy.)

1604/Cal/96 Tapati Paul. "Novel plant or apparatus and process for removal of undesirable organism and/or chemical from water."

1605/Cal/96 Siemens Aktiengesellschaft. "Decoder gate" (Convention No. 19537888.1 on 11-10-95 in Germany).

1606/Cal/96 Siemens Aktiengesellschaft. "Method for handling incoming calls to communications system having automatic call distribution when agent communications etc. (Convention No. 19535540.7 on 25-09-95 in Germany).

1607/Cal/96 Siemens Aktiengesellschaft. "Method for electrically connecting a semiconductor chip to at least one contact surface" (Convention No. 19535775.2 on 26-09-95 in Germany).

1608/Cal/96 Siemens Aktiengesellschaft. "Sram memory cell" (Convention No. 19535106-1 on 21-09-95 in Germany).

1609/Cal/96 Matsushita Electric Industrial Co. Ltd. "Washing Machine" (Convention No. 8-121294 on 16-05-95 in Japan).

1610/Cal/96 Merck Patent Geselleschaft Mit Beschrankter Haftung. "Biotin derivatives" (Convention No. 19534016.7 on 14-09-95 in Germany).

1611/Cal/96 Merck Patent Gesellschaft Mit Beschrankter Haftung. "Arylalkyl-Diazirone" (Convention No. P 19533975.4 on 14-09-95 in Germany).

1612/Cal/96 Merck Patent Gesellschaft Mit Beschrankter Haftung. "Flaky aluminum oxide and pearlescent pigment, and production thereof" (Convention No. P 19533975.4 on 14-09-95 in Japan).

1613/Cal/96 Georg Fischer Rohrleitungsysteme AG. "Connecting element for a pipeline piece".

1614/Cal/96 Likospol S.R.O. "Process, apparatus and microorganism strain for the manufacture of citric acid" (Convention No. PV 1131/95, 11/09/95, PV156/96 on 02-02-96 in Slovak Republic and 960786.8 on 16-04-96 in UK and 9607864.7 on 16-04-96 in UK).

1615/Cal/96 Chao-Yang Chen. "Toy doll and hanger assembly".

1616/Cal/96 LG Industrial Systems Co. ltd. "Electronic prepayment type electric Watthour meter" (Convention No. 29881/1995 on 13-09-95 in Republic of Korea).

The Gazette of India, December 21, 1996 (Agrahayana 30, 1918) pp. 1037–38

Alternation of date under Section 16

Patent No. 177295 (831/Mas/91) antedated to 13th January, 1989.
Patent No. 177299 (468/Mas/94) antedated to 22nd September, 1993.
Patent No. 177300 (675/Mas/94) antedated to 22nd January, 1993.

Complete specifications accepted

Notice is hereby given that any person interested in opposing the grant of patents on any of the applications concerned, may, at any time within four months of the date of this issue or within such further period not exceeding one month applied for on Form 14 prescribed under the Patent Rules, 1972 before the expiry of the said period of four months, give notice to the Controller of Patents at the appropriate office on the prescribed Form 15 of such opposition. The written statement of opposition should be filed alongwith the said notice or within one month of it state as prescribed in Rule 36 of the Patent Rules, 1972.

The classification given below in respect of each specification are according to Indian Classification and International Classification.

Typed or photo copies of the specifications together with photo copies of the drawings, if any, can be supplied by the Patent Office, Calcutta or the appropriate Branch Office and payment of the prescribed copying charges which may be ascertained on application to that office. Photo copying charges may be calculated by adding the number of pages in the specification and drawing sheets mentioned below against each accepted specification and multiplying the same by two to get charges as copying per page costs Rs. 2/-.

Ind. Cl. :	C007C	120/00	121/00	177261
	C008F	2/00	214/00	

Int. Cl.[4] : 32 E

An improved process for the preparation of nitrile containing group polymers

Applicant : COUNCIL OF SCIENTIFIC AND INDUSTRIAL RESEARCH, Rafi Marg, New Delhi.

Inventor: DURAIRAJ BASKARAN, PRADEEP KUMAR DHAL, SANJAY PURSHOTTAM KASHIKAR, RATNAPRABHA SADASHIV KHISTI, BABANRAO MAHADEO SINGE, SWAMINATHAN SIVARAM.

Application for Patent No. 223/DEL/90 filed on 08-03-90.

Appropriate office for filing the opposition proceedings (Rule 4, 1972) Patent Office Branch, Karol Bagh, New Delhi.

5 Claims

A process for the preparation of nitrile group containing polymers which comprises reacting a nitrile group containing vinyl monomer of formula $CH_2=C(Y)$ X, where X=CN and Y=CH_3, H,C_6H_5, $C_6H_5CH_2$ with an initiator of the general formula ($ArCR_1R_2R_3R_4R_5R_6$), wherein Ar = phenyl, substituted phenyl or a heterocyclic compound, $R_1 = R_4$ = H, ester, cyanol alkyl, aryl, 1, 3 oxazoline, N, N-dimethyl amide and other similar alpha activating groups, or combination of them, or one of R_1 or R_2 together with Ar, where Ar is a phenyl or a substituted phenyl, is a nitrogen atom containing heterocyclic compound and the other being a nitrile group, R_3, R_4, R_5 and R_6 may be same or different and represent substituted alkyl, cycloalkyl, arylalkyl or aryl or two of the R_3, R_4, R_5 and R_6 together with nitrogen atom form a heterocycle with the condition that the sum of all carbon atoms of all R_3, R_4, R_5 and R_6 is 50 and only one of the R_3, R_4, R_5 and R_6 is an aryl derivative in presence of dipolar aprotic solvent or solvent having either group in an inert atmosphere at a temperature not exceeding 60°C.

(Complete Specification 18 Pages Drawing Sheets Nil)

Ind. Cl. : 34 B. 177262

Int. Cl. : CO8B 5/00.

A process for preparing superior quality cellulose sponge

Applicant: DOM SHRIRAM INDUSTRIES LIMITED, Kanchanjunga, 18, Barakhamba Road, New Delhi 110 001.

Inventor : PREM SHANKAR SHARMA.

Application for Patent No. 351/DEL/90 filed on 09-04-90.

Appropriate office for filing opposition proceedings (Rule 4, 1972) Patent Office Branch, Karol Bagh, New Delhi 110 005.

11 Claims

A process for preparing superior quality cellulose sponge from cellulose pulp by treating cellulose pulp with alkali ageing and xanthating the alkali cellulose to obtain viscose solution, mixing with strength-giving fibers and pore formers as herein described in a kneader and extruding the same through rollers to obtain a sheet which is then coagulated and cellulose regenerated to obtain the sponge, washing to remove the impurities if necessary, treating with commonly known chemicals as shown in the art and cut into sizes, which is characterized in that

(a) preparing alkali cellulose of the following composition and bulk density:

% of cellulose	34–36
% of alkali as NaOH	14–16
	Bulk density 130 to 140 g /litre

by treating cellulose pulp with 18–20% sodium hydroxide solution for at least one hour at 20 to 22°C.

(b) ageing of alkali cellulose by maintaining the temperature and humidity as herein described in such a way so as to reduce the degree of polymerization of cellulose between 450 to 550.

(c) maintaining the concentration of carbon disulfide in xanthating reaction with 60 to 65% based on cellulose to prepare viscose solution.

(d) adding pre-swollen rayon staple fiber as strength-giving fibers to viscose solution and ripening the mixed mass for a period of 16 to 25 hours before addition of Glauber's salt as pore formers, and mixing uniformly at a temperature not exceeding 20°C before extrusion through rollers.

(e) coagulating and regenerating cellulose in two steps by first heating under infrared lamp and then by treating with 10 to 15% sulfuric acid.

(f) washing the coagulated mass with 1% sodium carbonate solution, water and then treating with 30 to 35% magnesium chloride solution containing 0.2 to 0.5% phenol, squeezing out the excess magnesium chloride and phenol and then dried.

(Complete Specification 14 Pages Drawing Sheets Nil.)

The Gazette of India, No. 51, December 21, 1996, (Agrahayana 30, 1918), p.1042

Ind. Cl. : 104 P. 177269

Int. Cl. : C08J/3/24

A process for producing a dynamically vulcanized composition

Applicant : ADVANCED ELASTOMER SYSTEMS, LP at 540 Maryvile Center Drive, PO Box 66735, St. Louis Missouri 63166-6735, United States of America.

Inventors : ROBERT CHESTER PUYDAK DONALD ROSS HAZELTON, BLAIR ALFRED GRAHAM, NARAYAN A SWAMI RAJA DHARMARAJAN.

Application for Patent No. 413/DEL/90 filed on 02-05-90.

Appropriate office for filing opposition proceedings (Rule 4, 1972) Patent Office Branch, Karol Bagh, New Delhi 110 005.

8 Claims

A process for producing a dynamically vulcanized composition having an improved balance of stiffness and impact resistance, which comprises the following steps:

(a) mixing together

i) from 10 to 90% by weight of a thermoplastic polyolefin resin, and

ii) from 10 to 90% by weight of an elastomer selected from the group consisting of butyl-rubber, halogenated-butyl-rubber, a copolymer of a C_{47} iso mono-olefin and a para alkylistyrene, a halogenated copolymer of a C_{47} iso mono-olefin and a para alkylityrene, ethylene-, propelene-, diensrubber, poly isoprene, styrene-butadiene, rubber, nitrilerubber, chlorosulfonated-polyethylene, and mixtures thereof;

(b) dynamically vulcanizing the elastomer component in the mixture of step (a) by the steps of:

i) heating the mixture to a temperature at or above the melting point of said polyolefin resin,

ii) adding a conventional curing agent for said elastomer and

iii) masticating the resulting mixture at a high shear rate until said elastomer is substantially vulanized and

(c) adding to the mixture of step (b) from 0.05 to 70 % of a solid particulate component selected from the group consisting of conventional filler, an additive and mixtures thereof, wherein said additive is selected from the group consisting of ultraviolet light stabilizers, pigments, antiblocking agents, coupling agents for fillers, and mixtures thereof;

thereby producing a composition having the major portion of said solid particulate component incorporated into the poly-olefin resin component of the composition.

(Complete Specification 35 Pages Drawing Sheets Nil.)

The Gazette of India, December 21, 1996 (Agrahayana 30, 1918) p. 1042

Ind. Cl. : 32 B 172770
Int. Cl. : C 07 C/7/10

A process for the manufacture of sweet hydocarbon fractions substantially free from mercaptans

Applicant : UOP, at 25 East Algonquin Road, Des Plains, Illinois, USA.
Inventor : JEFFERY C. BRICKER, USA, ROBERT R. FRAME, USA, BRYAN L. BENEDICT, USA, SHEILA L. POLIASTRINI, USA.
Kind of Application : Complete
Application for Patent No. 416/DEL/90 filed on 03-05-90.
Appropriate office for filing opposition proceedings (Rule 4, 1972) Patent Office Branch, Karol Bagh, New Delhi 110 005

6 Claims

A process for the manufacture of sweet hydrocarbons substantially free of mercaptans from a sour hydrocarbon fraction containing mercaptans which comprises reacting the said hydrocarbon fraction in the presence of an oxidizing agent of the kind such as herein described with an alkaline solution containing a metal chelate of the kind such as herein described and quaternary ammonium compound having the structure of the formula. (See Fig. AIV.1.)

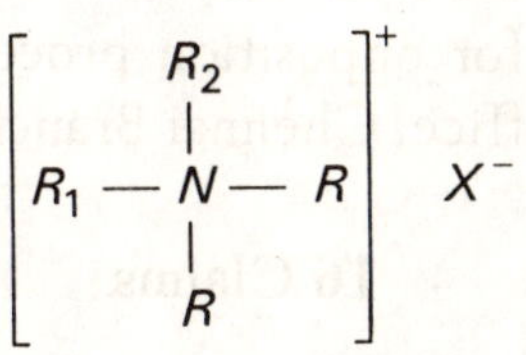

Fig. AIV.1 The molecular formula of the quaternary ammonium compound.

The Gazette of India, No. 51, December 21, 1996, (Agrahayana 30, 1918), p. 1050

Ind. *Cl.* : 38 Sc. 134-B 177283
Int. Cl^4. : F 16 G 13/00

An improved timing chain

Applicant : TI DIAMOND CHAIN LIMITED, Tiam House, 28, Rajaji Road, Chennai 600 001, Tamil Nadu, India, a company duly organized and existing urder the law of the union of India.

Inventor : GAJARAJ SUBRAMANIAN

Application No. 369/MAS/90 filed 15-05-90.

Appropriate office for opposition proceedings (Rule 4, Patent Rules, 1972), Patent Office, Chennai Branch.

2 Claims

An improved timing chain comprising inner and outer link plates, the said link plates in adjacent pitches being profiled to about against each other such that while the chain is enabled to flex inwards to wrap over sprockets, it is prevented by the profiled link plates from appreciably flexing outwards.

(Complete Specification 6 Pages Drawing Sheet 1).

Ind. Cl : 131-C 177284
Int. Cl.[4] : E 21 D 23/04

A Mine roof support

Applicant : GULLICK DOBSON LTD, British company, of PO Box 12, Ince, Wigan, Lancashire, England.

Inventor : TOM CARL BITHELL

Application No. 382/MAS/90 filed 17-05-90.

Convention dated 18-05-89, No. 8911468.0; U.K.

Appropriate office for opposition proceedings (Rule 4, Patent Rules, 1972) Patent Office, Chennai Branch.

16 Claims

A mine roof support comprising a base, a roof engaging canopy, jack means acting between the base and canopy, and auxiliary jack means connected to the base by means of a connection for lifting or lowering at least part of the base when the support advances, the said connection between the base and the auxiliary jack means being provided with lost motion means. See Fig. AIV. 2.

Ind. Cl. : 108-C_3
Int. Cl.[4] : C 21 B 13/00

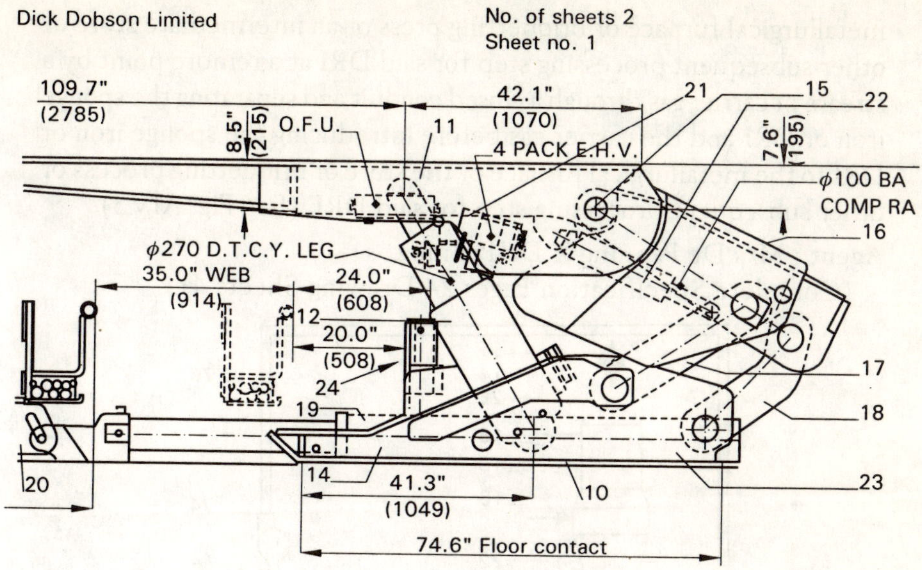

Fig. AIV. 2 The mine roof support

An improved method of producing iron and/or steel from iron ores composed of iron oxides

Applicant : HYLSA SA DE C.V., a corporation organized under the laws of the United Mexican States of Avenida Muncihy Calle Guerrero San Nicolas de Los Garza, Nuevo, Leon, Mexico.
Inventors : JORGE OCTAVIO BECERRA NOVOA, Mexico, RICARDO VIRAMONTES BROWN, Mexico, MARCO AURELIO FLORES VERDUGO, Mexico, JOSE JAVIER GARZA ONDARZA, Mexico.

Application No. 421/MAS/90 filed 29-05-90.

Appropriate office for opposition proceedings (Rule 4, Patent Rules, 1972), Patent Office, Chennai Branch.

23 Claims

An improved method of producing iron and/or steel from iron ores composed of iron oxides comprising direct reduction of the iron ores to sponge iron or DRI in a reduction reactor and subsequent processing such as in a metallurgical furnace, the improvement comprising conveying the sponge iron or DRI with at least 80% having a size greater than 0.5 cm and at least 50% having a size greater than 1 cm from the discharge point of the reduction reactor in the metallurgical furnace or briquetting press or an intermediate store or other subsequent processing step for said DRI at a remote point by a stream of carrier gas through a closed conduit and separating the sponge iron or DRI and the carrier gas before introducing the sponge iron or DRI to the metallurgical furnace or the store or briquetting process or other subsequent processing step for said DRI. (See Fig. AIV.3)

Agent : M/s De Penning & De Penning

(Complete Specification Pages 24 Drawing Sheets 4).

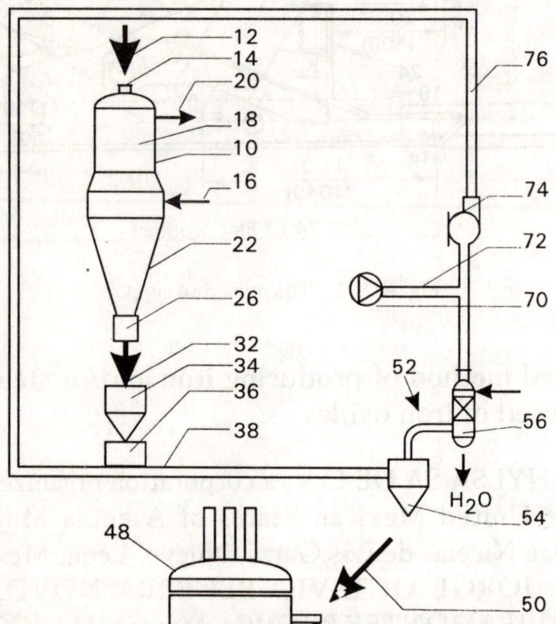

Fig. AIV. 3 The reduction reactor and metallurgical furnace

The Gazette of India, No. 51, December 21, 1996, (Agrahayana 30, 1918), pp. 1057–58.

Notice is hereby given that PACIFIC CHEMCIAL CO. LTD. of 181 Hankang-ro-2-Ku, Yongsan-Ku, Seoul, KOREA a Korean Company, have made an application under Section 57 of the Patents Act, 1970, for amendment of their application for Patent No. 140/ Mas/93 (175104) for "A patch for percutaneous administration of one or more skin-whitening materials".

The amendments are by way of correction. The application for amendment and the proposed amendments can be inspected free of charge at the Patent Office Branch, 61 Wallajah Road, Chennai 600 002, or copies of the same can be had on payment of the usual copying charges. Any person interested in opposing the application for amendment may file a notice of opposition on prescribed Form 30 within three months from the date of notification at the Patent Office Branch, Chennai. If the written statement of opposition is not filed with the notice of opposition, it shall be left within one month from the date of filing the said Notice.

Request for an amendment for change of the name of applicants Himant Incorporated of 2301 Centerville Road, New Castle Country, Delaware, USA Delaware Corporation, a corporation duly organized and exiting under the laws of the State of Delaware, USA to Montelle North America Inc., in the application for Patent No. 176311 as advertized in Part III, Section 2 of the Gazette of India dated 03-08-96 had no opposition within the stipulated period the said amendment has been allowed.

Notice is hereby given that HOOGOVENS GROUP BV PO BOX 10, 000 1970 CA IJMUIDEN, THE NETHERLAND, a Dutch company, have made an application under Section 57 of the Patents Act 1970, for amendment of application and their application for Patent No. 748/Mas/90 (177409) for "A shaft furnace".

The amendments are by way of correction. The application for amendment and the proposed amendments can be inspected free of charge at the Patent Office Branch, 61, Wallajah Road, Chennai 600 002 or copies of the same can be had on payment to the usual copying charges. Any person interested in opposing the application for amendment may file a notice of opposition on prescribed Form 30 within 3 months from the date of notification at the Patent Office Branch, Chennai. If the written statement of opposition is not filed with the notice of opposition, it shall be left within one month from the date of filing the said Notice.

Claim under Section 20(1) of the Patents Act, 1970

The claim made by ROCK WOOL MANUFACTURING COMPANY, and MINERAL PRODUCTS AND TECHNOLOGY, INC. in respect of Patent Application No. 453/Mas/90 (177286) has been allowed.

Cessation of patents

167469 167481 167516 167525 167531
167551 167561 167575 167578 167593
167594 167595 167649 167655 167656
167661 167678 167701 167728 167767
167780 167792 167808 167811 167827
167829 167850 167869 167874 167877
167892 167921 167922 167952

Renewal fees paid

157140 157579 158749 158826 159035
159327 159737 159740 159780 159971
160023 160029 160226 160813 160820
160868 161128 161465 161554 161818
161819 162011 162176 162345 162542
163435 163536 163662 164000 164018
164062 164355 164427 164593 164787
164889 165005 165352 165459 165739
165847 165902 165903 166158 166210
166304 166377 166762 166784 166785
166977 167159 167268 167651 167967
168088 168188 168204 168443 168578
168579 168630 168821 169011 169056
169062 169336 169425 169538 169560
169659 169675 169679 169733 169774
169809 169824 169930 170134 170471
170472 170481 170775 170922 171073
171080 171091 171129 171295 171324
171480 171472 171566 171698 171813
171814 171894 171915 172038 172039
172357 172385 172465 172483 172863
172895 173038 173053 173189 173190
173241 173242 173399 173513 173592
173663 173748 173749 173885 173973
174147 174191 174365 174394 174413
174425 174446 174525 174535 174667
174668 174754 174838 174917 175253
175396 175397 175398 175424 175429
175462 175544 175755 175913 175928

175935	175961	175972	175978	176041
176045	176046	176049	176050	176055

Patent sealed 22-11-96

175919*D	176106	176305	176367*	176372
176400*F	176412	176413	176415*	176416*
176417*	176433*D	176436*D	176440*D	176444*
176445*	176446	176448	176450*	176461*
176469*F	176470*D	176471	176472	176475*
176476				

CAL—02, DEL—20, MUM—04, CHE—NIL

*Patent shall be deemed to be endorsed with the words LICENSE OF RIGHT under Section 87 of the Patents Act, 1970 from the date of expiry of three years from the date of sealing.

D—Drug Patents, F—Food Patents

Registration of designs

The following designs have been registered. They are not open to inspection for period of two years from the date of registration except as provided for in Section 50 of the Designs Act, 1911.

The date shown in each entry is the date of the registration included in the entries.

Class 5. Nos. 170044 to 170046, Bharat Vadilal Parekh, Indian National, of Mehta Mansion, 176 Girgaon Road, Mumbai 400 004, Maharashtra, India "GAME", 17th October, 1995.

Class 5. No. 171006, Ganesh Energene Limited at Ganesh House, Marol, Andheri (East), Mumbai 400 059, Maharashtra, India. "PREGNANCY TESTING DEVICE", 28th March, 1996.

Class 5. No. 170005, Reemtsma Cigarettenfabriken GmbH., Parkstrasse 51, Hamburg-Othmarschen, Germany. "CIGARETTES PACKING", 11th October, 1995.

Class 5. No. 169710, LG Electronics Inc. incorporated in Republic of Korea and whose address is Daelim Woosung APT 2-1305, 762-21, Daelim 3 dong, Youngdungpo-Ku, Seoul, Korea. "PACKING BOX", 21st August, 1995.

Class 5. No. 170087, The Room & Co. Ltd., a corporation organized and existing under the laws of Japan, of 18-18, 2-chome Mita. Megu ro-Ku, Tokyo, Japan. "FOLDING HOUSEHOLD ALTAR", 30th October, 1995.

Class 5. No. 170970, Lotte Confectionery Co. Ltd., of 4 ka-23, Yangpyong-dong, Youngdeungpo-Ku, Seoul, Republic of Korea, a Korean company. "A PACKAGE FOR CONFECTIONERY", 26th March, 1996.

Class 5. No. 170061, Munch Food Products Limited, whose address is D 992, New Friends Colony, New Delhi 110 065, India. "A BOX", 20th October, 1995.

Class 5. No. 199127, Paul Associated Equipments Co., a regd. Indian partnership firm of 66, Kasthandanga Road, Calcutta 700 061, West Bengal, India. "CARTON" 5th May, 1995.

Class 5. No. 169938, The Assam Company Limited, having registered office at Green Wood Tea Estate, P O Dbrugarh 786 001, Assam, India, an Indian organization. "STRAINER FOR DISPOSABLE TEA CUP", 28th September, 1995.

Class 5. No. 169925, Reemtsma Cigarettenfabriken GmbH. Parkstrasse 51, Hamburg-Othmarschen, Germany, a Germany Company. "CIGARETTE PACKAGING", 26th September, 1995.

Class 6. No. 169419, Ginny Photo Products, Shop No. 8, Suman market, Esplanade Road, Delhi 110 006, India, an Indian proprietorship firm. "BAG", 27th June, 1995.

T. R. SUBRAMANIAN
Controller General of Patents, Designs and Trademarks

The Gazette of India, No. 49, December 7, 1996, (Agrahayana 16, 1918), p. 984

Opposition proceedings under Section 25

As per order of the Joint Controller dated 07-06-96 following drawings (2 sheets) in respect of Patent Application No. 168545 have been amended:

Amendment proceedings under Section 57

Notice is hereby given that SCHUBERT & SALZER MASCHINE-NEABRIK AKTIENGESELLSCHAFT, Friedrich-Elbert-Strasse 84, 8070 Ingolstadt, GERMANY have made and application under Section 57 of the Patents Act, 1970, for amendment of application and application of their application for Patent No. 517/MAS/89 (174891) for "A method and device for producing thread in an open end spinning means".

The amendments are by way of correction. The application for amendment and the proposed amendments can be inspected free of charge at the Patent Office Branch, 61, Wallajah Road, Chennai 600 002, or copies of the same can be had on payment of the usual copying charges. Any person interested in opposing the application for amendment may file a notice of opposition of prescribed Form 30 within 3 months from the date of notification at the patent office branch, Chennai. If the written statement of opposition is not filed with the notice of opposition it shall be left within one month form the date of filing the said Notice.

Notice is hereby given that AUSMELT PTY, LTD. a company incorporated under the laws of the State of Victoria, Australia, of 304 High Street, Kew, Victoria 3101, Australia have made an application under Section 57 of the Patents Act, 1970, for amendment of application and specification of their application for Patent No. 671/MAS/90 (176773) for "A process for smelting a metallurgical waste material to produce a slag product".

The amendments are by way of correction. The application for amendment and the proposed amendments can be inspected free of charge at the Patent Office Branch, 61, Wallajah Road, Chennai 600 002, or copies of the same can be had on payment of the usual copying charges. Any person interested in opposing the application for amendment may file a notice of opposition on prescribed Form 30 within 3 months from the date of notification of the Patent Office Branch, Chennai. If the written statement of opposition is not filed with the notice of opposition it shall be left within one month from the date of filing the said Notice.

Cessation of patents

166354 166408 166487 166516 166547 166580 166587 166631

166634 166643 166657 166660 166685 166697 166703 166744 166745 166782 166836 166847 166854 166857 166868.

The Gazette of India, No. 16, April 20, (Chaitra 31, 1918), p.298

Commercial working of patented inventions Electrical Engg. Industry List No. II

The following patents in the field of Electrical Engineering Industry are not being commercially worked in India as admitted by patentees in the statements filed by them under Section 146(2) of the Patents Act, 1970 in respect of calender year 1993, generally on account of want of request for licenses to work the patented invention. Persons who are interested to work the said patents commercially may contact the patentees for the grant of a license for the purpose.

Patent No.	Date of patent	Name & address of the patentee	Title of the invention
170111	07-06-88	AEG Kabel Aktiengesellschaft, of Bounenbroicher, Strasse, 2-14, D-4050, Monchengladbach, 2, West Germany.	An improved high frequency cable for the transmission of high frequency signals.
168765	26-11-87	Bailey Japan Co. Ltd., & NIP, of 551, Baraki, Nirayana-cho, Tagata-Gun, Shizuoka, Japan.	Electric actuator for a control valve.
171090	21-07-88	Bindicator company, 1915, Dave Street, Port Huron, Michigan 48060.	A system for indicating level of material in a vessel.
168677	01-04-89	Borden Inc. USA, of 180, East Broad Street, Columbus, Ohio 43215, USA.	Electrodes.
152282	23-02-80	British Aerospace of 100, Pall, London, SW1Y, SHR, England.	Improved VHF, antenna with tuned circuit.
168886	15-12-86	British Telecommunications PLC of 81, Newgate Street, London, ECIA, 7AJ, England.	A system for routing telecommunication traffic through a circuit switched network.

Continues

Continued

Patent No.	Date of patent	Name & address of the patentee	Title of the invention
170204	17-11-87	do.	A video coding apparatus.
170322	28-09-87	do.	An apparatus for translating phrases from a first language into a second language.
158794	04-06-83	do.	Optical transmission.
163795	12-06-85	do.	Electronic tracking system for micro-wave antennas.
171236	06-10-88	Ceda Spa Construcsioni Electromeccaniche, E. Dispsit of Via, Nazionale-34, 33042, Buttrio (UD), Italy.	Device to measure the level of liquid metal in a crystallizer of a continuous casting ingot mould.
155263	08-08-80	Degussa Ag. of Frankfurt/ Man-6450, Hononi, Post, fech-1345, F.R. Germany.	A process of producing an electrical contact based on silver and tin oxide.
153576	08-12-80	De Nora Permelec, SPA, of Via, Bistolfi, 35, 20134, Milan, Italy.	Electrode for electrolysis cells.
168827	24-11-87	Dr Allan Shaw, Professor, Rusellestcout., Luxton, of 5th Floor, Security House-233, Narth Terrace, Adelaide, Australia.	Air conditioners.
168952	12-08-87	Eaton Corporation, of 111, Superior Avenue, Cleveland, Ohio 44114, USA.	Electromagnetic contactor having improved structure and assembly.
169987	07-04-89	Electrometal Ltd., 3C, Camac Street, West Bengal, India.	Connector for cables.
164992	10-02-86	Energy Conversion Trust, of 5, The Parade, Edidge Road, Crowborough, Sussex, England	Energy converter.

Continues

Continued

Patent No.	Date of patent	Name & address of the patentee	Title of the invention
163477	19-02-86	Equipment Merchants, International Inc., of 1203, West 65th Street, Cleveland, Ohio 44102, USA.	Moding register system.
167867	25-09-87	Fabrique National Nonvelle, Herstal, en abrege, FNNH, Societe, anonyme, of voie de, liege, 33, 4040 Herstal Belgique.	Telescopic grenade.

The Gazette of India, No. 44, November 2, 1996 (Kartika 11, 1918), p. 861

Amendment proceeding under Section 57

Request for amendment for change of the name of the applicants Himont Incorporated of 2801, Centerville Road, New Castle Country, Delaware, USA, a Delaware corporation, a corporation duly organized and existing under the law of the State of Delaware, USA, to Montell North America Inc. in the application for Patent No. 176227 as advertized in the Part III Section 2 of the Gazette of India dated 15-06-96 had no opposition within the stipulated period; the said amendment has been allowed.

Restoration proceedings

Notice is hereby given that an application for restoration of Patent No. 165705 dated 14-08-96 made by Otto India Private Ltd. on 12-08-94 and notified in the Gazette of India Part III, Section 2 dated 22-10-94 has been allowed and the said patent restored.

Notice is hereby given that an application for restoration of Patent No. 172389 dated 29-01-90 made by Eaton Coporation on 10-01-90 and notified in the Gazette of India Part III, Section 2, dated 11-05-96 has been allowed and the said patent restored.

Notice is hereby given that an application for restoration of Patent No. 173746 dated 07-06-90 made by George Sidaway on 25-09-95 and notified in the Gazette of India Part III, Section 2 on 23-12-95 has been allowed and the said patent restored.

Renewal fees paid

156659 157720 158199 159525 159528 159603 159662 159848
160318 160431 161691 161868 162348 162776 163367 163484
163934 163966 164125 164143 164153 164283 164361 164532
164640 164857 165027 165611 166194 166572 166595 166937
166955 166985 167043 167045 167048 167084 167088 167089
167255 167267 167556 168095 168695 169156 169169 169207
169226 169227 169240 169301 169404 169513 169755 170556
170562 170678 170784 170798 170853 171030 171235 171304
171459 171606 171612 171702 171864 172123 172208 172238
172268 172376 172478 173057 173298 173367 173532 173653
173660 173682 173702 173972 173978 173979 173980 174149
174163 174450 174574 174747 174834 174899 174913 175058
175059 175062 175063 175064 175066 175067 175068 175070
175073 175074 175076 175077 175078 175080 175081 175082
175084 175085 175088 175090 175094 175109 175271 175872
175873 175876 175950

Cessation of patents

164052 164053 164061 164075 164082 164086 164087 164092
164159 164171 164191 164248 164276 164285 164302 164340
164406 164413 164452 164458 164472 164480 164506 164520
164562

Patent sealed on 04-10-96

169881 176299*D 176302 176303* 176306 176307 176310
176314 176317 176324

CAL—09, DEL—10, MUM—NIL, CHE—NIL

*Patent shall be deemed to be endorsed with the words LICENSE OF RIGHT under Section 87 of the Patents Act, 1970 from the date of expiry of three years from the date of sealing.

D — Drug Patent

Name Index of Application for Patents in respect of Patent Office Calcutta and its branches for the months of July 1994 to December 1994 (Nos. 517/Cal/94 to 1093/Cal/94, 303/Bom/94 to 665/Bom/94, 580/Mas/94 to 1299/Mas/94 and 831/Del/94to 1743/Del/94).

Name and Application No.
CALCUTTA
(517/Cal/94 to 1093/Cal/94).

—A—

ABB Air Preheater Inc.—1017/Cal/94.
ACS Dobfar SPA—584/Cal/94.
Aarti Healthy Wealthy Happy Life Co. (Pvt.) Ltd — 942/Cal/94. 943/Cal/94 & 944/Cal/94.
Adir Ascalon—877/Cal/94.
Agarwal, P. (Mrs.)—688/Cal/94.
Agrogene Ltd.—1037/Cal/94.
Ahmed, F.—541/Cal/94.
Aimbridge Pvt. Ltd.—671/Cal/94.
Aktsionernoe Obschestvo Zakrytogo Tipa "RNT"— 792/Cal/94.
All Systems Inc.—886/Cal/94.
American Cyanamid Company— 823/Cal/94, 828/Cal/94 & 854/Cal/94.
American Filtorna Corporation—1008/Cal/94.
Analogic Corporation—980/Cal/94, 981/Cal/94 & 982/Cal/94.
Anton Gunzinger—1091/Cal/94.
Applexion—931/Cal/94.
Apr Applied Pharma Research SA—540/Cal/94.
Arco Chemical Technology, LP—965/Cal/94, 1000/Cal/94 & 1085/Cal/94.
Armal S.A.—735/Cal/94.
Asahi Kasei Kogyo Kabushiki kaisha—626/Cal/94.
Ascour Tech Ag.—737/Cal/94.
As Sydvaranger—731/Cal/94.
Asta Medica AG—1022/Cal/94 & 1038/Cal/94.
Australian National University, The—734/Cal/94.
Austoft Industries Ltd.—851/Cal/94.
Autorobot Finland Oy—956/Cal/94.

—B—

B&J Manufacturing Company—644/Cal/94 & 676/Cal/94.
BHP Steel (JLA) Pvt. Ltd.—1068/Cal/94.
BTR PLC—595/Cal/94.
Babcock & Wilcox Company, The —553/Cal/94, 554/Cal/94, 759/Cal/94, 783/Cal/94, 856/Cal/94, 878/Cal/94, 1063/Cal/94, 1069/Cal/94 & 1070/Cal/94.

The Gazette of India, October 5, 1996
(Asvina 13, 1918), p. 776

Registration of assignments, licenses, etc. under Section 68/69 of the Patents Act, 1970

The number of each case is followed by the name of the parties claiming interests:

1. Patent No. 156355 registered deed of supplementary license agreement licensing non-exclusively to Indo Unique Flame Pvt. Ltd.
2. Patent No. 171945 registered deed of assignment assigning their entire right to Borealis Holding A/S.
3. Patent No. 171340 registered deed of assignment assigning their entire right to Hogoovens Technical Services & Environment B V.
4. Patent No. 170805 registered deed of assignment assigning their entire right to Nigu Chemic.
5. Patent No. 172740 registered deed of assignment registered their entire right to Colorcon Asia Pvt. Ltd.
6. Patent No. 171556 registered deed of assignment assigning their entire right to Applied Medical Research Ltd.
7. Patent No. 171518 registered deed of assignment assigning their entire right to New England Pharmaceuticals Inc.
8. Patent No. 164795 registered deed of assignment assigning their entire right to Aquapore Moisture Systems Inc.
9. Patent No. 138029 registered deed of assignment assigning their entire right to Dowthorpe Industries Ltd.
10. Patent Nos. 158858; 170328; 170391 and 171493 registered deed of assignment their entire right to Kmk Lizence Ltd.

Claim under Section 20(1) of the Patents Act, 1970

In pursuance of leave granted under Section 20(1) of the Patents Act, 1970 Application No. 29/DEL/89 (172605) of NATIONAL RESEARCH DEVELOPMENT CORPORATION and SHRI A. M. M. MURUGAPPA CHETTIAR RESEARCH CENTRE, CHENNAI 600 001 has been allowed to processed in the name of NATIONAL RESEARCH DEVELOPMENT CORPORATION only.

Cessation of patents

161772 161773 161782 161821 161852 161878 161888 161910
161919 161927 162053 162091 162135 162217 162228 162256
162259 162298

Renewal fees paid

157519 157704 158649 158655 158666 158945 158990 159007
159132 159153 159156 159277 159810 160150 160177 160181
160356 160512 160515 160516 160815 160845 161028 161236
161527 161865 161974 161975 162326 162352 162878 163118
164081 164264 164667 164707 165212 165465 165648 165809
165925 166484 166491 167490 167900 167976 168029 168055
168068 168139 168177 168579 168918 168933 169034 169259
169516 169577 169596 169597 169983 170077 170347 170588
170773 170839 171156 171642 171647 171792 171827 171943
171989 172009 172029 172193 172280 172377 172393 172511
172654 172851 172880 172980 172995 173281 173329 173758
173905 174181 174313 174317 174325 174326 174351 174353
174354 174357 174358 174359 174363 174653 174712 174808
175588 175627 175630 175744 175765 175766 175775 175777
175778 175831

Patent sealed on 06-09-1996

176278* 176282*D 176284 176286 176290 176291 176294

CAL—06, DEL—01, BOM—NIL, MAS—NIL.

*Patent shall be deemed to endorse with the words LICENSE OF RIGHT under Section 87 of the Patents Act, 1970 from the date of expiry of three years from the date of sealing.

F—Food Patents, D—Drug Patents

Registration of designs

The following designs have been registered. They are not open to inspection for period of two years from the date of registration except as provided for in Section 50 of the Designs Act, 1911.

The date shown in each entry is the date of registration included in the entries.

Class 1. No. 169865, Premier Industrial Drives Pvt. Ltd., an Indian company, of industrial estate, S. Vellaalpatti Post, Karur, Tamil Nadu, India, "MIXIE", 18th September, 1995.

Class 1. No. 170409, Freemans Tools, a registered partnership firm at B XXXV/1380 A, Barewal Raod, Ludhiana 141001, Punjab, India, "TOOL", 14th December, 1995.

Class 1. Pioneer Plastic Work (P) Ltd. having its principal place of business at 9, Ezra Street, Calcutta, W. Bengal, India. "LOCKING ELEMENT", 17th July, 1995.

The Gazette of India, December 14, 1996 (Agrahayana 23, 1918), p. 1002

Ind. Cl. : 40 F 177260
Int. Cl.[4] : C02 F 11/00

Stabilizer for sludge

Applicant : LENOX INSTITUTE FOR RESEARCH INC., of 101 Yokun Avenue, Lenox, Massachusetts 01240, USA

Inventor : MILOS KROFTA

Application for Patent No. 221/DEL/90

Appropriate office for filing the opposition proceedings (Rule 4, 1972) Patent Office Branch, Karol Bagh, New Delhi 110005.

13 Claims

A stabilizer for sludge having a solid content in the range of 3 to 8% dry solid content comprising;

- at least one hollow reactor tank (10, 10) having an inlet and an outlet for the sludge,.
- flow control means (28, 30) connected to said tank inlet and outlet (14) for controlling flow of sludge through said tank (10, 10) so that the tank (10, 10) is substantially filled with the sludge at a hyperbaric pressure,
- feed means (18, 20, 22, 24) connected to said rank (10, 10) for introducing microscopic bubbles of oxygen and/or ozone gas into the sludge within said tank (10, 10),
- a mixer (34) mounted within said tank (10, 10) to work said gas bubbles into contact with the sludge, said mixer (34) being in

cooperation with respect to the interior of said tank (10, 10) so that the sludge is carried by the mixer (34) into contact with any accumulation to said gas at the upper interior portion of said tank (10, 10), and

- driving means (48, 50) connected to and for driving said mixer (34). See Fig. A IV. 4

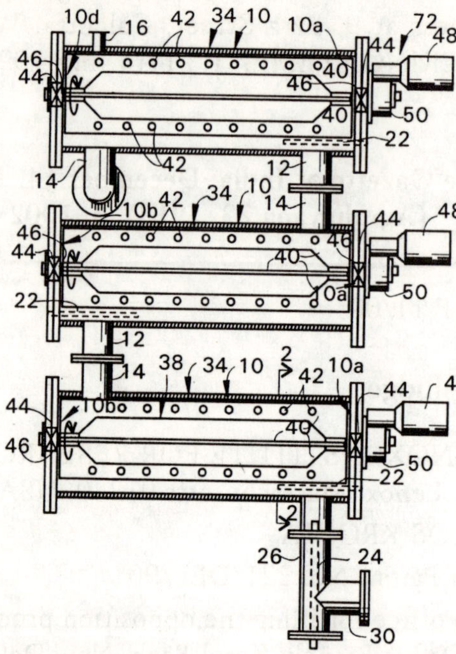

Fig. A IV. 4 The stabilizer for sludge

Restoration proceedings

Notice is hereby given that an application for restoration of Patent No. 162127 dated 10-01-84 made by National Dairy Development Board on 24-11-95 and notified to the Gazette of India Part III, Section 2, dated 06-04-96 has been allowed and the said patent restored.

Notice is hereby given that an application for restoration of Patent No. 169370 dated 06-04-87 made by Dorrenberg Edelstahl GmbH on 16-02-96 and notified in the Gazette of India Part III, Section 2, dated the 11-05-96 has been allowed and the said patent restored.

Notice is hereby given that an application for restoration of Patent No. 172234 dated 07-11-88 made by T. R. Unni on 29-09-95 and notified in the Gazette of India Part III, Section 2, dated the 23-12-95 has been allowed and the said patent restored.

Renewal fees paid

157937 157958 158583 158699 158820 160085 160246 160723
160817 160818 160847 161074 161384 161512 161816 162558
163636 163946 163970 164139 164193 164410 164635 164714
164742 164767 164820 164822 165738 165901 166123
166523 166603 166869 166988 167102 167175 167189 167215
167216 167250 167315 167333 167432 167433 167441
167693 168686 169008 169053 169289 169484 169523 170175
170178 170319 170416 170540 170558 170559 170683 170848
170876 171026 171052 171090 171162 171234 171478 171710
171738 171940 171954 172209 171348 172396 172432 172440
172567 172872 173051 173134 173201 173223 173230 173235
173263 173535 173642 173643 173648 173668 173781 173832
173845 174073 174074 174283 174284 174334 174463 174591
174634 174711 175690 175834 175951 175967 175973

Cessation of patents

166958 166982 167025 167119 167169 167170 167202 167218
167254 167279 167334 167360 167371 167427 167440 167450
167465

Patents sealed on 15-11-96

175164 176255*D 176341* 176349*D 176371 176374 176377
176379 176383 176384 176386 176391 176397 176401
176402* 176403 176410* 176447 176449* 176451 176452
176453* 176454 176455 176456*D 176457*D 176462*
176463 176465 176468*

CAL—NIL, DEL—19, BOM—10, MAS—01

*Patent shall be deemed to be endorsed with the words LICENSE OF RIGHT under Section 87 of the Patents Act, 1970 from the date of expiry of three years from the date of sealing.

D—Drug Patents, F—Food Patents

The Gazette of India, No. 3, January 20, 1996 (Pausa 30, 1917), pp. 36–37

Ind. Cl. : 174 F 176089
Int. Cl.[4] : F 16 F 13/00

Air cushioned shock absorbers

Applicant & Inventor : SATISH KUMAR DAS, of 7/7, Krishna Nagar, G. T. Road, Kanpur 208 007, India an Indian national.

Application for Patent No. 614/DEL/89 filed on 11-07-89.

Appropriate office for opposition proceedings (Rule 4, Patent Rules, 1972) Patent Office Branch, New Delhi 110 005.

4 Claims

An air cushioned shock absorber comprising an upper mounting (2) spaced from a lower mounting (1) with a main spring (9) held there between, an outer tube (3) held to said lower mounting (1), an inner tube (4) having hydraulic fluid therein being provided coaxially within said outer tube (3), characterized in that an orifice body (21) having a housing, a spring loaded plunger (19) disposed displacably within said housing, an orifice or passage (18) extending

614/Dec/89
Satish Kumar Das

2 sheets
sheet 1

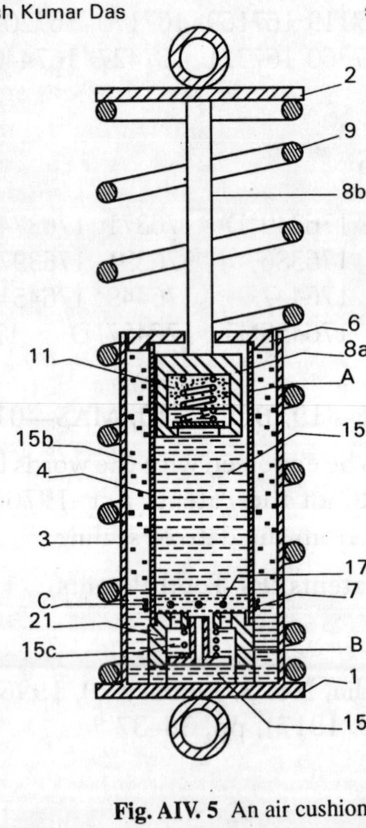

of L.S.Davar & Co.
APPLICANTS AGENT

Fig. AIV. 5 An air cushioned shock absorber

through said plunger (19), being provided for preventing a negative impact from being transmitted to said upper mounting (2). See Fig. AIV. 5.

Ind. Cl. 104F 176090
Int. Cl.^{4} : 08 K, 5/17

A method for the preparation of a vulcanized rubber at an increased rate of vulcanization

Applicant: THE GOODYEAR TIRE & RUBBER COMPANY, of 1144 East Market Street, Akron, Ohio 44316-0001, United States of America.

Inventors : CARL RAMSEY PARKS, RICHARD MICHAEL D'SIDOCKY, MARTIN PAUL COHEN.

Application for Patent No. 644/Del/89 filed on 21-07-89.

Appropriate office for opposition proceedings (Rule 4, 1972) Patent Office Branch, Karol Bagh, New Delhi 110 005.

7 Claims

A method for the preparation of vulcanized rubber at an increased rate of vulcanization which comprises subjecting a sulfur vulcanizable rubber to a vulcanization reaction in the presence of a methyl trialkyl ammonium salt in an amount ranging from 0.05 to 5.0 phr said methyl trialkyl ammonium salt having the formula (See Fig. AIV. 6):

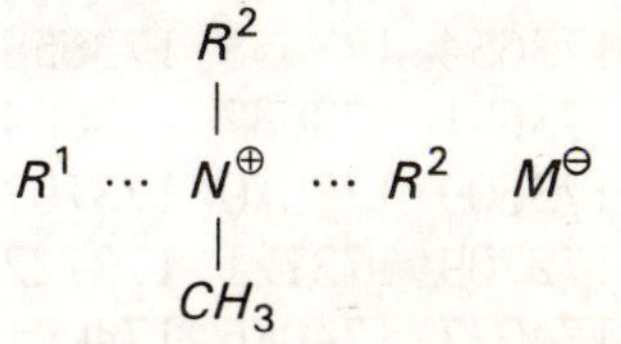

Fig. AIV. 6 The methyl trialkyl ammonium salt

wherein R^1, R^2 and R^3 are independent alkyl radicals having 8 to 10 carbon atoms and M is selected from the group consisting of Cl, Br, $CH_3\ SO_4$ and HSO_4.

Complete Specification 21 Pages Drawing Sheets Nil

Restoration proceedings

Notice is hereby given that an application for restoration of Patent No. 171, 490 dated 22-04-91 made by JCI India Limited on

24-05-95 and notified in the Gazette of India Part III, Section 2, dated the 29-07-95 has been allowed and the said restored.

Claim under Section 20(1) of the Patents Act, 1970

The claim made by Metallgesllechaft Aktiengesellschaft under Section 20 (1) of the Patents Act, 1970 to proceed the application for Patent No. 172169 in their name has been allowed.

Renewal fees paid

156185 156351 156698 156827 157122 157123 157124 157151
158818 159039 159051 159072 160367 160693 160821 161036
161356 161534 161834 162266 162599 163094 163488 164249
164378 164465 164593 164888 164907 164912 164913 164958
164959 165077 165263 165270 165308 165546 165548 165584
165614 165618 165610 165664 165734 165739 165775 165948
167176 167179 167283 167389 167391 167448 167449 167543
167633 167815 167820 167845 167880 167881 167882 167905
168073 168125 168332 168369 138370 168977 169056 169159
169566 169619 169724 169726 169790 169907 169978 169989
170679 171164 171180 171276 171374 171511 171592 171660
171663 171739 171909 171964 171969 171979 172528 172617
172705 172706 172707 172824 172852 173134 173220 173370
173414 173572 173574 173576 173577 173578 173580 173604
173607 173608 173610 173611 173613 173615 173617 173620
173646 173649 173654 173655 173658 173671 173676 173677
173679 173680 173681 173682 173684 173686 173687 173689
173693 173697 173609 173670 173703 173704 173705 173706
173707 173708 172709 173721 173722 173724 173729 173730
174030 174070 174077 174086 174091 174125 174130 174143
174145 174195 174260 174287

List of printed specification published

A limited number of printed copies of the undernoted specification are available for sale from the Patent Office, Calcutta, and its branches at Mumbai, Chennai and Delhi at Rs. 30/- per copy.

(1)

165411 165412 165413 165414 165415 165416 165417 165418
165419 165420 165421 165422 165423 165424 165425 165426

165427 165428 165429 165430 165431 165432 165433 165434
165435 165436 165437 165438 165439 165440

(2)

165441 165442 165443 165444 165445 165446 165447 165448
165449 165450 165451 165452 165453 165454 165455 165456
165457 165458 165459 165460

(3)

165461 165462 165463 165464 165465 165466 165467 165468
165469 165470 165471 165472 165473 165474 165475 165476
165477 165478 165479 165480 165481 165482 165483 165484
165485 165486 165487 165488 165489 165490

(4)

165491 165492 165493 165494 165495 165496 165497 165498
165499 165500 165501 165502 165503 165504 165505 165506
165507 165508 165509 165510 165511 165512 165513 165514
165515 165516 165517 165518 165520 165521 165522 165523
165524 165525 165526 165527 165528 165529 165530 165531
165532 165533 165534 165535 165536 165537 165538 165539
165540 165541 165542 165543 165544 165545 165546 165547
165548 165549 165550 165551 165552 165553 165554 165555
165556 165557 165558 165559 165560

Cessation of patents

166884 166885 166893 166912 166915 166924 166934 166935
166942 166961 166989 166997 167008 167010 167027 167050
167064 167085 167099 167104 167112 067113 167114 167120
167131 167148 167158 167183 167186 167193 167196 167201
167232 167262 167278 167288 167294 167295 167307 167322
167347 167349 167366 167372 167381 167388 167415 167422
167434 167436 167446 156166 157958 160611 168776 170340
171004

Patents sealed on 22-12-95

175245 175249*F 175250*F 175258 175267 175268 175276*
175303 175304 175305 175306 175307 175309 175310
175313 175314 175316 175317 175320 175322 175323

175324 175325* 175326 175327 175329 172330*175331
175332 175333 175334 175336 175337* 175338 175339
175340 175343* 175344 175347

CAL—10, DEL—23, BOM—06, MAS—NIL

*Patent shall be deemed to be endorsed with the words LICENSE OF RIGHT under Section 87 of the Patents Act, 1970 from the date of expiry of three years from the date of sealing.

D—Drug Patents, F—Food Patents.

Application Number Index of complete specifications accepted during the year 1994.

(Nos. 172901—174540)

Application No.	Patent No.	Application No.	Patent No.
1986		288/Del/87	173496
316/Del/86	172981	289/Del/87	173083
387/Del/86	172982	327/Del/87	173497
433/Del/86	173932	357/Del/87	173483
505/Del/86	174011	371/Del/87	173084
590/Del/86	172941	407/Del/87	173498
602/Del/86	172933	409/Del/87	173322
618/Del/86	173490	435/Del/87	173499
989/Del/86	174201	445/Del/87	172983
1047/Del/86	173492	466/Del/87	173752
1121/Del/86	173521	484/Del/87	173441
1122/Del/86	173560	549/Del/87	172972
1987		551/Del/87	174181
60/Cal/87	174114	560/Del/87	172973
33/Del/87	173522	575/Del/87	173622
39/Del/87	172942	601/Del/87	173935
59/Del/87	173553	627/Del/87	173401
77/Del/87	173082	646/Del/87	174182
119/Del/87	172971	672/Del/87	173936
164/Del/87	173321	685/Del/87	173484
166/Del/87	173481	700/Del/87	172974
187/Del/87	173554	711/Del/87	173086
190/Del/87	173494	719/Del/87	172975
217/Del/87	173482	729/Del/87	173557
229/Del/87	174012	788/Del/87	173442
245/Del/87	173555	806/Del/87	173331

812/Del/87	173332	1016/Del/87	173556
827/Del/87	174261	1040/Del/87	173445
834/Del/87	173443	1049/Del/87	173526
835/Del/87	173444	1051/Del/87	173902
842/Del/87	172984	1072/Del/87	172961
856/Del/87	173623	1091/Del/87	173903
860/Del/87	173793	1104/Del/87	173085
861/Del/87	173486	1106/Del/87	173001
863/Del/87	173487	1118/Del/87	173561
905/Del/87	172976	1130/Del/87	173446
909/Del/87	173488	1140/Del/87	173524
921/Del/87	172985	1155/Del/87	173447
934/Del/87	173523	1156/Del/87	173448
939/Del/87	173937	1162/Del/87	173333
962/Del/87	173402	1163/Del/87	173002
965/Del/87	173489		

Appendix V

Sample on-line search

Two sample searches using the Derwent Database to illustrate how to obtain relevant information related to patents

Patent search I

This search is on Kevlar — a speciality material used in the manufacture of space vehicles' parts. The search attempts to identify significant patents in this field, including major patent holders and patent assigness' reports have also been downloaded on-line to illustrate its usefulness. Full text, including the various codes, illustrate other features of the information available.

Note: Files 350 & 351 contain data from 1963–1980 & 1981–1995 respectively.

File 350 : Derwent World Pat.
1963 – 1980 / UD = 9445
File 351 : Derwent WPI
1981 – 1995 / UD = 9503; UA = 9444; UM = 9440

Set	**Items**	**Description**
? e kevlar		
Ref	Items	Index-term
E1	1	KEVERS
E2	2	KEVLAN
E3	620	*KEVLAR
E4	1	KEVLARNOMEX
E5	1	KEVLARR
E6	1	KEVLARTM
E7	2	KEVLAS

E8	1	KEVLAT
E9	8	KEVLER
E10	3	KEVLON
E11	4	KEW
E12	2	KEWAY
S1	620	"KEVLAR"

Searching key words rocket, satellite, shuttle.
Note: Boolean "or" is used to cover all the above terms.

? s (rocket ? or satellite ? or shuttle ?)

	3223	ROCKET ?
	12935	SATELLITE ?
	4066	SHUTTLE ?
S2	20040	(ROCKET ? OR SATELLITE ? OR SHUTTLE ?)

Searching for type, alternate, substitute.
Note: again "or" is used. Also use of "?" at the end of the word searches the expanded terms, e.g. alternate, alternates, alternative, etc.

? s (type ? or alternate ? or substitute ?)

	349813	TYPE ?
	55508	ALTERNATE ?
	45584	SUBSTITUTE ?
S3	442452	(TYPE ? ALTERNATE ? OR SUBSTITUTE ?)

? s s1 and s2 and s3

	620	S1
	20040	S2
	42452	S3
S4	3	S1 AND S2 AND S3

Search combines Kevlar with rocket, shuttle, satellite, type, alternate, substitute, etc.

? s (application ? or use ?)

	120236	APPLICATION ?
	2552251	USE ?
S5	2583349	(APPLICATION ? OR USE ?)

? s s1 and s5

	620	S1
	2583349	S2
S6	438	S1 AND S5

```
? s  (fiber ? or laminate ? )
            3682       FIBER ?
           76282       LAMINATE ?
   S7      79818       (FIBER ? OR LAMINATE ?)
? s  s1 and s7
             620       S1
           79818       S7
   S8         81       S1 AND S7
```

Gets 81 hits for Kevlar and fiber/laminate.

```
   S9          3       Sort S4 / ALL / PA.
```

Sorts S4 with respect to all patent asignees.

```
?   sort s6 / all / pa
   S10       438       Sort S6 / ALL / PA
?   sort s8 / all / pa
   S 11       81       Sort S8 / ALL / PA
?   report s9 / assignee / all
```

Patent assignee report as per sorting in S9

BASIC
BASIC
No.
PATENT
PATENT

PA PATENT NUMBER	ASSIGNEE IPC	DATE
2	(SHOW -) SHOWA HIKOKI KOGYA KK JP 5237954 B29C - 043	930917
	JP 5237953 B29C - 043	930917
1	(STHD) STEEL HEDDLE MFG CO US 4487234 D03J - 005	841211

Total : 2 PATENT ASSIGNEE (s)

Patent assignee report as per sorting in S11 (only a few have been listed)

BASIC
BASIC
No.
PATENT

PATENT PA PATENT NUMBER	ASSIGNEE IPC	DATE
2	(MITO) MITSUBISHI JUKOGYA KK US 5042358 B63B - 035	910827
	GB 2187680 B63B - 035	870916
2	(SANK -) SANKYU INC US 5042358 B63B - 035	910827
	GB 2187680 B 63B - 035	870916
2	(USAF) US SEC OF AIR FORCE US 6623873 F41F - 000	841127
	US 6614905 F41F - 000	841030
2	(USAS) NASA US NAT AERO and SP US 5302351 G01J - 001	940412
	US 8111321 G01L - 000	940301
2	(USSA) US SEC OF THE ARMY US 4573647 F41G - 007	860304
	US 6470749 F41F - 000	830802

Example of a full record downloaded on-line

DIALOG (R) File 351 : DERWENT WPI

(c) 1995 Derwent Info Ltd. All rights reserv.

009637486 WPI Acc No : 93-331035 / 42

XRAM Acc No. : C93 -146466

XRPX Acc No. : N93 - 255579

TI : Curved-surface honeycomb panel prodn. for rockets, etc. — by sandwiching the honeycomb core material between inner and outer surfaces sheets through mould and press-moulding.

PA = Patent Assignee	:	(SHOW -) SHOWA HIKOKI KOGYA KK
Number of Patents	:	001
Number of Countries	:	001

Patent Family :

CC	Number	Kind	Date	Week
JP	5237954	A	930917	9342

(Basic)
Priority Data (CC No Date) : JP 9275211 (920226)
Abstract (Basic) : JP 05237954 A

The method produces a curved-surface honeycomb panel with a predetermined curvature which is composed of a honeycomb core as a core material, and an inner surface sheet and an outer surface sheet bonded to the opposite sides of the honeycomb core. Previously, with a mould having a predetermined curvature, a spacer panel is produced by press-moulding. The spacer panel comprises a honeycomb core for a spacer and FRP boards bonded to the opposite sides of the honeycomb core for a spacer, having a thickness smaller by the thickness of the inner surface sheet than that of the curved-surface honeycomb panel to be produced. The outer surface sheet is produced by press-moulding with the mould. The spacer panel is placed on the inner surface of the mould, and the inner surface sheet is produced by press-moulding, using the outer side of the spacer panel. Then, the honeycomb core as the core material is sandwiched between the inner surface and the outer surface through an adhesive, and press-moulded with the mould. The inner-outer-surface sheets are unidirectional base material made of glass, "Kevlar", carbon, etc. fibers and an epoxy-modified, phenol type, etc. resin.

Use/advantage

Used for outer walls of rockets, various appts., structural materials, etc. Even when inner surface sheets containing unidirectional base materials composed of warps only, and a resin are used, the honeycomb panel is prevented from being cracked. The panel is superior in tensile strength and elasticity. The spacer panel is lightweight, has high stiffness, hardness, heat resistance, smoothness, durability, etc.

Derwent Class : A32; A93; P73;
Int Pat Class : B29C-043 / 14; B29C-065 / 54; B29C-065 / 70; B29C-069 / 02;
B29K-105-08; B29L-009-00; B32B-003 / 12
Manual Codes
(CPI / A-N) : All - B09A2; A12-R06; A12-S08; A12-T03

Plasdoc Key Serials : 0011 0147 0150 0153 0205 0229 0231
1277 1282 1990 2213
2214 2215 2220 2344 2419 2488 2491
2492 2522 2600
2613 2616 2622 2628
2646 2654 2657 2661 2718 2852 0016
0034 1283 2212 2219

Polymer Fragment Codes (AM) :
* 001 * 014 03 - 04- 08 and 10 - 140 15- 17 and 17- 226 229 23 and 231 308 309 331
371 376 431 441 446 46 and 465 477 502 541 551 552 555 560 561 566 575 581
596 597 598 602 654 661 722 723 725
* 002 * 014 141 151 273 308 309 311 654 722

PLASDOC Coding :
(01) * 001 * PO464 - R; M9999 M2391; S9999 S1581
* 002 * PO226 P0282-R; S9999 S1581
* 003 * P0000; S9999 S1354
* 004 * ND07; ND01; N9999 N7192 N7023
N9999 N6600; J9999 J2904; Q9999
Q7818-R; N9999 N5721-R; K9892;
N9999 N6042-R; K9698 K9676;
Q9712 K9676; Q9999 Q9245 Q9212;
B9999 B5243-R B4740; B9999
B3849-R B3838 B3747; B9999 B4842
B4831 B4740; B9999 B4079 B3930

Using the above-mentioned codes an information expert can provide targeted information on the searched subjects.

Patent search II

This search is also done on Derwent Database to illustrate how useful information on patents can be extracted. The search is targeted at identifying developments in the field of computer peripherals and special applications such as the ATM cards and in traffic signalling.

An information expert can help in the process of technology mapping, monitor competition or indicate technology and R&D trends.

File 350: Derwent World Pat. 1963-1980/UD=9628
(c) 1996 Derwent Info Ltd
File 351: DERWENT WPI 1981-1996/UD=9630; UA=9626; UM=9618

Search	Author's remarks on the search
(c)1996 Derwent Info Ltd	
Set Items Description	Author's remarks on the search
S1 192982 DC=T01	T01 — *code for digital computers*
S2 129383 DC=T04	T04 — *code for Computer peripherals*
>>> PAUSE started.	
?_s s1/1990:1996; pause ^ M	*records between*
Searching	*1990–1996 being searched*
>>> PAUSE ended.	
Processing	
192982 S1	
2982392 PY=1990 : PY=1996	
S3 123300 S1/1990:1996	*search result for 1990–1996*
>>> PAUSE started.	
?_s s1/1995:1996 ^ M	*search for records during the period 1995–1996*
>>> PAUSE ended.	
192982 S1	
883153 PY=1995 : PY=1996	
S4 49579 S1/1995:1996	*search result for 1995–1996*
?_s s1/1996 ^ M	
192982 S1	
312393 PY=1996	*search for records only in 1996*
S5 18824 S1/1996	*search result for 1996*
?_e ud=96 ^ M	*search for weekly breakup of the results in 1996.*
Ref Items Index-term	*weekly breakup from 50th week of 1995 to latest week in 1996*
E1 22463 UD=9550	*UD is the code for*
E2 22468 UD=9551	*Derwent week.*
E3 UD=9600	*UD = 9601 means the*
E4 26817 UD=9601	*1st Derwent Week in*
E5 23244 UD=9602	*1996.*
E6 29491 UD=9603	
E7 25774 UD=9604	
E8 22690 UD=9605	
E9 22340 UD=9606	
E10 23018 UD=9607	

E11 20654 UD=9608
E12 23399 UD=9609
E13 23598 UD=9610
E14 21410 UD=9611
E15 26435 UD=9612
E16 27621 UD=9613
E17 27156 UD=9614
E18 26579 UD=9615
E19 23361 UD=9616
E20 25710 UD=9617
E21 24660 UD=9618
E22 22543 UD=9619
E23 28034 UD=9620
E24 24637 UD=9621
E25 25536 UD=9622
E26 21182 UD=9623
E27 22913 UD=9624
E28 24673 UD=9625
E29 20956 UD=9626
E30 21387 UD=9627
E31 21508 UD=9628
E32 20457 UD=9629
E33 24380 UD=9630
E34 24403 UD=9999
E35 1 UE=BR
E36 2 UE=E

?_e dc=t01 ^M
E1 3 DC=TO4
E2 1 DC=TO6
E3 192982 *DC=T01
E4 13227 DC=T02
E5 109521 DC=T03
E6 1 DC=T03-V04-W04
E7 129383 DC=T04
E8 35138 DC=T05
E9 93993 DC=T06

Looking for subjectwise breakup of the records from 1990–1996.
Such a search helps to map the level of activity in a particular field and also to identify the areas of intense competition and overlap.

Code Subject
T01 — Digital Computers
T02 — Analog and Hybrid
T03 — Data recording
T04 — Comp. peripherals
T05 — Counting, Checking

E10 6862 DC=T07 — *T07 — Traffic signals and controls, etc. Vending, ATM and AOS systems*

E11 3 DC=T08

E12 1 DC=T09

(T05) in 1996 — *Searching for records*

?_s e8/1996^M

35138 DC=T05

312393 PY=1996

S6 3531 DC="T05"/1996 — *Results of the search on T05*

?_rank pa^M

Started processing RANK — *Ranking the assignees as per the number of patents in their names.*

Completed Ranking 500 of 3531 records — *Ranking of the 3531 records according to the assignees*

DIALOG RANK Results

RANK: S6/1-3531 Field: PA= File(s): 350,351

(Rank fields found in 3531 records — 3251 unique terms)

RANK No. Items

No.	Ranked	Term
1	205	TOKE
2	205	TOSHIBA KK
3	103	FJIE
4	103	FUJI ELECTRIC CO LTD
5	87	OKID
6	87	TODK
7	85	OKI ELECTRIC IND CO LTD
8	82	HITA
9	82	TOKYO ELECTRIC CO LTD
10	80	HITACHI LTD
11	77	NIPPON SIGNAL CO LTD
12	77	NIUG
13	65	KUBI
14	65	KUBOTA CORP
15	56	OMRO
16	56	SAOL
17	53	SANYO ELECTRIC CO LTD

Listing of the top 40 patent holders for T05

This indicates 205 patents in the name of Toshiba, 102 patents of Fuji, and so on. There are ways of avoiding double hits. An information expert can help in achieving this. (note that the same organization may have appeared two times, once in full and once abbreviated.)

```
18  51   FUIT
19  51   FUJITSU LTD
20  50   OMRON KK
21  49   PITB
22  48   NSM AG
23  48   NSMA-
24  47   PITNEY BOWES INC
25  43   AMTT
26  36   MARS INC
27  36   MRSC
28  36   SIEI
29  34   NIDE
30  32   SOFI-
31  32   SOFIA KK
32  30   NICO-
33  28   GLOR
34  28   GLORY KOGYO KK
35  26   ACE DENKEN KK
36  26   ACED-
37  26   NIPPON CONLUX CO LTD
38  24   NATC
39  24   NEOP-
40  24   NIPQ
?_t /3/1-2 ^ M
```

Looking for a few abstracts and some basic information from the search S6 on T05

7/3/1 (Item 1 from file: 351)
DIALOG(R)File 351:DERWENT WPI
(c)1996 Derwent Info Ltd. All rts. reserv.
010803904 WPI Acc No: 96-300857/30

Image available

Visual financial clearing operation system - has 'hand-key' unit to identify client according to recorded data of wrist parameters and uses circular data transmission device to transmit new information to all accounting and service centres after transaction.

Patent Assignee: (BLIT=) BLITS-CENTRE STOCK CO
Author (Inventor): BOBYR J A; BOLOVINTSEV J M; KAMSHITSKY I J; KOCHUASHVILI K Z; KOZLOVSKY S V; LEVCHENKO A I; LEVITIN V A; PROKIP A Z; PROKOFIEV J A; SARYAN V K; TAKHIRI A M; TROFIMOV E N; ZAKHAROV O V
Patent Family:

CC Number Kind Date Week
WO 9618981 A1 960620 9630 (Basic)
Priority Data (CC No Date): WO 94RU273 (941214)

7/3/2 (Item 2 from file: 351)
DIALOG(R)File 351:DERWENT WPI
(c)1996 Derwent Info Ltd. All rts. reserv.

010803903 WPI Acc No: 96-300856/30
Related WPI Accession(s): 96-160507
Image available
Vending machine detection system with credit card reader uses control lines to connect control device to vending machine for controlling operation of latter
Patent Assignee: (USTE-) USA TECHNOLOGIES INC
Author (Inventor): KOLLS B
Patent Family:
CC Number Kind Date Week
WO 9618980 A1 960620 9630 (Basic)
Priority Data (CC No Date): US 489682 (950613); US 354207 (941212); US 381119 (950131)
Applications (CC, No, Date): WO 95US16054 (951212)
?_s dc=t07 ^ M — *Searching for T07 in the latest Derwent week.*
S8 6862 DC=T07
?_s s8/1996 ^ M
6862 S8
312393 PY=1996
S9 594 S8/1996
?_s s9 and ud=9999 ^ M
594 S9
24403 UD=9999
S10 46 S9 AND UD=9999
?_rank pa ^ M
Started processing RANK
DIALOG RANK Results — *Completed ranking 46 records*

RANK: S10/1-46 Field: PA= File(s): 350,351
(Rank fields found in 46 records — 74 unique terms)

RANK No.Items — *listing of the top 20 patent assignees*

No.	Ranked	Term
1	11	TELE-
2	11	TELEDRIVE TELEMATIK IM VERKEHR GMBH

```
3    2      KUST-
4    2      KUSTOM SIGNALS INC
5    2      SUME
6    2      SUMITOMO ELECTRIC IND CO
7    2      TOKE
8    2      TOSHIBA KK
9    2      TOYOTA JIDOSHA KK
10   2      TOYT
11   1      ADAM/
12   1      ADAMS C
13   1      APPLIED CONCEPTS INC
14   1      BALA/
15   1      BALARAMAN A
16   1      BRER
17   1      BROTHER KOGYO KK
18   1      CONC-
19   1      FASE-
20   1      FASEROPTIK HENNING GMBH
```

?_exs ^ M
Executing TB204
?_ds ^ M

Set	Items	Description	
S1	192982	DC=T01	
S2	129383	DC=T04	
S3	123300	S1/1990:1996	
S4	49579	S1/1995:1996	
S5	18824	S1/1996	
S6	3531	DC="T05"/1996	
S7	234	S6 AND UD=9999	
S8	6862	DC=T07	
S9	594	S8/1996	
S10	46	S9 AND UD=9999	
S11	**3531**	**S6**	
S12	**138281**	**PA="TOKE"**	*looking for the patent assignee Toshiba*
S13	101984	PA="TOSHIBA KK"	*abbreviated as "TOKE"*
S14	18743	PA="FJIE"	
S15	4659	PA="FUJI ELECTRIC CO LTD"	
S16	16386	PA="OKID"	
S17	4009	PA="TODK"	

S18	6830	PA="OKI ELECTRIC IND CO LTD"
S19	132186	PA="HITA"
S20	3643	PA="TOKYO ELECTRIC CO LTD"
S21	37150	PA="HITACHI LTD"
S22	371	PA="NIPPON SIGNAL CO LTD"
S23	542	PA="NIUG"
S24	9911	PA="KUBI"
S25	4756	PA="KUBOTA CORP"
S26	6781	PA="OMRO"
S27	25983	PA="SAOL"
S28	6985	PA="SANYO ELECTRIC CO LTD"
S29	84554	PA="FUIT"
S30	84297	PA="FUJITSU LTD"
S31	964	PA="OMRON KK"
S32	1655	PA="PITB"
S33	159	PA="NSM AG"
S34	248	PA="NSMA-"
S35	1545	PA="PITNEY BOWES INC"
S36	7509	PA="AMTT"
S37	261	PA="MARS INC"
S38	359	PA="MRSC"
S39	48306	PA="SIEI"
S40	124569	PA="NIDE"
S41	324	PA="SOFI-"
S42	153	PA="SOFIA KK"
S43	1106	PA="NICO-"
S44	166	PA="GLOR"
S45	197	PA="GLORY KOGYO KK"
S46	293	PA="ACE DENKEN KK"
S47	308	PA="ACED-"
S48	132	PA="NIPPON CONLUX CO LTD"
S49	2344	PA="NATC"
S50	226	PA="NEOP-"
S51	8373	PA="NIPQ"
S52	**631000**	**S12:S51**
S53	**1282**	**S11 AND S52**

Note : S12 is TOSHIBA S51 is NIPPON Proceeding to monitor Toshiba & Nippon.

?_s dc=t05^M

S54 35138 DC=T05 *Detailed breakup of patents only within*

?_s s11 and s52^M 3531 S11 631000 S52 **S53 1282 S11 AND S52**	*T05 for Toshiba & Nippon in the latest Derwent week*
?_rank ic^M Started processing RANK ...Ranking 500 of 1282 records ...Ranking 1000 of 1282 records Completed Ranking 1282 records DIALOG RANK Results	*Ranking of 1282 records as per the international subject classification IC. This would help to map the technology portfolio of these companies*

RANK: S53/1-1282 Field: IC= File(s): 350,351
(Rank fields found in 1282 records — 733 unique terms)

RANK No.	No.Items Ranked	Term	
			Presenting the top 10 classifications as per the number of patents
1	167	G07D-009/00	*in these subjects.*
2	144	G06F-019/00	
3	106	G06F-017/60	*These results can be used*
4	94	G07B-015/00	*to map various fields as*
5	75	G07G-001/12	*per their patent densities.*
6	72	G07B-001/00	*Note : Each IC code indicates*
7	67	G07F-007/08	*a specific technology.*
8	65	G07F-009/10	
9	58	G07F-009/00	
10	57	A63F-007/02	

A patent information expert uses a judicious combination of on-line tools and off-line facilities such as CD-ROM databases to provide relevant information in a cost-effective manner.

Appendix VI

List of WTO convention countries

Ministry of Industry (Department of Industrial Development)

Notification

New Delhi, 3rd January, 1995

5.0.7 (E) – Whereas the countries specified in the Table given below (hereinafter referred to as the said countries) have ratified the agreement for the establishment of World Trade Organization including the Agreement on Trade Related Intellectual Property Rights, to which India is also a signatory country;

and whereas for the fulfilment of arrangements with the said countries as per the said Agreement the said countries would afford to applicants for patents in India or to citizens of India similar privileges as are granted to their own citizens in respect of the grant of patents and the protection of patent rights, it is necessary to do;

now, therefore, in exercise of the powers conferred by Sub-section (1) of Section 133 of the Patents Act, 1970 (39 of 1970), the Central Government hereby declares each of the said countries to be a convention country for all the provisions of the said Act. See Table AVI.1.

Table AVI. 1 Name of the country

Antigua & Barbuda	Argentina	Austria	Bahrain
Bangladesh	Barbados	Belgium	Belize
Botswana	Brazil	Brunei	Chile

Continues

Appendix VII

Collection centres

International Depository Authority as per the Budapest Treaty

Sr. No.	Culture collection	Address
1.	Agricultural Research Service Culture Collection (NRRL)	1815 North University Street, Peoria , Illinois 61604, U.S.A.
2.	American Type Culture Collection (ATCC)	12301 Parklawn Drive Rockville, Maryland 20852, U.S.A.
3.	Australian Government Analytical Laboratories (AGAL)	New South Wales Regional Laboratory 1, Suakin Street, Pymble, NSW 2073 Australia.
4.	Belgium Coordinated Collections of Micro-organisms (BCCM)	Prime Minister's Services, Science Policy Office, Rue de La Science, 8 B-1040, Brussels.
5.	Institut d'Hygiene et d'Epidemiologie Mycologie (IHEM)	Rue J. Wytsman, 14 B-1050, Brussels.
6.	Universiteit Gent Laboratorium voor Moleculaire Biologie-Plasmiden collectie (LMBP)	K.L. Ledeganckstraat, 35 B-9000, Ghent.
7.	Universiteit Gent Laboratorium voor Microbiologie-Bacterienverzameling (LMG)	K.L. Ledeganckstraat, 35 B-9000, Ghent.
8.	Mycotheque de l'Universite Catholique de Louvain [Collection referred to hereinafter as (MUCL]	Place Croix du Sud, 3B-1348, Louvain-la-Neuve.
9.	Belgium Co-ordinated Collections of Micro-organisms (BCCM)	
10.	Centraalbureau voor Schimmelcultures (CBS)	Oosterstraat 1, Postbus 273, NL - 3740 AG, Baarn.

Continues

Table AVI. 1 *Continued*

Columbia	Costa Rica	Côte d' Ivoire	Czech Republic
Denmark	Dominica	Finland	France
Gabon	Germany	Ghana	Greece
Guyana	Honduras	Hong Kong	Hungary
Iceland	Indonesia	Italy	Japan
Kenya	Korea	Kuwait	Lesotho
Luxembourg	Macau	Malaysia	Malta
Mauritania	Mauritius	Mexico	Morocco
Myanmar	Namibia	Netherlands	Nigeria
Norway	Pakistan	Paraguay	Peru
Philippines	Portugal	Romania	Senegal
Singapore	Slovak Republic	South Africa	Spain
St. Lucia	St. Vincent	Surinam	Swaziland
Sweden	Tanzania	Thailand	Uganda
United States	Uruguay	Venezuela	Zambia

Author's note

India is already part of a convention which includes UK, Ireland, New Zealand, Sri Lanka, Australia and Canada.

Continued

Sr. No.	Culture collection	Address
11.	China Centre for Type Culture Collection (CCTCC)	Wuhan Universitiy Wuhan, 430072, People's Republic of China.
12.	China General Microbiological Culture Collection Centre (CGMCC)	China Committee for Culture, Collection of Micro-culture, Collection of Beijing, 100080, People's Republic of China.
13.	Coleccion Espanola de Cultivos Tipo (CECT)	Departmento de Microbiologia, Facultad de Ciencias Biologicas, E-46100, Burjasot (Valencia).
14.	Collection Nationale de Cultures de Micro-organisms (CNCM) Institut Pasteur	28 rue du Dr Roux F-75724, Paris (Cedex 15), France.
15.	Culture Centre of Algae and Protozoa (CCAP)	(i) Institute of Freshwater Ecology, Windermere Laboratory, Far Sawrey, Ambleside, Cumbria, United Kingdom, LA22 0LP. (ii) Dunstaffnage Marine Laboratory, PO Box 3 Oban, Argyll, United Kingdom, PA34 4AD.
16.	Culture Collection of the Commonwealth Mycological Institute (CMICC)	NB. This organization has been renamed as "International Mycological Institute (IMI)" and is now included at a later point in this chapter.
17.	Czech Collection of Micro-organisms (CCM)	Ceskoslovenska sbirka mikro-organismu, Masarykovy university, ul. Tvrdeho c. 14 602 00, Brno, Czech Republic.
18.	Collection of Yeasts (CCY)	Ceskoslovenska sbirka kvasinek pri chemickem ustavu, Slovenske akademie ved, Dubravska cesta 9 842 38 Bratislava, Slovakia.
19.	Deutsche Sammulung von Mikro-organismen und Zellkulturen (DSM)	Mascheroder, Weg 1b D-38124, Braunschweig, Germany.
20.	European Collection of Animal Cell Cultures (ECACC)	Porton Down, Salisbury, Wiltshire, SP4 0JG, United Kingdom.
21.	Fermentation Research Institute (FRI)	
22.	Forschunginstitut Borstel, Institut fur experimentelle Biologie und Medizin (FIB)	D - 2061 Borstel, Federal Republic of Germany.

Continues

Continued

Sr. No.	Culture collection	Address
23.	Institute for Fermentation Osaka (IFO)	17-85, Juso-honmachi 2-chome, Yudogawa-ku, Osaka 532, Japan.
24.	Institute of Micro-organism Biochemistry and Physiology of the USSR Academy of Science (IBFM)	USSR Collection of Micro-organisms, Institute of Micro-organism Biochemistry and Physiology of the USSR Academy of Science, Puschchino -na-Oke, 142292 Moscow Region, Russian Federation.
25.	International Mycological Institute (IMI)	Bakeham Lane Englefield, Green Egham Surrey TW20, 9TY United Kingdom.
26.	In Vitro International Inc (IVI)	7885 Jackson Road, Ann Arbor, Michigan 48103, USA.
27.	Korean Cell Line Research Foundation (KCLRF)	Seoul National University, . College of Medicine 28, Yungon-dong, Chongno-gu, Seoul 110-799 Republic of Korea.
28.	Korean Culture Center of Micro-organisms (KCCM)	College of Engineering, Yonsei University, Sodaemum gu, Seoul 120 - 749, Korea.
29.	Korean Collection for Type Cultures (KCTC)	Genetic Engineering Research Institute, Korea Institute of Science and Technology, 305-333, 1 Oun-Dong Yusong-Gu Taejon Republic of Korea.
30.	Mezogazdasagi es Ipari Mikro organizmusok Magyar Nemzeti Gyujtemenye (Hungarian National Collection of Agricultural and Industrial Micro-organisms (MIMNG) (also known as by the initials 'NCAIM')	Kerteszeti Egyetem, Mikrobiologiai Tanszek. (Department of Microbiology, University of Horticulture.) Somloi ut 14-16 H-1118 Budapest.
31.	National Bank for Industrial Microorganisms and Cell Cultures (NBIMCC)	125 Lenin Blvd Block 2, Sofia, Bulgaria.
32.	National Collection of Food Bacteria (NCFB)	Agricultural and Food Research Council, Institute of Food Research Reading Laboratory, Shinfield Reading RG2 9AT United Kingdom.
33.	National Collections of Industrial and Marine Bacteria Ltd (NCIMB)	23, St. Machar Drive, Aberdeen AB2 IRY, United Kingdom.
34.	National Collection of Type Cultures (NCTC)	Central Public Health Laboratory 61, Colindale Avenue, London NW9. 5HT England, United Kingdom.

Continues

Continued

Sr. No.	Culture collection	Address
35.	National Collection of Yeast Cultures (NCYC)	AFRC Institute of Food Research, Norwich Laboratory, Colney Lane, Norwich NR4 7UA, Great Britian.
36.	National Institute of Bio-science and Human Tech-nology (NIBH), Agency of Industrial Science and Technology, Ministry of International Trade and Industry	1-3, Higash, 1-chome, Yatabe-machi, Tsukuba-shi, Ibaraki-ken 305, Japan.
37.	USSR Research Institute for Antibiotics of the USSR Ministry of the Medical and Micro-biological Industry (VNIIA)	Collection of Micro-organisms, USSR Research Institute for Antibiotics, Nagatinskaya Street 3-a, 113105 Moscow, Russian Federation.
38.	Russian National Collection of Industrial Micro-organisms (VKPM)	GNII Genetica, Dorozhnaya Proezd, 1, Moscow 113545, Russian Federation.

Appendix VIII

Glossary

1.	Assignee	:	The inventor or inventors who legally transfer their rights (in part or whole) to the invention to another person or organization.
2.	Breeder's Privilege	:	Permits use of one protected variety to breed another new variety without authorization of the original plant breeder.
3.	Claim	:	Defines the monopoly claimed in the patent and is used to decide infringement. What is not claimed is open to others.
4.	Complete Specification	:	Generally follows the provisional specification. Is a detailed specification: disclosure of the invention, its novelty with respect to prior art, demonstration of the invention through worked examples, results, diagrams, etc. The invention must be within the scope of what is described in the provisional specification.
5.	Controller (CGPDT)	:	Controller General of Patents, Designs and Trademarks.
6.	Convention application	:	India is a part of the World Trade Organization (WTO). The Indian Patents Act now recognizes 78 "member countries" patents as a belonging to a "Convention". An application submitted first in any convention country can be filed as a "Convention Application" (within 12 months) in India claiming the priority date of the original application of the convention country.

7. Date of Patent : Date of filing the complete specification.
8. Defendant : The person(s) being sued for infringement constitutes the "defendant".
9. EPC : European Patent Convention.
10. EMR : Exclusive marketing rights.
11. Farmers' privilege : Entitles a farmer to use farm-saved seeds for growing subsequent crops on his own land or on leased land or for traditional exchanges in the village community.
12. Final injunction : After the trial of the suit, orders may be passed by the court to stop the "defendant" from continuing the act(s) of infringement.
13. GATT : General Agreement on Tariff and Trade.
14. Granting of patent : If a patent application is not opposed after advertisement in the Gazette within the prescribed period, the patent gets "granted". However, if there is opposition, the patent is granted to the applicant only if the decision is in his favour.
15. Importation : When a product is imported into the country for which a patent (product or process) has been granted in the country . For example, if a patent is granted in India for a product or a process to manufacture the product and if the same product is imported into India, it would be importation. Importation would not be considered as having "worked" the patent in India.
16. Intellectual property : "Intellectual goods" generated by creative and innovative human endeavour.
17. IPR : Intellectual property rights.
18. Intellectual property rights : Formal state-run system exists where the "intellectual goods" are protected in various forms such as patents,trademarks, copyright, designs, utility patents, trade secrets, geographical indications.

19. Interlocutory injunction : As a part of an infringement proceeding the plaintiff may pray for "interim relief" to restrain the defendant from continuing the act of infringement till the case is completely heard and disposed of. This is called an interlocutory injunction.

20. Invention : A new and useful article, method or substance produced by manufacture.

21. Inventive step : It is that feature of the invention which relates to a solution of a problem which has eluded earlier attempts. Earlier work may have suggested directions, but the present work has transcended the idea stage and the solution is arrived at through extensive experimentation, the results of which lead to the solution to the problem.

22. Inventor : A person who first made the invention and applied for the patent.

23. Lapsed patent : A patent is considered "lapsed" when the renewal fee is not paid within the prescribed time.

24. License : It is a legal permit given by a patentee to other(s) to make, use or exercise the invention. The legal document needs to be registered with the Patent Office.

25. License of right : A patent may be endorsed with the words "license of right" three years after it is sealed. In such cases any person may obtain, as a matter of right, a license without having to establish a case for a compulsory license. In India all patents related to foods/drugs are automatically endorsed in this category within three years of their sealing.

26. Member states : All signatories of the GATT are members of RHW WTO. The member countries are also called "member states".

27. Mosaicing of Publications: : An invention may be a judicious combination of various components or features, where each of the aspects is probably known. Mosaicing is a process by which an attempt is made to combine

bits and pieces of the information from diverse sources to show that the alleged invention in a patent is not novel but is obvious to any unimaginative person.

28. Opposition : After a patent application is examined by the Patent Office it is accepted if the Controller is satisfied that it has cleared all the tests of patentability under the Act. This is published and is open to "interested persons" to challenge its grant. The opposition proceedings that may follow are held in the Patent Office by the Controller.

29. Patent : Exclusive right to use an invention granted to a person for a limited time.

30. Patentee : The owner of a patent as entered in the Register of Patents.

31. Patent agents : Patent agents need certain qualifications to practise. They have to clear the exam for patent agents which is conducted by the Patent Office in India.

32. PCT : Patent Cooperation Treaty.

33. Person interested : Is a person or organization engaged in or having business stakes in the field or doing/funding R&D work in a specified field. The "interested person" has to establish "his" bonafides (*locus standi*) while opposing a patent application.

34. Pipeline protection : A provision under the GATT in which countries not presently granting product patents are required to create an intermediate provision of exclusive marketing rights for five years based on product patents granted in any of the member states.

35. Plaintiff : The patentee or his assignee can file a suit in the High Court for infringement of his patent. They constitute the "plaintiff".

36. PBR : Plant breeding rights.

37. Priority : When a patent application is filed at the Patent Office it gets a priority as of that date. Convention countries can claim the priority of the

first filing of the patent in any of the member countries within 12 months. In all countries except the USA "first to file" gets the priority.

38. Prior art : This refers to anything known in the public domain. This could be in the form of lectures, broadcasts, newspapers, reports, books, patent specifications, etc. Even public use is considered to be prior art. This is very important while determining the novelty of the invention.

39. Provisional Specification : A patent application is filed to obtain priority. The applicant is expected to disclose the essential features with a description of the invention, its field of application and usefulness. In India claims need not be included in a provisional specification.

40. Register of Patents : This is a register maintained by the Patent Head Office in Calcutta. It has records of names, addresses, the invention, number of the patent, date of sealing, all details of assignments, transmission amendments, revocations, licenses, and all other information on the propriety/validity of the patent.

41. Revocation : A patent is granted by the Patent Office after examining it within the framework of the Patents Act. This, however, does not guarantee the validity of a patent. Its validity can be challenged under prescribed grounds. If the challenge is upheld by the High Court the patent becomes "invalid" and is "revoked". The entire process is called revocation.

42. Sealing of patent : This follows the grant of a patent. The patent is considered sealed when its details are entered in the Register of Patents administered by the Patent Head Office in Calcutta.

43. Synergy : The arthmetic sum of the effects of the individual components is less than the combined effect of these components in a composition or formulation.

44. *Sui generis* : A system of its own. This has been used in TRIPS as an option given to the member countries of

		WTO to evolve their own systems for plant protection within the GATT framework.
45. Term of a patent	:	It is a period for which a patent is "entitled to be in force" provided the renewal fees are paid within a prescribed time. In India it is 14 years from the date of patent for all patents except for those relating to food, drug and medicine, for which it is seven years from the date of patent or five years from the date of sealing, whichever is shorter.
46. TRIPS	:	Trade Related Intellectual Property Rights.
47. UPOV	:	Union for Protection of Plant Varieties.
48. Working of a patent	:	When a patent is exploited and put to use commercially.
49. World patent	:	There is no such thing as a world patent. A patent is a national right.
50. WTO	:	World Trade Organization.
51. "Wrongful obtaining"	:	A term used when the invention is obtained (fully or partially) by someone by wrong or unfair means from the inventors/assignees.

Appendix IX

Select readings

Select titles for further reading

1. Warshofsky Fred, *The Patent Wars : The Battle to Own the World's Technology*, 1994, John Wiley and Sons Inc.
2. Cornish, W.R., *Intellectual Property*: *Patents, Copyright, Trademarks and Allied Rights*, 2nd edn. and 3rd Indian reprint, 1995, Universal Book Traders, New Delhi.
3. Pearson, Hilary E. and C. G., Miller, *Commercial Exploitation of Intellectual Property*, 1st Indian edn., 1994, Universal Book Traders, New Delhi.
4. Narayanan, P., *Law of Copyright and Industrial Designs*, 2nd edn., 1995, Eastern Law House, Calcutta.
5. Wegner, H. C., *Patent Law in Biotechnology, Chemicals and Pharmaceuticals*, 2nd edn., 1994, Stockton Press, USA.
6. Yound D., Watson A., Thorley S. and Miller R., *Terrell on Law of Patents*, 1994, Sweet and Maxwell, London.
7. Byrne, Noel, *Licensing Technology: Drafting and Negotiating Agreements*, 1994, Stockton Press, USA.
8. Narayanan, P., *Patent Law*, 2nd edn., 1985, Eastern Law House Pvt. Ltd., Calcutta.

Recent articles of interest on patents

(These excerpts have been compiled by Mr John Peter of Administrative Staff College of India, Hyderabad.)

MacLean, Kurt A, "Avoiding patent problems through proper planning", *Pharmaceutical Executive*, **15** (2), 1995, pp. 76–80.

Pharmaceutical companies can realize significant advantages by making patent laws part of their R&D strategy from the outset.

In addition to being a source of legal information, patent attorneys can help research programs that account for a company's broader market goals as well as the potential for effective patent protection with their strong technical backgrounds. Additionally, a preliminary patent search at the outset of any R&D program is critical since a company may identify a protected compound or process that it might incorporate into its final product under a licensing arrangement. The company's bargaining position will be much stronger if it negotiates early in its research. Meanwhile, as international markets grow, it becomes economically necessary that R&D efforts avoid being at cross purposes with patent laws and procedures in countries where the product will be sold. Companies should consider international patent issues throughout the product development process.

Hanson, David, "New rules ease biotech patent requirements", *Chemical and Engineering News*, **73** (1), 1995, pp. 7–8.

The US Patent and Trademark Office has issued new guidelines that will make it easier for biotechnology companies to patent potential drugs.

Kawaura, Akihiko and J La Croix Sumner, "Japan's shift from process to product patents in the pharmaceutical industry: An event study of the impact on Japanese firms", *Economic Inquiry*, **33** (1), 1995, pp. 88–103.

Japan changed its patent law by introducing product patents for newly developed chemical and pharmaceutical products. An analysis uses rate-of-return data from the Tokyo Stock Exchange for Japanese pharmaceutical companies to examine the impact of the change in the patent law. The empirical findings indicate that the passage of the new patent law induced an excess return of approximately 26% to a portfolio of large pharmaceutical companies. Companies with R&D programs specializing in new product development experienced large gains, while companies with R&D programs specializing in imitative patents experienced no gains.

Hornsleth, Henrik, "Danish intellectual property", *International Financial Law Review*, 1995, pp. 15–9.

In Denmark, IPR are based almost solely on statutory law, and the assertion of these rights can only be carried out pleading the relevant statute. Yet remedies for proprietors of the different IPR are essentially the same. The legislation on trademarks is laid down in the Danish Trademark Act, consolidated as Act No. 341. A trademark right, as a rule, provides protection only against unauthorized use of the trademark with regard to services within the same or similar type of goods. Danish patent legislation is set out in Act No. 587. Patents can be obtained on inventions representing technical innovations and must be registered with the Directorate of Patents. The Danish Copyright Law is contained mainly in the Danish Copyright Act, Act No. 714.

Kleinberg, Norman C and Ronald, Abramson, "Intellectual property", *International Financial Law Review*, United States Litigation Supplement, 1995, pp. 27–33.

Litigation of copyright, patent, or trademark claims in USA often presents procedural and substantive issues not found in other types of litigation in US courts. USA has been slow to harmonize its copyright laws with those of the rest of the world. In 1989, the US finally became a signatory to the Berne Convention for the Protection of Literary and Artistic Works. The implementation of the North American Free Trade Agreement and approval of the Uruguay Round revisions to the GATT will further harmonize domestic copyright related issues with those of the international intellectual property community. Under the US Copyright Act, non-US works covered by the Berne Convention are exempted from the registration requirement. Section 43(a) of the Lanham Act is a significant weapon for the owners of unregistered trademarks.

Kemppinen, Seppo and Jyrki Nikula, "Finnish intellectual property", *International Financial Law Review*, 1995, pp. 27–9.

One means of disclosing the strategic features of a technology through simple analysis of complementary patents is presented. The methodology shows how it is possible to bring to light the specific dynamics of a technology during conception and industrial application. Obviously, technologies find themselves at different strategic stages depending on the partnerships involved — research laboratories, the market, competing or complementary companies. Similar technology may be strategic at different times: from an academic research point of view, from an industrial applications point of view, or from a commercial point of view. In each case, analysis of solidarity network technologies will make this possible. The advantage of working with technology networks, based on the analysis of words associated by patent sets, is that it makes it possible to focus on the features of strategic variables according to the reference network. A certain technology may be strategic for a company or series of companies without being strategic from the point of view of the field being considered or the opposite.

Barton, John H., "Adapting the intellectual property system to new technologies," *International Journal of Technology Management*, **10** (2/3), 1995, pp. 151–72.

An examination is made to determine whether the system of protecting IPR is capable of adapting to the changes taking place in the new technologies. Biotechnology, computer software and computer databases are used as examples of fundamentally new technologies. The new issues posed by these technologies are described, and the approaches taken to adapt the intellectual property system in each case are reviewed. The performance of this adaptation process is evaluated, looking at 3 levels:

1. The mechanisms for developing doctrine.
2. The systems (e.g. Patent Offices) that grant IPR.
3. The formal systems (primarily courts) and informal systems (e.g. cross-licences) that enforce IPR and shape their practical economic implementation.

In a number of areas, the analysis is international and comparative. The conclusions are meant to be international as well.

Challu, Pablo M., "Effects of the monopolistic patenting of medicine in Italy since 1978", *International Journal of Technology Management*, **10** (2/3) 1995, pp. 237–51.

The effects that the patenting of medicine in Italy has had since the current legislation was passed in 1978 are discussed. It is shown that:

1. Prices of patented pharmaceuticals in Italy have undergone an average increase of about 200% on probable prices of the

same products in competitive conditions which can be attributed to patent monopoly.

2. Owing to the enforcement of the new pharmaceutical patent law, national laboratories have gradually lost their market share, starting from 48.10% share in 1979, slightly increasing to 49.20% in 1980, dropping to 41.32% in 1988, and then continuing to decrease.
3. The number of drug inventions dropped in Italy after patent monopoly implementation.
4. The trade balance of the pharmaceutical sector has been deteriorating rapidly since the implementation of monopolistic patenting in Italy.

Subramanian, Arvind, "Putting some numbers on the TRIPS pharmaceutical debate," *International Journal of Technology Management*, **10** (2/3), 1995, pp. 252–68.

The changes in prices, profits and social welfare arising from increased patent protection for pharmaceuticals in a number of developing countries are estimated. Two market structures are proposed and comparisons are made between the situations where there is no patent protection and after the introduction of patent protection. The monopolist model of the post-patent market structure is refined by introducing a Nash–Bertrand duopoly, with non-patentees acting under compulsory licenses and the same comparisons made. Gaps between the adoption of legislation and its impact are discussed and the effects of retroactive legislation are compared with non-retroactive patenting. Prices of patented drugs in three countries are then compared and possible price changes are discussed. For larger countries, or a group of small countries, the effects of patent protection are calculated for the same scenarios and the incentives for increased research and development are examined. It is concluded that the effects of patent protection are sensitive to assumptions about market structure and price elasticity.

Yusuf, Abdulqawi A., "Intellectual property protection in the countries of Africa", *International Journal of Technology Management*, **10** (2/3), 1995, pp. 269–92.

The state of IPR and their protection and exploitation in African countries is examined. Listed are the coverage of intellectual property laws, the subject matter of protection and the scope of rights conferred. It is shown that African legislation is generally comparable to that in developed countries with regard to terms of protection, compulsory licensing, subject matter and government and public interest use. A comparison is made between developed countries and African members of the GATT in regard to fields excluded from protection. The results of surveys of some individual African countries give the extent of registration of patents and technology transfer to these countries. The possible impact of new legislation, especially in the context of the TRIPS negotiations of the Uruguay round, is considered.

Taylor, Susan, "The US Patent and Trademark Office: A case study in business process reengineering", *National Productivity Review*, 14 (1), 1995, pp. 85–96.

Inspite of Al Gore's initiative, few federal government agencies have actively embraced the concept of business process reengineering. One notable exception is the Patent and Trademark Office (PTO) of the Department of Commerce. Already one of the best managed agencies in the federal government, the PTO is revamping the application process for both patents and trademarks and expects to save tens of millions of dollars every year once the redesigned systems are fully implemented. The new process will take full advantage of electronic technology to achieve huge reductions in labor and printing costs, as well as allow innovative and flexible management techniques such as work-at-home programs. Responsibility and authority will be concentrated in fewer employees through job enrichment and restructuring, and the level of service provided to PTO's customers will improve. The redesigned trademark application process will also meet emerging international trademark requirements.

Griliches, Zvi and Iain Cockburn, "Generics and new goods in pharmaceutical price indexes", *American Economic Review*, 84 (5), 1994, pp. 1213–32.

When the patent on a drug expires, there are substantial welfare gains to those consumers who, like the Food and Drug

Administration, regard branded and generic versions as perfect substitutes. Standard price indexes fail to reflect this, since they treat generics as distinct goods and link them in with fixed weights. Alternative calculations are presented, using detailed data on the wholesale prices of two anti-infective drugs. Significant differences are found: for one of the drugs studied the standard price index rose by 14% over 45 months following patent expiration, while the preferred alternative index fell by 48%.

Pohl, Mark J., "Patents in business: A primer for bankers", *Banking Law Journal*, **111** (6), 1994, pp. 583–602.

Patent law provides that discoveries must meet several requirements to be patentable:

1. The discovery must be new.
2. The discovery must be adequately disclosed.
3. The discovery must be proper subject matter (useful).

The requirement that the discovery be useful refers to the ability of the discovery to foster economic development. Economic development is a central theme in defining what types of discoveries are patentable. Patents are useful to protect proprietary business processes and machinery. Using patent protection may protect against the skill losses associated with employee mobility. Patents may better enable firms to increase earnings by developing licensing revenues. Patent protection may also provide a useful marketing strategy to deal with competitors using similar technology.

Mazurek, Martin J., "Creeping genericism infects trademarks", *Pharmaceutical Executive*, **14**(11), 1994, pp. 32–4.

With some countries seeing a weakening in patent law enforcement, industries are counting on trademarks to retail intellectual property protection. Yet, at the same time, there is an emerging effort to remove trademarks. The creeping genericism that could encourage displacement of pharmaceutical trademarks by generic terms is found in several isolated proposals, resolu-tions and recommendations emanating from various agencies that together pose a serious threat to the pharmaceutical industry. The activities in question focus primarily, in the pharmaceutical industry, on multisourced off-patent products — medications that several different companies market after the patent has expired for the innovative manufacturer. The concern is that those activities may quickly affect newly discovered, patented and protected products. Trademark-related proposals from the World Health Organization, FDA and US Pharma-copeia and their potential impact on the pharmaceutical industry are discussed.

Kingston, William, "Compulsory licensing with capital payments as an alternative to grants of monopoly in intellectual property", *Research Policy*, **23**(6), 1994, pp. 661–72.

Historically, intellectual property has consisted of grant of monopoly rights, but such rights have been criticized on the grounds that important inventions demand multiple agents if they are to be innovated on the optimum scale and as rapidly as possible. Compulsory licensing would seriously damage incentives to innovate because royalties cannot fully compensate for the risks an innovator takes. However, the shortcomings of compulsory licensing might be dealt with by additional payment of a prescribed capital sum on grant of a license. Arbitration would also be compulsory if the parties cannot agree on a royalty rate. Results from the US Small Business Innovation Research Programs are used to obtain an indication of what such payments might be in the patent area. The analysis indicates that such payments might satisfactorily replace uncertain rewards from a monopoly grant, since an innovator would get them in advance from as many licenses as the invention justifies.

Burton, Deron, "Bringing theory into practice: Predictable scope for functional patent claims", *UCLA Law Review*, **42**(1), 1994, pp. 221–61.

The doctrine of equivalents and the use of functional language developed independently in response to threatened or actual imbalances between the competing policies underlying the patent system. Both have been recognized as performing distinct and essential roles in the patent law, helping to ensure that patent law achieves its goals of promoting the progress of the useful arts. To preserve the usefulness of both functional claim language and the doctrine of equivalents, a clear distinction must be upheld. The strict, element-level analysis of the federal courts in a 1987 case, Pennwalt Corp. vs Durand–Wayland, Inc., reduces this distinction to a theoretical nicety too fine to be of practical help. To preserve the balance-keeping effect of both the doctrine of equivalents and Section 112(6) of the US Patent Code, there needs to be a place for "as a whole" analysis in the doctrine of equivalents, and literal infringement of a means-plus-function claim should be narrowly construed to require strict structural equivalents.

Gentzoglanis, Anastassios, "Sunk costs, innovation, and spillover effects in R&D-intensive industries", *Journal of Applied Business Research*, **10** (4), 1994, pp. 1–11.

A theoretical relationship is established between the sunkcosts of a firm' and its degree of innovation, as measured by the number of patents and trademarks introduced in the market. Departing from the assumption that incumbents and potential entrants are risk-averse, the presence of sunk costs is demonstrated not to be a barrier to entry, as it is usually considered to be, but it acts as a stimulus to R&D activities. The empirical results confirm this assertion for the sample and the period examined. In the light of these results public policies encouraging R&D activities such as tax credits and grants should be reexamined carefully.

Merges, Robert P., and Richard, Nelson R., "On limiting or encouraging rivalry in technical progress: The effect of patent scope decisions", *Journal of Economic Behavior and Organization*, **25** (1), 1994, pp. 1–24.

The scope of the claims of a patent determines the ability of competitors to produce substitutes without fear of infringement suits, and hence the real "monopoly power" of the patent holder. It is argued that this depends on the topography of technical advance in a field, in particular on how inventions are linked to each other, and on the extent to which rapid technical advance requires a diversity of actors and minds, as contrasted with being facilitated by express coordination of inventive activity. The areas where rival inventors appear to have seen opportunities in similar ways are in what can be called sciencebased technologies. In the cumulative-systems-technology cases, broad, prospect claiming, pioneer patents, when their holder tried to uphold them, caused nothing but trouble. Other parties often were more active or creative than the pioneer patent holder and suits slowed down their ability to put their inventions into practice, and undoubtedly dampened the interests of other talented people.

Hill, Eileen, "Strong IPR protection is important for high-tech trade", *Business America*, 115(8), 1994, pp. 23–5.

Copyrights, patents, and other IPR are the keys to current and future US competitiveness in high-technology industries. Millions of dollars invested in R&D can be lost overnight if a company fails to protect its discoveries under the IPR laws of the US and other potential country markets. The US government has put much emphasis on IPR in its trade policy over the past decade. US interests have found that while their IPR can be enforced at home, they often have little recourse against infringers under the laws of US trading partners. Intensive discussions by the US to upgrade worldwide IPR protection began in the early 1980s with several trading partners in the Pacific Basin where US companies were experiencing the biggest losses. Discussions have now spread across all continents and the topic of effective IPR protection occupies an important spot on the agenda for US trade talks with almost every country in the world.

La Manna, Manfredi M.A., "Research vs Development: Optimal patenting policy in a three-stage model", *European Economic Review*, 38 (7), 1994, pp. 1423–40.

To produce a new product or process, firms have to go through two distinct stages. Research is discontinuous and stochastic: a prototype is a success (failure) with probability p (1 – p). Development is non-stochastic and continuous, quality improvements being a concave deterministic function of development inputs. A study shows how patent policy affects market structure and welfare. Under a single-patent regime, granting patents to research prototypes is unambiguously welfare-improving, whereas under a multiple-patent regime, granting patents only to developed products or processes may be more beneficial in so far as it reduces entry, which tends to be excessive under the prototype-protection regime.

Vishwasrao, Sharmila, "Intellectual property rights and the mode of technology transfer", *Journal of Development Economics*, 44 (2), 1994, pp. 381–402.

Transferring technology in an environment where patent protection is uncertain can pose significant risks to an innovating firm's ability to appropriate rents. An analysis incorporates asymmetric information in a screening game where the innovating firm has the choices of licensing a new product at arm's length to a foreign firm, exporting it, or licensing it to a subsidiary. Subsidiary production avoids the risk of imitation but involves higher costs for the innovating firm. The gains to the southern country from the lack of IPR protection may be offset by strategic behavior by northern firms that opt for technology transfer via subsidiary or monopoly production. The theoretical model suggests that the effect of patent infringement on the mode of technology transfer would be to cause the foreign firm to try to internalize the cost by opting for foreign direct investment rather than arm's length licensing.

Keep, William W, Glenn, S Omura and Roger, J, Calantone., "What managers should know about their competitors' patented technologies", *Industrial Marketing Management*, **23** (3), 1994, pp. 257–64.

The present study applies industrial organization theory to the study of the technological process that leads to patenting by examining the industry structure/industry performance relationship. The results indicate that a greater number of competitors increases patent activity in a technological area. The regression results indicate that patent activity in a technological area declines as research concentration increases. A longer competitor lead time does not appear to lower the patent activity in the technological area. A greater technological focus in a specific technological area will not result in higher patent activity in that area. Greater technological complexity will lower the patent activity in a technological area.

Snow, Bonnie, "Drug patent extension information on-line: Monitoring post-approval regulatory developments", *Online*, 18 (4), 1994, pp. 95–100.

Proposed healthcare reforms in the US have spurred many new types of information requests, requiring medical searchers to expand their horizons beyond the clinical databases. For example, demands for drug cost containment and third-party-induced price sensitivity have focused renewed attention on the flow of less expensive generic drugs onto the market. That flow is governed by the time-table of brandname drug patent expirations and subsequent approval of generic alternatives. At the same time, patent protection ensures a constant flow of new chemical entities into the R&D pipeline to meet new disease challenges. Companies are more likely to continue investing in risk projects if they are guaranteed market exclusivity to exploit the products of their proprietary R&D. Thus, queries that were once the purview of law firms or intellectual property departments are now on the medical searcher's desk, along with clinical information requests. Tips for locating drug patent extension information on-line are presented.

Harter, John F. R., "The propensity to patent with differentiated products", *Southern Economic Journal* , **61**(1), 1994, pp. 195–201.

An examination is made of the patenting decision of a firm when a patent would allow non-inventors to learn more about how the product is made, potentially hurting the profits of the inventor. While this is a sub-game of a larger, differentiated-products game which would include the choices of product varieties by the firms, the patent issue must first be addressed and is an interesting topic on its own. The result is a framework for explaining a propensity to patent between zero and one which acts as a complement to Hortsmann, MacDonald and Slivinski (1985). It is shown that, if the non-innovator will not use the information contained in the patent grant in order to imitate, then the innovator will patent. It is also shown, however, that situations exist when the innovator might not wish to patent. The decision on whether or not to patent will depend on the intended actions of the non-innovator in the particular equilibrium being played.

Schmoch, Ulrich and Thomas Schnoring, "Technological strategies of telecommunications equipment manufacturers: A patent analysis", *Telecommunications Policy*, **18** (5), 1994, pp. 397–413.

Patent analysis on a company level leads to many insights into the technological strategy of telecommunications manufacturers. European companies are usually focused on telecommunications, whereas Japanese companies put higher emphasis on other fields such as data processing or audiovisual electronics and enter telecommunications from this angle. This might be important for the future markets. European companies target European markets and North America, neglecting Japan. US companies are oriented to both European and Japanese markets. Japanese patents are mainly aimed at the US market and on a lower level, the European. International trade and patent patterns correlate with each other.

Littell, Candace L., "Innovation in medical technology: Reading the indicators", *Health Affairs*, **13** (3), 1994, pp. 226–35.

Investment in medical technology innovation has enabled significant advances in patient care. An understanding of the dimensions and measures of innovation is critical in fully assessing the implications of many policy initiatives under debate. Several indicators are presented of inputs and outputs associated with medical device innovation, including public- and private-sector research and development investment, patent activity, product regulatory clearance patterns, and market acceptance trends. Changes in these selected indicators point to a potential shift occurring in both the nature of and the investors in the innovation process.

Lerner, Joshua, "The importance of patent scope: An empirical analysis", *Rand Journal of Economics*, **25** (2), 1994, pp. 319–33.

An analysis examines the impact of patent scope on firm value. It develops a proxy for patent scope based on the International Patent Classification scheme. Using a sample of 535 financing rounds at 173 privately held venture-backed biotechnology firms, the analysis shows that the breadth of patent protection significantly affects valuation. A one standard deviation increase in average patent scope is associated with a 21% increase in the firm's value. Broad patents are more valuable when substitutes in the same product class are plentiful, a finding consistent with theoretical suggestions.

McConville, Daniel J., "Intellectual property gains respect", *Industry Week*, **243** (5), 1994, pp. 33–8.

The owners of patents, copyrights, trademarks, trade secrets, and other intellectual properties have never before enjoyed so much government protection and financial reward. Microsoft founder Bill Gates can be credited with sounding the wake-up call for intellectual property protection in 1976. Others cite creation of the Court of Appeals of the Federal Circuit in 1983 as a crucial turning point. Under the GATT's trade-related intellectual property safeguards, patent protection will be extended to 20 years. Late in January 1994, the US patent community was shaken by an unexpected announcement that the Patent Office would stick with its system of awarding patents on the date of invention, rather than switching to the first-to-file basis used by all other industrial nations. The vast majority of inventors are hired hands, and in many cases, breakthrough technology is the result of team work. Most companies' research and development is done in-house, although companies sometimes engage in joint-venture research with customers.

Perrotta, Debra, "Estate planning for owners of patents and copyrights", *Estate Planning*, **21**(2), 1994, pp. 94–103.

Not only are the exclusivity lives for copyrights and patents different, these assets have separate tax treatments. The special tax rules applicable to each of these assets should be kept in mind when designing an estate plan involving either a copyright or a patent. During the life of a patent, the owner has the right to determine who, if anyone, will have the right to the patent. The law does not require that the owner put the patent to use, but failure to do so may be counterproductive both to technology and to the owner financially. The basic property concept of copyright is originality. The parallel in patent law is novelty. To value a copyright or a patented work, it is necessary to project the future earning capacity of the work or invention.

The estates of intellectual property holders typically consist of their works or inventions, copyrights or patents, and perhaps various royalty rights for the exploitation of their works. The creators of intellectual property should first decide whether to retain or divest control. Then, the parties should examine problems regarding value and liquidity.

Engelsman, E. C. and A. F. J. van Raan, "A patent-based cartography of technology", *Research Policy*, **23**(1), 1994, pp. 1–26.

Bibliometric methods and techniques are used to develop a cartography of technology. Two types of maps are presented: co-word maps, and co-classification maps. Both types of maps have been constructed for the entire domain of technology, i.e. the ensemble of all fields of technology in their mutual relations. Time series clearly illustrates the changing relations between the major clusters of technology, and in particular the changing role of fields which act as a bridge between clusters, or as a center of technological activities within a specific cluster. In order to have measures of the relative strength of relations between fields of technology, the concept of affinity between fields is developed. First attempts are also made to map the science and technology interface by a specific combination of publication and patent data. Conclusions are presented.

Chakrabarti, Alok K., and Israel, Dror, "Technology transfers and knowledge interactions among defense firms in the USA: An analysis of patent citations", *International Journal of Technology Management*, 9 (5/6/7), 1994, pp. 757–70.

The role of military R&D in the civilian economy has been a controversial one. With rapid changes in the geopolitical power structure, the debate about the defense technology has assumed a higher level of significance. The defense sector has been a driving force in many new technologies, such as developments in microelectronics, computers, semiconductors, and aviation. While one can marvel at the contributions of these technologies to the growth of the civilian economy, one can argue about the effectiveness of defense R&D in producing and diffusing technology suitable for the civilian sector. The pattern of transfer of technology between defense firms and other organizations is investigated. The patents for eight large defense contractors, including Boeing, Lockheed, and McDonnell Douglas, are analyzed.

Correa, C. M., "Intellectual property rights and foreign direct investment", *International Journal of Technology Management*, Special Issue on the Management of International Intellectual Property, **10** (2/3), 1995, pp. 173–99.

This paper discusses the relationship between foreign direct investment and IPR. It aims to provide an analytical framework with which to understand this relationship and to deal with it. The multiple variables that affect the relationship, the industries involved and the degree of development of countries are first considered. The main developments in legislation, the WIPO, the UPOV and the GATT that have recently taken place are outlined with regard to strategies and decisions for foreign direct investment. An analytical framework is then presented and the significant differences it exposes when applied to different types of intellectual property are exemplified by case studies.

Frischtak, C. R., "Harmonization versus differentiation in international property rights regimes", *International Journal of Technology Management*, Special Issue on the Management of International Intellectual Property, **10** (2/3), 1995, pp. 200–13.

This paper argues that IPR in any country are protected according to the perceived national interest of that country. It discusses the relative merits of a differentiated system of IPR, *vis-a-vis* a homogeneous regime, depending on the stage of industrial development within a country. Illustrative examples of the level and range of protection given by different regimes are given and models of IPR regimes, giving optimum protection, are discussed.

de Almeida, P. R., "The political economy of intellectual property protection: Technological protectionism and transfer of revenue among nations", *International Journal of Technology Management*, Special Issue on the Management of International Intellectual Property, **10** (2/3), 1995, pp. 214–29.

This paper discusses the differing attitudes of developing and developed countries to protection of IPR and the effects on international trade negotiations. It highlights the trend in industrialized countries towards technological protectionism and the economic and social costs for developing countries. Finally, suggestions are made as to how these difficulties may be resolved.

Barbosa, D. B., "Letter from the Gama World", *International Journal of Technology Management*, Special Issue on the Management of International Intellectual Property, **10** (2/3), 1995, pp. 230–36.

This paper argues that an international system of patenting is needed to protect interests of countries in high technology. It discusses the aims of the "new economic order" and attempts to discriminate positively in favour of under-developed countries. Proposals for sharing technology by active intervention are outlined and the problems associated with technology transfer discussed. Changing attitudes of the OECD countries, led by USA, are attributed to globalization of the world market, leading to legal uniformity. Finally, the paper predicts that developed countries will require a more efficient international legal structure.

Menzler-Hokkanen, I., "Multinational enterprises and technology transfer", *International Journal of Technology Management*, Special Issue on the Management of International Intellectual Property, **10** (2/3), 1995, pp. 293–310.

The diversity of the roles played by foreign R&D in multinational enterprises (MNEs) is demonstrated in this paper. In many MNEs R&D has taken its place among the key internationalized functions. It is recognized that this enhances MNEs' ability to utilize diverse sources of scientific input efficiently, to meet globalized competition. In formulating their attitudes to multinationals' R&D units the host countries also need to acknowledge the diversity of the roles such units play, and thus also to consider the range of potential benefits and costs which they bring. The granting of world product mandates to subsidiaries in particular merits further investigation as a possible means whereby multinationals may create production facilities which possess independent innovation potential of their own.

Menon, U., "Access to and transfer of genetic resources", *International Journal of Technology Management*, Special Issue on the Managementof International Intellectual Property, **10** (2/3), 1995, pp. 311–24.

This paper gives a brief outline of the work of FAO and the Consultative Group on International Agricultural Research (CGIAR), with regard to free access to the world's genetic resources of plants. It reports on various meetings held to discuss regulation and attitudes towards the protection of IPR and the free exchange of technology, with a diversity of opinions between the developed and developing countries. Two examples of the problems facing this issue [involving India and the US Agency for International Development (USAID), and Costa Rica and Merck] are discussed in detail. Finally, the paper suggests an approach that both recognize the need for free access to genetic resources and private rights.

McNaughton, W. P. and Dooley, B., "Demonstration projects for diffusion of multifaceted technology: Characterization and strategy", *International Journal of Technology Management*, Special Issue on the Management of International Intellectual Property, **10** (2/3), 1995, pp. 325–42.

The key factors for successful transformation of laboratory discoveries into commercial and consumer application are well-documented. However, the critical success factors for transfer of technical knowledge as represented by methods, processes and technical philosophies have not been so completely characterized. This paper explores the use of demonstration projects for the transfer of these "non-product" technologies. Recent case studies, covering two of the most important reliability issues facing the US utility industry, are examined. From these case studies, a list of key questions and strategic implications that can be applied to future technology diffusion and demonstration projects are developed.

Liyanage, S. and Mitchell, H., "Management of intellectual property rights in Australian Cooperative Research Centres", *International Journal of Technology Management*, Special Issue on the Management of International Intellectual Property, **10** (2/3), 1995, pp. 343–64.

The ownership and exploitation of rights to intellectual property are major factors that determine the viability of cooperative research relationships. Australian cooperative research centres primarily deal with pre-competitive research and are involved in the commercialization of research results. The issue of IPR has emerged as a major area of concern for all partners involved in collaborative research. Differing views of how intellectual property should be treated and how such decisions affect commercial development in centre activities are discussed in this paper. It is argued that an over-emphasis on intellectual property can act as an impediment in the commercialization of collaborative research. Established practices amongst partners for the management of intellectual property are important and should not be disregarded in favour of new legal arrangements. This paper examines different approaches proposed for managing intellectual property in Australian Cooperative Research Centres.

Index